PRAISE FOR

Eight Flavors

"A unique and surprising view of American history. . . . Richly researched, intriguing, and elegantly written."

—*The Atlantic*

"Engaging narrative. . . . [Lohman] writes with passion and insight."

—*USA Today*

"It is a nifty idea, cleverly executed and well written—the kind of book that makes the reader annoy her family by constantly exclaiming 'Gosh! Did you know. . .?'"

—*Financial Times*

"Very cool. . . . A breezy American culinary history that you didn't know you wanted."

—*Bon Appétit*

"One part travelogue, one part history, and one part recipe book . . . *Eight Flavors* is a fascinating and thought-provoking tour of the history of America as told through the lens of its culinary innovations. . . . Lohman's book will stay with readers."

—*Christian Science Monitor*

"Warning: This book may make you hungry."

—*Bustle*

"Lohman's delectable book illustrates the deep connections between culture and food, reminding us that the flavors that enhance our foods represent the people who cook it."

—*BookPage*

"[Lohman] is a quirky but lovable guide through some of the least considered aspects of American history. . . . Endlessly fascinating and compulsively readable."
—*Fredericksburg Free Lance-Star*

"A compulsively readable, surprising, and deeply researched culinary history."
—*Brooklyn Based*

"In this convivial book, Lohman tells the stories of eight popular flavors. . . . Lohman makes the stories of these flavors fascinating, and by focusing on the influence of immigrants, brings a fresh, original perspective to American culinary history."

—*The National Book Review*

Eight Flavors

The Untold Story of American Cuisine

Sarah Lohman

Simon & Schuster Paperbacks

New York   London   Toronto   Sydney   New Delhi

Simon & Schuster Paperbacks
An Imprint of Simon & Schuster, Inc.
1230 Avenue of the Americas
New York, NY 10020

First Simon & Schuster trade paperback edition November 2017

SIMON & SCHUSTER Paperbacks and colophon are
registered trademarks of Simon & Schuster, Inc.

For information about special discounts for bulk purchases, please contact
Simon & Schuster Special Sales at 1-866-506-1949 or business@simonandschuster.com.

The Simon & Schuster Speakers Bureau can bring authors to your live event.
For more information or to book an event, contact the
Simon & Schuster Speakers Bureau at 1-866-248-3049 or
visit our website at www.simonspeakers.com.

Interior design by Ruth Lee-Mui
Illustrations by Peter Van Hyning

Manufactured in the United States of America

1   3   5   7   9   10   8   6   4   2

The Library of Congress has cataloged the hardcover edition as follows:

Names: Lohman, Sarah, author.
Title: Eight flavors : the untold story of American cuisine / Sarah Lohman.
Description: New York : Simon & Schuster, [2016]
Identifiers: LCCN 2016040059 (print) | LCCN 2016043818 (ebook) |
ISBN 9781476753959 (hardcover) | ISBN 9781476753966 (trade pbk.) |
ISBN 9781476753980 (ebook) | ISBN 9781476753980 (eBook)
Subjects: LCSH: Cooking, American. | Flavor. | LCGFT: Cookbooks.
Classification: LCC TX715 .L795 2016 (print) | LCC TX715 (ebook) | DDC 641.5973—dc23
LC record available at https://lccn.loc.gov/2016040059

ISBN 978-1-4767-5395-9
ISBN 978-1-4767-5396-6 (pbk)
ISBN 978-1-4767-5398-0 (ebook)

This book is dedicated to the memories of

DR. CHARLES BERGENGREN

and

JOSH OZERSKY

Contents

Introduction

History Has a Flavor

IT WAS THE year 2000, and I celebrated post–high school freedom by driving my light-blue-and-rust-colored Toyota Corolla maybe a little too fast and playing my Ben Folds Five album just a little too loud. I was eighteen and headed to my summer job, a job that allowed me to travel back in time.

Those June mornings were beautiful. I descended down winding country roads into Ohio's Cuyahoga River Valley, the sun's rays the electric peachy color of dawn, the air already thick with the rising humidity. The smell of hay and manure breezed in through my rolled-down window when I finally pulled into the parking lot.

I would emerge from my car and smooth the front of my light pink and blue paisley dress, which reached to the floor. To make the skirt stand out to the appropriate proportions, I wore a large, poufy crinoline—of the type that goes under a wedding dress—topped by several starched petticoats. The dress was never meant for driving, and cramming my skirts around the gear shift proved challenging. One morning I unknowingly drove all the way to work with my hem slammed in the door.

It was a unique uniform, but appropriate. I worked at a large, outdoor museum—a collection of historic houses, brought together from all over northeastern Ohio, for the purpose of preservation. Set about a village green, they functioned as a fabricated historical town, a re-creation of what life was like in 1848. We—those of us driving into the valley in our petticoats and waistcoats—were employed as denizens of this town, "living history" characters. Our stories were fictionalized, but created from the factual lives of real people from the past. I spent five days a week, eight hours a day, in costume, in character, in this museum.

That was how I spent the first four summers of my employable life. Putting on petticoats, learning cross-stitch (I loathed it), and pretending it was perfectly normal to have hundreds of tourists a day stop by for a visit. I had a "home," with an assigned family group—who are still like brothers and sisters to me—and the woman who played my mother *was* my mother. I spent so much time living in the past that aspects of my work life began to slip into my real life. Like the time I greeted my server at Applebee's with a hearty "Good day!" instead of "Hello!"

In high school history classes, I had learned about the past as a series of dates, laws, and battles. But my job immersed me in history, and taught me that the past was three dimensional; I could only begin to understand it by using all of my senses. The most important place in my workday life was the kitchen of my historic home. We cooked on a wood-burning stove every day, using recipes from the mid-nineteenth century. When the morning was chilly, we gathered in the kitchen to watch my "brother" light the fire. The kitchen smelled like wood smoke, fresh coffee, and my brother's cigarettes.

Each morning, we sipped tea and made plans for the day, until the first museum visitor came knocking at our door. Then the house's cook took over the kitchen table, her red hair swept back in a bun, her sleeves rolled up. She spread out her ingredients and scrutinized 150-year-old recipes. By lunch, we would sit around the table, eating buttery macaroni and cheese flavored with a generous grating of nutmeg, fricasseed chicken with marjoram, and hunks of cake full of raisins and currants, perfumed with brandy and rose water.

One day the cook was out sick, and I begged to take her place. The foodways director didn't usually welcome newcomers in the kitchen, but this time she said yes to me. I busted my butt to produce the most perfect pound cake that day—accomplished, mind you, with 1840s technology and in front of the probing eyes of the visiting public. It was nerve racking. When the director came back that afternoon to inspect my work, she gave me the subtlest nod of approval. I can't say that I was "in" after that—especially since, immediately afterward, I burnt an entire tray of cookies to an unidentifiable crisp. But I was granted permission to cook from time to time. The experience of working with those nineteenth-century recipes changed the way I thought about American food.

What stuck in my head about that first 1848 cake I baked was that it wasn't flavored with vanilla. It had all of the other ingredients of a modern cake, from white sugar to butter, but it was flavored with a teaspoon or more of *rose water*.

I had never encountered the flavor of rose water before. It imparted a bright, citrus note to the cakes and cookies I baked. I found out later that it's made by distilling a mixture of alcohol, water, and damask rose petals. The alcohol and essential oils evaporate, leaving behind rose-scented water used to flavor food. Brought to Europe during the Middle Ages from the Middle East—in the cultural exchange following the Crusades—rose water was used in English cooking for hundreds of years before colonists brought it to North America. Bakers in the late eighteenth and early nineteenth centuries used rose water the same way we use vanilla today: a teaspoon in a cake, a dash or two in pumpkin pie, even a tablespoon with stewed fruits. Today we associate rose water only with imported or immigrant foods—like yogurt drinks and milk-based desserts from India—with no memory that in 1800, using a tablespoon in apple pie would have been as "American" as the apple pie itself.

Every dish I made in that historic kitchen had its own distinctive taste, unique to the time. By the end of four summers there, I could easily rattle off the spices we used to cook: nutmeg, mace, black pepper, savory, and marjoram. But every dish was also flavored with the taste of wood smoke from our stove. I didn't notice it while at work, but if I packed up leftovers and ate them at home, the flavor of the smoke was overpowering. The food seemed out of place in modern surroundings—a relic of the past, but made just a few hours ago.

After that summer, I moved out from my parents' house to start my first year at the Cleveland Institute of Art. I tried to ignore my love of butter churns and wood-burning stoves. But I kept revisiting history, in assignment after assignment, fascinated by the interpretation of the past. In my final year at art school, I traveled to the East Coast to assemble research for my senior thesis. I visited a museum that was similar to the one I had worked in as a teenager, and discovered it boasted a restaurant that served cuisine from the 1830s. I was thrilled.

I reserved a table for lunch. A waitress sauntered over, wearing a generic, old-timey blouse with a sort of dirndl thing on top—all polyester. She greeted me and handed me a laminated menu. I pored over it . . . and was instantly disappointed. There was no Beef à la Mode or Marlborough Pudding, dishes I remembered from mid-nineteenth-century cookbooks. Instead, the restaurant offered beef stew and apple pie. Dishes that, yes, would have existed in the 1830s, but that are also still familiar today. When I ordered, I was doubly disappointed: the beef stew tasted like the beef stew from any modern restaurant. Where was the marjoram, the savory, the cloves and mace? Dessert was a delicious apple pie, but without rose water, white wine, and nutmeg, it wasn't an apple pie from the 1830s.

In that moment, I realized the same dish made in 1800, or 1900, or 2000, had different ingredients and different flavors. And I wondered why.

My trip to this restaurant inspired my senior thesis: I opened a pop-up restaurant for a week that served Revolutionary War–era food, seasoned with the flavors I encountered in historical cookbooks. There was a carrot soup pureed with cream, flavored with the spicy zing of mace. I roasted squab with a maple syrup glaze as a stand-in for the now extinct passenger pigeon, once an easy and affordable game meat for all Americans. And for dessert, I served green tea–flavored ice cream over a delicate rose-water sponge cake. Ginger beer and cider accompanied the meal, and smoky Lapsang souchong tea and French-roast coffee brought it to a close. Consumed around a communal table, in a space constructed to look like the dining room of an abandoned mansion, the meal was like a dinner eaten with ghosts of the past.

The restaurant was a success, but at the time—2005—my professors warned me there wasn't an audience in Cleveland for the work I was doing. They told me to go to New York City.

In January 2006, a handful of days before my twenty-fourth birthday, I packed the matching luggage my parents gave me for Christmas. I boarded a plane that lifted off from a cornfield in Akron, Ohio, and landed at LaGuardia Airport in Queens, New York. I remember that it was a clear winter day when I flew over the city, and I could easily pick out the tiny green action figure of the Statue of Liberty in the harbor. She greeted me as she had greeted my father's mother, all four of my mother's grandparents, and the millions of immigrants like them.

I landed my first job in Manhattan—predictably in food services, selling fancy chocolate on Park Avenue. Then I sold fancy men's suits on the wealthy Upper East Side. And then I found a job coding animated features for *New York* magazine's website, which (after the fashion director dramatically fired the videographer) led to filming and editing video features, many of which focused on New York's culinary scene.

On assignment in some of the city's best restaurants, I witnessed chefs mining the past for inspiration. Like a potato dish from a Michelin-starred restaurant, where the spuds were set in a cast-iron

Dutch oven, nestled in hay. The whole thing was then placed on a hot burner and the burning hay imbued the potatoes with a smoky flavor that took me right back to my 1848 kitchen. And there was the trend for Ossabaw pork from pigs descended from a very old breed left by Spanish conquistadors on an island off the coast of Georgia in the sixteenth century. Even Chipotle introduced corn tortillas that were "based on a 3,500-year-old recipe." Each dish I encountered reminded me of my own love of food history.

I realized the combination of my "living history" job experience and art school education gave me a unique perspective on food. I began to devour old cookbooks, always dreaming about how the recipe would taste and look when I made it. In my reading, I stumbled across a reference to the first cocktail guide ever published, Jerry Thomas's *How to Mix Drinks; or the Bon-vivant's Companion*, published in 1862. Thanks to the wonder of the modern era, the book was online in its entirety. As I digitally flipped through its pages, the old historical food itch came back to me. I didn't want to just read about these 150-year-old drinks, I wanted to taste what my great-great-grandfather—a Union cavalryman—sipped during the Civil War. Unless he was a teetotaler.

I decided to invite a few friends over to sample the historical cocktails. I made some phone calls and sent an evite—and, okay, there was a website, too, with photos, because I was excited. I expected a half-dozen patronizing acquaintances to attend. Instead, thirty people showed up. In costume: soldiers, troubadours, and mountain men. Long before old-timey mustaches were the latest Brooklyn fashion trend, they made an appearance at my apartment in Queens.

We got drunk and debauched, 1860s style. There's a photo of me giving the camera the peace sign while wearing petticoats and a corset. The image is snapped from up high, a photo of my kitchen swirling with a bizarre assortment of costumed characters, sipping ale flips, green tea punches, and peach brandy mint juleps. My apartment was sticky with simple syrup and hellish to clean the next morning, but I couldn't wait to throw another party.

After the party, I decided to launch a blog called *Four Pounds Flour*. Within a year I watched my life go from a series of odd jobs to even odder jobs: "Can you cater this 1860s St. Patrick's Day party?" "Can you come and cook a Revolutionary War–era Thanksgiving dinner?" "Can you make eighteenth-century cookies for my museum's bake sale?" Well . . . sure! I cobbled together a career based on what was in the bellies of historical Americans. It became apparent that my obsession with the flavors of the past was just as intriguing for others as it was for me.

Unexpectedly, the deeper I delved into the history of American food, the broader a perspective I gained on what Americans eat today. I realized American food is greatly influenced by where the cook grew up and where their family originally emigrated from. These differences in regionality and ethnicity result in an extremely diverse culinary nation.

But if I looked past these differences, I wondered what united America's culinary culture? I thought of rose water and vanilla: rose water, at one time, was used all over the United States; and vanilla, regardless of a family's ethnicity, is consumed all over the country today. I realized the key to defining American cuisine was to break it down to the basic flavors we all use, like vanilla.

Flavor is a concentrated mixture of aromatic compounds that provide all or part of the sensory experience of a food or a beverage. Some flavors are liquids (like vanilla extract) and others are dry powders (like curry powder). All flavors are chemicals. Eight to twelve chemicals make up the flavor of a garlic clove, while over two hundred chemicals work together to make up the flavor of a vanilla bean.

Flavor is primarily a combination of taste and aroma. There are at least five basic tastes: sweet, salty, bitter, sour, and savory (or umami). Each has an evolutionary trigger tied to survival: for example, sweet signals the presence of carbohydrates, which provide energy; while bitter can indicate the presence of poisons that could lead to sickness or even death. Chemicals in our food trigger taste receptors in our mouth; our brain then interprets information about which foods are good to eat, and which are not.

Humans can detect only a handful of tastes but can identify about one trillion different scents. Scent is caused by chemicals evaporating off our food and entering our nasal cavity. To understand the importance of aroma, try this experiment I learned from visiting the *Flavor: Making It and Faking It* exhibit at the Museum of Food and Drink (MOFAD) in Brooklyn: chomp on a Crunchy Flamin' Hot Cheeto with your nose pinched closed. When I plugged my nose, my tongue detected salty— a basic taste—and the chemical irritation of "spicy," from the capsaicin present in hot peppers. When I unplugged my nose, I suddenly could appreciate the aromas of cheesy and herby. Together salty, spicy, cheesy, and herby created the flavor of the Cheeto.

The physiological signals of flavor are interpreted in our brain's frontal lobe, the part of the brain where emotional reactions are processed and personality is formed. Personal experience, memories, and emotions all inform the experience of flavor.

Flavor preferences and aversions are learned. Since every cuisine around the world employs specific flavors in its cooking, flavor preferences could be considered the signature of a cuisine and can be used to interpret culinary culture. So American food, and how it has changed over time, can be illustrated by its most commonly used flavors.

When I began my research, I made a timeline of recipes from my respectable collection of cookbooks, dating from Amelia Simmons's *American Cookery*, the first cookbook published in this country in 1796, all the way through modern American standards like *How to Cook Everything* by Mark Bittman. I flipped through these cookbooks from different eras: the 1800s, 1850s, 1900s, and 1950s, selecting the most influential tomes from those periods, like Mary Randolph's *The Virginia Housewife*; Fannie Merritt Farmer's *The Boston Cooking-School Cookbook*; and James

Beard's *The Fireside Cook Book*. I looked for ingredients that significantly affected the flavor of the recipe. After I made a list of commonly used flavors, I plotted them on a graph with the help of Google's Ngram Viewer, which visualizes the frequency of words in all the books Google has digitized. I set the sample size to American books from 1796 to 2000. When I built the graph of American flavors, it revealed which ones were used the most frequently in text (and for all practical purposes, were the most popular), when flavors entered our lexicon, and how some grew in popularity while others disappeared. After all was said and done, the results revealed eight winners—flavors that were the most popular, and had never waned in their popularity.

I didn't so much choose the flavors that appear in this book, as discover them: black pepper, the dried berries of a tropical vine; vanilla, the fruit of a Central American orchid; chili powder, ground dried chilies with spices; curry powder, the Westernized version of an Indian spice blend; soy sauce, the salty-savory runoff of fermented soybeans; garlic, the odorous leaf of a European herb; monosodium glutamate (MSG), the umami-rich glutamic acid salt; and Sriracha, the California-made hot sauce that has captured American's hearts. I've excluded two common flavors, chocolate and coffee, simply because so much has already been written about them. I wanted to tell the stories of the equally popular but less recognized flavors of American food.

I've organized this book chronologically, in the order that these flavors appeared in American kitchens, from black pepper just after the Revolutionary War, to the Sriracha boom of the last decade. Our current pantry is cumulative: as flavors have arrived in this country, some earned a permanent place in the kitchen.

But at the end of the day, the study of culinary history isn't about food—it's about the people who prepare and consume this food. The individuals who brought these flavors to America's table don't usually get a page in the history books. We have black pepper because of enterprising New England merchants who treated the indigenous people of Sumatra with respect. Vanilla is here thanks to a twelve-year-old slave who figured out a botanical secret no one else knew. Chili powder spread across the country because of entrepreneurial Texan-Mexican women who fed soldiers and tourists—and a clever German immigrant who was looking for a culinary shortcut. Curry powder's popularity was due to sailors craving flavors they had tasted in the Far East, but also because of America's first Indian chef (who was a kind of bad boy). Soy sauce came thanks to immigrants from China—although we started using it more broadly because of the Japanese; and garlic, thanks to immigrants from Italy—although we started using it more broadly because of the influence of French cuisine. MSG was discovered in a homemade soup by an inquisitive Japanese scientist, and Sriracha was created by a refugee from Vietnam as a sauce for pho. Each flavor became American as a result of three main factors: an event that created the desire for each flavor, followed by increased availability, paired with a biological preference.

This book tells the stories of these flavors, the stories of the people behind them, and, consequently, the story of our country. You can find these eight flavors in kitchens from New York to California, used by families whose ancestors came from everywhere, from Italy to Vietnam. And through these eight flavors, I learned that American food has a complicated, continuously evolving identity—just like Americans themselves.

Eight Flavors

Black pepper

One

Black Pepper

AMERICANS HAVE COOKED with black pepper for hundreds of years, and it will be a part of our pantries for hundreds of years to come. It's integral to American cuisine: the United States is the largest black pepper importer in the world. According to Al Goetze, McCormick's spice buyer of more than thirty years, black pepper is currently the number one selling spice in America, representing 10 percent of all retail spice sales, and Americans use more than 158 million pounds of it per year. *Slate* recently wondered if there was a spice or seasoning that would better serve as salt's accompaniment. In a reader vote, 34 percent of people voted to keep pepper in its place, the largest percentage. A few of the runners-up—garlic (powder), MSG, and Sriracha—are featured later in this book.

Until recently, I took black pepper for granted. But in the late eighteenth century, black pepper was difficult to come by. In 1801 a merchant from Salem, Massachusetts, named George Crowninshield and his son, John, made plans to seek out pepper at its source. The black pepper trade would make them some of the richest men in America. Because of the Crowninshields and other Salem merchants like them, black pepper became the American pantry staple it is today.

I cooked with black pepper never thinking about its origins until a frigid day in February 2011. I was visiting the Brooklyn Botanic Garden, gathering ideas for a class I was teaching in the spring. I decided to seek refuge from the outdoor arctic temperatures in the Tropical Pavilion, a great, glass-domed greenhouse where the season never changes. I pushed through the door, and into the humid air, dense and pungent with the scent of earth. When I entered this world, it felt both familiar and alien, an island of the Tropics in the middle of the city.

As I walked through the Pavilion, I came across a deep-green vine climbing up the trunk of a palm, its foliage so dense it could be mistaken for the tree itself. Teardrop-shaped leaves reached out from a ropelike stem that spiraled upward. The color range would have made Pantone proud: everything from the purest spring greens to the deepest forest hues. Amidst this frenzy of emerald were strings of ruby berries, growing on stalks. This botanical specimen, native to southern India, was *Piper nigrum*—a black pepper plant, the first I had ever seen in person. I would later learn that a peppercorn is this plant's dried berry, with a husk, pulpy middle, and a seed in the center.

As I examined the plant, a large family of tourists came around the trail. As they peered at the vine, I gathered they weren't sure what they were supposed to be looking at. I gently tapped a woman about my age on the shoulder and pointed out the cherry-red berries. She looked at me, amazed, as if I had performed a magic trick. She showed the fruit to her family, who flashed their cameras and exclaimed to one another in at least two languages. I wasn't the only one who was fascinated by this spice in its natural state.

That day, when I got home, I unscrewed the top of my pepper grinder and rolled a few peppercorns into my hand. I examined the dry, wrinkled berries closely for the first time. I tossed one in my mouth and bit down:

a hot, burning sensation covered my tongue and the back of my throat; I coughed. When the heat was gone, the aromatics remained—floral and earthy.

I felt driven to understand this plant better, but it's difficult to fully comprehend the cultivation of an exotic species half a world away. I scratched my head reading paragraphs of advice on loamy soil and light requirements. I decided there must be a better way to learn how pepper grows. So I bought a pepper plant.

A month after my visit to the Botanic Garden, I did some Googling and I found a greenhouse in Delaware that would deliver a baby pepper vine to my door. My excitement built as I tracked the plant in transit. When the postman finally arrived with a telltale box, I treated him as if he were the stork delivering a newborn.

"He's adorable!" I chirped when I unwrapped my little pepper vine from the cozy newspaper packing. No more than four inches tall, my vine had five stems, each topped by a cheery leaf that stretched upwards, searching for the sun.

Pepper plants can be grown from a seed, but the seed has to be un-processed, so you can't just plant a kitchen peppercorn and expect it to grow. My baby pepper vine was grown the way most are cultivated—from a cutting. I gave him water and set him in a windowsill. He doubled in size in less than a week. Pepper-farming guides recommended setting up a post for him to start climbing right away, so I moved him to a large pot, equipped with a six-foot stick for him to ascend.

He was happiest the year he summered in Ohio with my parents. He baked in 90-degree heat on their asphalt driveway and exploded in dark green foliage. When the weather changed, he returned home to my Queens apartment; and with him came soil gnats, which required an in-tensive treatment that nearly killed my other houseplants. But my pepper vine seemed largely unaffected. I babied him, while my roommates (and cat) swatted bugs and slowly went insane from the infestation.

And then to my great surprise, one October morning, I saw a pepper spike amongst his leaves. A pepper spike is about an inch long, shaped like a rounded pyramid, and covered in rows of very light green, miniscule buds that would eventually fruit. I had no idea if black pepper vines could self-pollinate, or what sort of help they might need to do so. I blew on the pepper spikes, rubbed them between two fingers, and did any number of other ill-informed and vaguely erotic gestures that I hoped would result in pollination. The flower buds shriveled, and then swelled and looked promisingly like pepper berries. But eventually the spikes died and fell off. To this day, I haven't had any luck growing my own pepper berries, though my plant still sits near my window, now four feet tall and growing.

It's likely I had so much difficulty reaping a pepper harvest because the vines are much more comfortable in their native climate of Southeast Asia. Pepper was first collected wild on the Malabar Coast of India long before modern records began. Pepper vines were first brought to Sumatra, a large Indonesian island just southwest of the Malay Peninsula, from India sometime before the seventh century. This island is where American merchants like the Crowninshields originally imported their black pepper.

Pepper is harvested the same way in Sumatra today as it has been for at least two hundred years. Small family landowners produce the bulk of the crop and large, commercial farms are rare. When pepper berries ripen, they turn from bright green to yellow to Christmas red. Male workers lean wood ladders against the trees or posts that support the pepper plants, then ascend to harvest the berries by hand. A pepper vine produces four types of pepper, depending upon when its berries are harvested: green, black, white, and red.

Three different peppercorns are sold in the multicolor pepper grinders, which can be found in grocery stores. Green peppercorns are freeze-dried, unripe berries. They taste fruity and are not too hot, although chomping down on a green peppercorn still makes my eyes water. White pepper is harvested when the pepper spike is almost fully ripened and all the berries are red or yellow. These berries are soaked in water, historically in a running stream, and the outer husk and pulp is degraded by bacteria. In the final stage of the process, the husk is rubbed off, leaving behind only the grayish seed of the pepper. White pepper has a distinctive funky taste from the slight fermentation, which reminds me of stinky feet. Red peppercorns are fresh berries and are used as a condiment in areas where pepper is grown. But don't confuse them with the pink "peppercorns" that are sometimes included in multicolor pepper mixes. These are not peppercorns at all, but the seeds of an unrelated shrub native to South America, *Schinus terebinthifolius*—more commonly (and festively) known as Christmas berry or Florida holly. This invasive species produces berries that more closely resemble rose hips than peppercorns, but their heat can nicely round out a pepper blend.

Black pepper is harvested when only a few berries on the spike have turned yellow, the midway stage of ripeness. Aromatics decrease as the berries ripen, so the slightly unripe berries are more flavorful than a fully ripe berry. After harvesting, the pepper berries are either blanched briefly in boiling water or left in piles to ferment for several days; each process is particular to the producer and results in different coloration and flavor profiles in the final product. Then, women and children spread the berries on a concrete floor or bamboo mats and leave them to dry in the sun. The pepper berries are turned with feet, hands, or rakes, working through the peppercorns like black sand to ensure the pepper dries evenly. As the peppercorns dry, the outside husks turn black, while the pulpy inside remains light.

Once properly dried, the harvested pepper is collected and usually sold to a large export house, which sorts, washes, and bottles the peppercorns before they're sent to grocery stores around the world.

There are many different varieties of black pepper, each with their own distinct flavor. At New York City's spice and condiment mecca Kalustyan's, I found six different types of black pepper. Overwhelmed by choice, I organized a pepper tasting: I taught a class on the history and uses of black pepper at the Brooklyn Brainery, a learning center that offers "casual classes for curious adults" on everything from macramé to . . . well, the history and uses of black pepper. I asked my fifteen students to taste six types of pepper. It was an awful idea. We were all beading sweat and breathing fire by the time we were done. It's funny, because you don't think of black pepper as being "hot," but black pepper packs the punch of *piperine*, a chemical irritant that is responsible for bite, pungency, and the sneezy sensation in your nose. An essential oil called oleoresin contributes to black pepper's aromatic qualities, in combination with up to 135 other compounds.

My tasters and I were shocked to discover that not all black pepper tastes the same. Malabar pepper, from India, had intense heat but with hints of coriander and a tannic, tealike flavor. Sarawak pepper, native to Malaysia, had distinct lemon and ginger notes. And Lampong pepper, from Sumatra, was the hottest, due to a high piperine content. It's one of the most popular peppercorns in America today.

Colonial Americans were just as unfamiliar with black pepper's origins as I was when I first saw that vine in the Brooklyn Botanic Garden. Although black pepper had been used in Western cooking since the Roman Empire, it wasn't until the end of the seventeenth century, when the British East India Company established reliable trade routes with Asia, that pepper became relatively affordable. American colonists bought most commodities, including pepper, through England and had little idea where it originated.

What were Colonial Americans cooking with all that pepper? To find out, I turned to the recipes of one of the period's leading ladies: Martha Washington. The future first lady was a widow when she married George; she got hitched to her first husband, Daniel Custis, in 1750. When she was married, she received a stack of recipes from her in-laws as a wedding present. The manuscript is known to scholars as "A Booke of Cookery," and it features recipes from the tail end of the Middle Ages through the

Colonial Era. Copied and passed down by Washington's in-laws in the kitchens of early America, it reveals clues about what Americans ate long before the first cookbook was published. And the way black pepper was used in these recipes surprised me.

In a manuscript of over five hundred recipes, black pepper is used about fifty times, usually in combination with other spices. Most of these mentions occur in recipes for meat, poultry, and fish, including sausage and pickled seafood. But the entry I found the most intriguing was called "To Make Pepper Cakes That Will Keep Good in Ye House for a Quarter or Halfe a Year." Oddly, as the title suggests, these "cakes" could hang out in your house for six months. The spicing reflects a holdover from the Middle Ages: a time when pepper was used the same as any other spice, in the sweet as well as the savory. Although the recipe's name includes black pepper, it is strangely omitted from the ingredients—though in the 1996 reprinted manuscript, culinary historian Karen Hess argued that it might have been left out accidentally. The recipe combined black pepper, ginger, coriander, and caraway with candied fruit, orange zest, and molasses.

The cakes are formed into "pritty large cakes about an intch and halfe thick at moste." In shape and texture, they're what we'd call a cookie today. They were then baked and could be stored for four to six months. I cooked a batch and, after half a year of sitting in the back of my pantry, they seemed oddly unperturbed by the passage of time. I took a bite. They were dense, sticky, and heavily spiced. With nearly as much ground seasoning as flour in the recipe, their flavor was overpowering.

But I found Washington's "Pepper Cakes" inspiring. I love to look to the past to inform my contemporary kitchen. Often historical documents can be used as a jumping off point for new recipes that feel modern, despite being grounded in history. A little tinkering in the kitchen and I came up with a version of Washington's cakes that blended black pepper harmoniously with other spices.

Black Pepper Brown Sugar Cookies

I chose to use Sarawak peppercorns from Indonesia, as the pepper has notes of citrus and coriander that lend itself well to desserts. But any black pepper you have will do. The result is a chewy cookie, speckled with pretty bits of black pepper.

Yield: makes 3 to 4 dozen, depending on the size of the cookie

4 cups flour

1 teaspoon baking soda

1 teaspoon salt

1 teaspoon freshly ground pepper, plus more to top the cookies

1 teaspoon ginger

1 teaspoon coriander

3/4 cup (1 1/2 sticks) unsalted butter, room temperature

2 cups packed light brown sugar

Zest of one orange

Juice of 1/2 an orange (about 1/4 cup)

2 large eggs

1. In a large bowl, whisk together dry ingredients and spices.

2. In the bowl of an electric mixer, add butter, sugar, and orange zest. Using the paddle attachment, beat on medium-high until light in color. Add the orange juice, and then add eggs one at a time, beating well after each addition.

3. With mixer on low, add the dry ingredients slowly. Stop and scrape the bowl, then continue mixing until combined. Divide dough in half, wrap in plastic wrap, and chill at least 1 hour and as long as overnight.

4. Preheat oven to 350 degrees. On a generously floured work surface and with a floured rolling pin, roll dough 1/8 inch thick. Using a pepper

grinder, crack fresh pepper over the surface of the dough and then gently press the pepper in with the rolling pin.

5. Cut into desired shapes using a cookie cutter or knife. Bake on a cookie sheet 10 to 12 minutes, rotating the cookie sheet halfway through, until the cookies are brown around the edges. Allow to cool completely on wire racks.

Black pepper was a common flavor in eighteenth-century American kitchens, but when the colony broke ties with England, the spice was harder to come by. After the Revolutionary War, no one in America knew where black pepper came from. The British, by exporting the commodity from England, had kept it a secret. Until their secret was discovered—and the Crowninshield family of Salem, Massachusetts, took advantage of it.

I visited the Crowninshields' home town of Salem in June 2012. I approached the city by driving down Chestnut Street, an avenue lined with mansions. Built in the Federal style of two hundred years ago, the exteriors are simple by today's standards, but subtle gilding, carving, and Flemish Bond—one of the most expensive ways to lay brick—whisper "wealth" to those in the know. These were the residences of the richest people in Salem: traders, merchants, and sea captains. From the widow's walks, they would have watched their ships come in to the port below.

Patriarch George Crowninshield's childhood home still stands, although now it's owned by the Peabody Essex Museum of Salem, and was moved from its original site to a tiny village of historic buildings near the museum. It's modest compared with the Chestnut Avenue mansions: two and a half stories with wood siding painted a cheerful yellow. Touring it with a museum guide, I saw that the house still included signs of the Crowninshield family's journeys abroad: in a corner of the study sat a massive clam shell, dragged back from some tropical port, that looked worthy of Aphrodite. Next to a bed was a nightstand with a shaving mirror, a basin to hold water to wash the face, and a chamber pot, all in a wooden cabinet that could be closed up and loaded aboard a ship, ready to sail for distant shores.

It's unlikely George spent much of his boyhood running around the halls of this home. George Crowninshield turned fifteen the same year Martha Washington received her stack of recipes; by then, he had already been sailing on trade ships for seven years. That wasn't uncommon at the time: boys as young as nine were admitted into the U.S. Navy.

Eight years later, in 1757, at the age of twenty-two, Crowninshield married into big money: he won the hand of Mary Derby, sister to Salem's wealthiest merchant. The Derby family's wharf is preserved in Salem, a testament to their economic power 250 years ago. Mary's brother Elias— or "King" Derby, as he was nicknamed—was a successful merchant who became even richer by operating a fleet of privateers during the Revolutionary War.

Crowninshield and Mary Derby had a batch of children together, eight of whom survived infancy: six boys and two girls. Crowninshield's time at sea left him rough in appearance and language, and by all accounts, he grew into a grouchy patriarch. A guest once recalled breakfast at the Crowninshield house; each of the children wanted something different to drink: tea, milk, water, hot chocolate, and so on. Irritated by his sons' and daughters' individual requests, George asked a servant to bring a cup of each and a large bowl. He poured the drinks all together, stirred them up, and said, "Now, children, help yourselves."

By the time of the Revolutionary War, the Crowninshield family became moderately successful merchants. As the boys grew older, they were expected to become sailors, like their father. George Crowninshield dreamed of building a trade empire with the partnership of his sons. Some took to it better than others. The youngest son, Edward, was known to be timid and introverted. Sent to sea by his father at the age of eighteen, he was brutalized by the ship's captain and later committed suicide. The incident was seldom spoken of by the family.

Other sons survived their father's tyranny to work in the family business. After the war, Salem-based merchants, including the Crowninshields, wanted to expand their interests to the Far East. The pepper trade was potentially lucrative—but how to break in when no one knew where pepper plants grew?

Finally, around 1790 the source of pepper was revealed when a Salem captain named Jonathan Carnes was docked in Sumatra. He received a hot tip that pepper grew wild on the island's northwestern coast. With this bit of information in hand, Carnes returned home and convinced a wealthy merchant named Jonathan Peele to fund an expedition to search for black pepper. Carnes's ship, the *Rajah*, left Salem in 1795; the crew kept its destination a secret. When the ship returned to port eighteen months later, it had pepper "shoveled right into her hold like gravel." The crew brought home an estimated 100,000 to 150,000 pounds of pepper, which sold for 37 cents a pound—an astounding 700 percent profit. This shipment was the first load of pepper ever imported directly to the United States from Sumatra.

It would have been to Peele's and Carnes's advantage to keep the source of the pepper secret, like the British East India Company had; but someone on their staff or crew let the cat out of the bag. Old Crabby Crowninshield caught wind that pepper could be found in Sumatra. Crowninshield dispatched his son John to Sumatra in 1801 as captain of a black pepper expedition.

Blond and blue-eyed, John was considered handsome at twenty-nine years old when he departed Salem on the *America III*. On July 2, 1801, he laid eyes on Sumatra. It was a sight that only a few Americans had witnessed: green mountains ascended from the rocky sea and disappeared into the mist. On these volcanic slopes grew pepper vines, entwined around the trunks of jungle trees.

I imagine John was as captivated as I was by the pepper vine when he first laid eyes on it. Here was the key to his family's budding fortune. But if he was, he didn't mention it in the journal he kept of his expedition. What he did talk about was how much he liked the local people, the Acehnese.

When a ship like the *America III* sidled up to a town along the coastline

John Crowninshield

of Sumatra, such as Rahnoo or Telloo Gootupang (both known as "considerable pepper ports"), a rowboat was sent ashore to inquire if pepper was available for sale. Ships would stay in port until they could purchase a full hold of pepper, which could take an entire year.

In Sumatra, pepper wasn't traded: it was bought with gold and silver, the price determined by the *picul*, a unit of measurement in Southeast Asia equal to about 133 pounds. The precious metals were then used in local commerce, either stamped into coins or weighed out in dust. The Acehnese adorned themselves with gold jewelry, in the form of headpieces, bracelets, and necklaces.

John tried two ports before he found enough pepper at a fair price—$8 for a *picul*—and struck a deal. A handkerchief was filled with pepper and eight pieces of silver, "kept sacred as a prooff of the bargain until all is finished," John wrote in his journal. He and his crew waited for weeks as thousands of pounds of dried pepper were loaded aboard. In the meantime, they hung out with the Acehnese. Initially intimidated by the curved swords the men wore, John came to respect his trading partners. "They treat us with the greatest politeness," he wrote. "The people on shore are remarkably civil to us & behave in every respect with the greatest propriety . . . they are by no means a vicious set of people, quite the reverse."

If John sounds astonished in his writings, it's because in the West, the Acehnese were often portrayed as primitive but cunning—and sometimes violent. Part of this depiction can be attributed to xenophobia, but it was also carefully crafted by the English to keep other traders away. In reality, the Acehnese had a monarchy with a lavish, central palace; their homes were comfortable and well adapted to the climate; and although they wore a simple loincloth for work, they also possessed fine sets of layered clothes made from cotton or locally produced silk. John Crowninshield told the Acehnese leaders before he left that "the reason the Americans had not traded largely with them before . . . was from the bad character we had heard of them." He suspected "this information has been given by those whose interest it was to deceave with the view of keeping trade in their own hands."

"They were very much surprised," John wrote, "And said they hoped I would not tell any such bad stories . . . that between nations thinking so different as we do there always must be great misunderstanding . . . I told them I thought very favourable indeed of them." When John was ready to return home, he left not only with a full cargo of pepper but also with a feeling of respect for the Acehnese people.

John had the right idea. The key to stealing trade from the English was to be *nice* to the local population. Before the English arrived, the Acehnese had little motivation to cultivate the pepper plant; small crops were harvested, but they were worthless on the local market. The English moved in on Sumatra in the late seventeenth century, which gave the Acehnese an outlet for their pepper. But the English also *literally* moved in by forming settlements on the island. Agents of the East India Company paid off local tribal leaders to "compel" their dependents to cultivate pepper: "The inhabitants of the districts were obliged to plant a certain number of vines: each family 1,000 and each young unmarried man 500." If the pepper crop failed to reach the East India Company's estimated yield, "punishments" were doled out.

This imperialistic agreement between the East India Company and the tribal chiefs included a guarantee to ensure that the pepper crop was sold exclusively to England. This arrangement allowed the English to keep the prices low and keep the locals in poverty—in 1780 the English were paying $15 for 500 pounds of pepper. When the Americans arrived, they offered a much better price: John, as I mentioned above, paid $8 for 133 pounds—double what the English offered—and by 1803, Americans were paying $10, and bringing hulls full of peppercorns back to Salem.

When I visited Salem, I imagined sailing ships docked along the waterfront. I walked out to the end of Derby wharf, property of the incredibly wealthy in-laws of the Crowninshields'. The Crowninshields' own wharf no longer exists, although the family commissioned a painting of it during its busiest years for posterity. Built of stone and earth, it stuck out into the port across from the customhouse, where incoming goods would have been assessed and taxed. I stood on the end of Derby wharf and thought about John, traveling home after eight months at sea and navigating the narrow, shallow bay as his ship came into port. If I had been there, waiting for him, I would have smelled his cargo even before he docked. An army of workers would have descended to unload the 844,918 pounds of black pepper he had acquired.

John paid around $50,800 in Sumatra for his pepper, and at the customhouse, he was charged a comparable amount of duties. The cargo sold on the market for about $282,000, which meant that the family earned around $180,400 in profit. Consider that in 1802, the average man made about $1 a day, and you'll begin to understand the vastness of the wealth the Crowninshields amassed. The *America III* turned right back around and returned to Sumatra; the next year, it brought back 760,000 pounds of pepper, which fetched $250,000. George Crowninshield dispatched a second ship to Sumatra, the *Belisarius*, which, during 1801 and 1802, brought home an additional 600,000 to 700,000 pounds of pepper. The pepper sold for around $206,366, as the market became flooded, and the price began to drop.

In the span of two years, George Crowninshield & Sons—as their partnership was now officially known—brought over 1.5 million pounds of black pepper into the United States, which yielded over $400,000 in profits. It's no surprise the Crowninshields haughtily called Sumatra "our pepper gardens."

The Crowninshields grew prosperous, but remained notoriously ill-tempered. A relative once said she knew of "No . . . Crowninshield . . . distinguished for intellect or piety. They were all marked by haughtily knit brows and intense hauteur of Manners." There was constant infighting amongst the siblings. In 1809 Crowninshield & Sons was reorganized so that John could strike out on his own. A sum just shy of $1 million was distributed among the four partners. George wrote to them: "Now Sons, I think You will Possess Ample Fortune Enough to Make you all Happy if . . . Pease & Union amongst you all is Cultivated, As I think it is not too late to Attempt & which is My Earnest wish to See Established Before I Bid you a Lasting Farewell. Your Father, George Crowninshield."

George Crowninshield died in 1815, a millionaire from the pepper trade—but with his children squabbling over his will around him.

The Crowninshields had fueled America's passion for black pepper and inspired other merchants to set their sights on Sumatra. As more ships sailed from Salem to Sumatra, their owners and captains followed the Crowninshields' example: American captains respected the Acehnese, if for no other reason than it was a wise business decision. The continual opportunity for competitive prices allowed the Acehnese to distance themselves from their English trading partners. By 1813, the East India Company abolished its mandatory cultivation rules and forgave debts in an attempt to win back the populace. But by 1830, only two pepper plantations remained under English rule. American merchants had stolen the pepper trade, and they had done it without conquest or colonization.

John Crowninshield lived until 1842; by the time he passed, the shipping trade had almost disappeared from Salem. The last boatful of pepper docked in Salem in 1846; after that, boats sailed directly from Sumatra to the larger harbors of Boston or New York. By then, fifty million pounds of pepper had been imported into Salem, worth over $25 million at the time.

With the American market flooded with pepper, it became more affordable and, soon, a staple in everyone's kitchen. But it was more than simple availability that made black pepper an important flavor in American cuisine: this spice has beneficial properties. A bizarre story recounted in the 1949 book *Pepper and Pirates: Adventures in the Sumatra Pepper Trade of Salem* alludes to one of black pepper's unique qualities: a seafaring man from the Crowninshields' time died far from home and "was shipped back to Salem in a coffin filled with pepper." Apparently his body returned only a little worse for wear.

The story could be true, because black pepper has antimicrobial properties. A 1998 study by Cornell University's Paul W. Sherman and Jennifer Billing showed that black pepper kills up to 25 percent of bacteria it comes into contact with. The alkaloids in black pepper's piperine affect the membrane permeability of bacteria. The microbes either lose or absorb liquid, depending on the salinity of the environment around them. They shrivel or pop, and die. Colonial recipes like Martha Washington's that included pepper in pickles and sausages suggest some awareness of the spice's preservative properties.

I was amazed to find that many flavors in this book have antimicrobial properties: the components of curry and chili powder, the jalapeños in Sriracha, and in particular, garlic, which, in one study, killed 100 percent of bacteria it came into contact with. Cornell researcher Sherman theorized the antimicrobial properties of these spices is one of the reasons humans like the taste of spicy food. Foods cooked with these spices were better preserved, and in a time before refrigeration, the people who ate them were at a lower risk of food-borne illness. They were healthier and lived longer than people who did not consume spicy food, so they had more children. Natural selection favored those who ate spicy food, because they survived, and the preference for spicy food became a dominant trait in humanity.

A recipe I found in Martha Washington's manuscript emphasized this connection between heavy seasoning and health. It was a preparation of venison, where the meat was stuffed with lemon peels and crusted in an enormous quantity of black pepper, salt, and lemon juice.

To Season a Venison

Take out ye bones & turne ye fat syde downe upon a board. yn take ye pill
of 2 leamons & break them in pieces as long as yr finger & thrust them into

every hole of yr venison. then take 2 ounces of beaten pepper & thrice as much salt, mingle it, then wring out ye juice of lemon into ye pepper & salt & season it, first taking ye leamon pills haveing layn soe a night. then paste it with gross pepper layd on ye top & good store of butter or muton suet.

If you have trouble understanding the recipe as written, try reading it out loud.

This recipe called for an entire haunch of venison, seasoned then crusted in pastry. It was possibly one of the older entries in the manuscript. The great quantity of pepper used here was common in medieval meat preparations, where a protein was crusted in expensive spices—including "sweet" spices like cinnamon and cloves. As I read it, I recalled the grade-school myth that heavy spicing hid the taste of spoiled meat. But as spices were costly in the middle ages, the story can't be true—someone who could afford to cook with these spices could also afford fresh meat. Instead, the old legend might simply be misinterpreted. The antimicrobial properties of the spices used in recipes like Washington's—as well as the salt and lemon juice, two other powerful antimicrobials—would have helped to preserve the meat and keep it fresh longer.

Lemon-Pepper Venison

This recipe has been reinterpreted with a smaller venison roast in mind, but it captures the beautiful blend of lemon and cracked peppercorns from the original recipe. The salt and clarified butter (or ghee) in this recipe keep moist what can be a lean, dry meat and the pepper keeps it flavorful. Grind the pepper fresh and as finely as possible; a spice grinder or a coffee grinder works best.

Recipe adapted from Washington's manuscript by Jill Paradiso.

Yield: serves 4 to 6

1 lemon

1.5- to 2-pound venison roast

1 tablespoon sea salt

1 ounce freshly ground black peppercorns

4 tablespoons clarified butter or ghee

1. Peel the lemon using a vegetable peeler, taking care to remove only the zest and not the bitter white pith. Juice the lemon and refrigerate the juice.

2. Use a paring knife to pierce the venison roast all over, leaving about an inch between cuts. Insert a piece of lemon peel into each hole. Cover and refrigerate at least 6 hours, or overnight—the longer the better.

3. Remove the venison roast from the refrigerator and allow it to come to room temperature, between 1 to 2 hours, depending on size of roast. This will ensure more even cooking.

4. Preheat oven to 325 degrees. Remove all the lemon peel from the venison. Mix together salt and pepper and coat the top of venison completely.

5. Heat a cast-iron skillet or heavy-bottomed fry pan over medium-high heat for 5 minutes. Add 2 tablespoons of clarified butter to the pan and put in venison, crust side down. Cook 3 minutes. Add the last 2 tablespoons of butter to the pan and flip the venison over, so the crust side is up. Tilt pan to one side and spoon butter repeatedly over top of the venison for about 10 seconds. Return the pan to level position and continue cooking for another 3 minutes. Sear the remaining sides of the venison 1 minute each. Turn off the flame, and pour off the pan juices and butter and reserve for sauce.

6. Place skillet in the oven and cook 4 to 6 minutes or until desired internal temperature is reached: 130 degrees for rare, 140 for medium-rare. Cooking times will vary depending upon size of roast.

7. Remove the venison from the oven and transfer to a cutting board. Allow to rest 10 minutes. While the venison is resting, prepare the sauce by adding the lemon juice to a pan with the butter and venison juices. Cook over low heat until just simmering, taking care not to reduce the sauce too much. It's finished when the sauce is thick enough to just coat the back of a spoon.

8. Cut the venison into ¼-inch slices and serve with lemon sauce.

This pepper-heavy treatment of venison was recommended in cookbooks throughout the nineteenth century to offset the strong, gamey flavor of the meat. It became known as Steak a la Diane, named after the Roman goddess of the hunt. As the dish evolved, noisettes, or small, round cuts of meat, were dressed in a rich, black pepper sauce called sauce poivrade. By the twentieth century, the venison was replaced with beef, and renamed steak au poivre. The pepper-covered steak became all the rage when Julia Child published her recipe in the 1960s. Child used filet mignon pressed in crushed black, green, and white peppercorns. She recommended that home cooks set the meat aside for an hour "so the flavor of the pepper will penetrate the meat." Today when I crust a steak in salt and cracked peppercorns, I think about how it's a cooking technique that has descended from medieval methods of meat preservation.

It was the combination of availability and biological preference that first made black pepper an important part of American cooking. But how Americans have used this spice has changed over time. If I purchased pepper in the time of the Crowninshields, I would have always bought whole peppercorns and then cracked them at home in a spice mill, with a mortar and pestle, or even with a rolling pin. For most of the nineteenth century, consumers avoided purchasing pre-ground pepper because it was easy to adulterate. It could be mixed with cheap substances to increase weight and, therefore, the supplier's profit. The least insidious of these methods was the addition of the ground husks from white pepper production. A lower-grade concoction was made from mixing in "pepper dust," which were the sweepings from the floor of a pepper warehouse. Sometimes, the mix-in wouldn't be pepper at all but ground olive pits, fruit stones, or simply burnt toast crumbs.

Additionally, when black pepper is pre-ground, its aromatic compounds evaporate over time, leaving behind only the spicy piperine. The pre-ground spice was hot, but not flavorful.

To alleviate some of the drudgery of pepper grinding, dedicated home pepper grinders appeared in the marketplace in the nineteenth century: in 1874 Peugeot (today better known for making cars) produced the first modern pepper grinder. A short, ceramic tube fed peppercorns into a small rotary mill; a top nut could be turned one way for a course grind, the other for a fine grind. But despite pepper mills like Peugeot's, by the end of the nineteenth century, many home cooks began to choose boxes of ground pepper. McCormick & Company, established in 1889, reassured consumers that its Bee Brand black pepper was "absolutely pure." Fannie Farmer's 1896 *Boston Cooking-School Cookbook*—the defining cookbook of American food at the turn of the twentieth century, which sold 360,000 copies between 1895 and 1914—called for ground pepper frequently. It is difficult to find a savory recipe in her book that *doesn't* use ground pepper, a clear sign of how ubiquitous black pepper had become. By the mid-twentieth century, Julia Child's steak au poivre would have been unique in calling for whole, cracked peppercorns.

That changed in 1993, when a new cable channel encouraged Americans to rethink how they used pepper. The Food Network allowed every American with a cable box to cook along with some of the country's greatest chefs and food personalities like Mario Batali, Emeril Lagasse, Rachael Ray, and Ina Garten. Although black pepper wasn't a new ingredient, the way the cooks of the Food Network used it was different. Kitchens on the Food Network almost always included a pepper mill, which the cooks used to grind fresh pepper over everything. These chefs assured us that everyone had the ability to make flavorful food from the freshest, finest ingredients—and only fresh cracked pepper would do.

Pepper mills began appearing in home kitchens, as cooking enthusiasts replicated what they saw on TV; they finished pasta, salads, and steaks with a few twists of fresh cracked pepper. Soon fresh ground pepper became synonymous with quality and became the standard of even midpriced restaurants. Spice companies like McCormick responded to the growing demand by introducing disposable plastic pepper grinders, which rapidly replaced the traditional pepper shakers both in restaurants and at home.

In the two decades since the Food Network was launched, black pepper consumption has increased by 40 percent in America. And in the twenty-first century, we're buying it whole and grinding it fresh, just like Martha Washington and the Crowninshields did.

Another aspect of how Americans use black pepper today recalls its Colonial past: the tradition of using black pepper as a sweet, instead of savory, spice—like Martha Washington's pepper cakes—has made a comeback. In recent years, I've sampled black and white pepper gelato and black pepper chocolate chip cookies. The Dutch, chef Andrew Carmellini's restaurant in New York City, formerly featured a Devil's Food Cake with Boiled Black Pepper Icing created by pastry chef Kierin Baldwin. Fresh ground black pepper was whipped into a meringue frosting at the last minute and used to top a rich chocolate layer cake. The top was then brûléed with a tiny kitchen torch until it tasted like crisp, fire-toasted marshmallows. Food columnist Melissa Clark published a riff on this recipe in the *New York Times* in 2014, adding fresh ground black pepper and vanilla seeds to a meringue and butter frosting, before spreading it between a six-layer chocolate cake.

Along with the desire for uniquely flavored recipes, contemporary cooks have become curious about where their food comes from—in a sense, like Americans after the Revolution. Two years after I first visited the Tropical Pavilion at the Brooklyn Botanic Garden, I launched an "edible" tour of plants there. Dozens of home cooks, professional chefs, and families found refuge from the winter chill in the Pavilion's eternal summer, and followed me around the greenhouse as I revealed the exotic origins of pantry staples. We crowded around the black pepper vine, and I pointed out its blossoms and berries, and shared the story of how black pepper came to be an American flavor. A spice as "ordinary" as pepper is actually extraordinary: a tropical berry from a half world away sits in every American's kitchen, the result of trade routes established by enterprising American merchants two centuries ago.

Red Wine Chocolate Cake with Black Pepper Ganache

I challenged cake historian Jessica Reed, of the blog Cakewalk, to come up with her own take on the chocolate-cake-meets-pepper trend. She presented this rich chocolate cake with a touch of red wine; the bittersweet chocolate ganache is made with cream infused with black peppercorns. The flavor of the ganache can be tweaked to suit your own tastes by adjusting the amount of time the peppercorns soak.

Yield: serves 6 to 8

For the cake:
1 cup all-purpose flour
$^1\!/_2$ cup plus 1 teaspoon Dutch-processed cocoa powder
1 teaspoon baking powder
$^1\!/_4$ teaspoon salt
$^3\!/_4$ cup red wine (I like to use Cabernet Sauvignon or Malbec, but any heavier red wine will work)
$^1\!/_2$ teaspoon vanilla
$^1\!/_2$ cup (1 stick) unsalted butter
1 $^1\!/_4$ cups dark brown sugar
2 large eggs

For the ganache (recipe below):

4 ounces heavy cream

2 teaspoons freshly ground black pepper

4 ounces bittersweet chocolate, chopped

1. Preheat oven to 350 degrees. Liberally grease the bottom of a 9-inch round cake pan.

2. Sift together all the dry ingredients and set aside. It's especially important to sift in order to break up any lumps of cocoa.

3. Combine wine and vanilla.

4. In the bowl of a stand mixer fitted with the paddle attachment, cream the butter and sugar on medium-high speed until fluffy, about 3 to 4 minutes. Add the eggs, one at a time, beating in each for about 1 minute. Don't forget to stop to scrape down the sides of the bowl!

5. On low speed, mix in the dry and wet ingredients in three parts, beginning and ending with the dry. Stop the mixer when most of the flour has disappeared. Using a silicone spatula, finish folding the batter by hand until all of the flour is incorporated.

6. Spoon the batter into the prepared pan, smooth the top with a spatula, and put in the oven. Bake for 30 minutes or until a tester comes out clean. Let cool in the pan for 5 minutes before removing to a rack to cool completely.

To make the ganache:

1. Pour the cream into a small saucepan set on the stove top. Whisk in the pepper and heat on medium until bubbles start forming around the edge. Make sure to whisk frequently while waiting.

2. Once you see bubbles, remove the pan from the heat and let the mixture steep for 15 to 20 minutes. (The longer it steeps, the stronger the flavor.) Strain out the pepper.

3. Once the cake is cool, put the chopped chocolate in a medium-sized bowl. Reheat the cream to a simmer and then pour over the chocolate. Let it sit for 5 minutes and then stir until you have a glossy, beautiful ganache. Spread over the cake, letting it ooze down the sides if you wish.

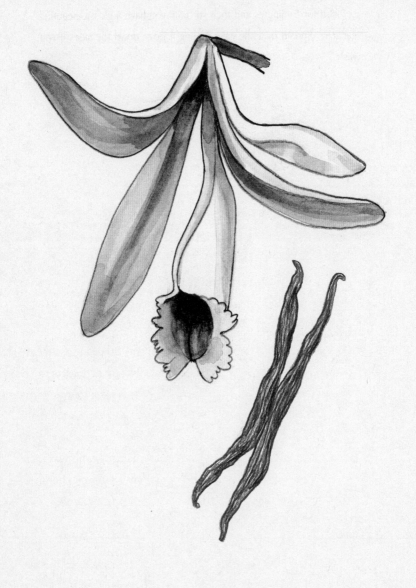

Vanilla

Two

Vanilla

WHEN I LIVED in the nineteenth century—back in my other life as an employee at a living history museum—we always had black peppercorns on hand to throw into a soup or to season a roast. Black pepper was plentiful in that century. Vanilla was not. Until the 1840s, vanilla was incredibly expensive: wanted by all, but only the elite could afford it. To make vanilla available to every American, it first took a genius botanist—who was then a twelve-year-old slave—and, later, the explorations of flavor chemists. America had to wait for science to catch up with our craving; now it's an addiction we can never break.

I wanted to see a vanilla plant in person like I had the pepper vine. Vanilla beans are the fruit of an orchid native to Central America, and the plant is still grown in its ancestral home. In July 2013 I flew to Mexico City and hopped into a rental car to drive five hours east, to the coastal state of Veracruz. I was traveling with my husband at the time, and although we are now divorced, this adventure would not have been possible without him.

We were headed to a part of Mexico where Americans don't normally go. When we stopped for lunch, pulling off a main road exactly in the middle of nowhere, we approached the elderly proprietress of a tiny cinder-block restaurant. She was agog the moment we opened our mouths and gave ourselves away for what we were—*"My God, Americans! I have not seen an American in five years!"*

She insisted we try her "Especial Americano": steak, French fries, and *nopalitos*—slivers of grilled cactus—cooked over a wood fire. The portion was ample, which is one of the reasons I think it was "Americano." We ate our meal on a red-checkered tablecloth at a picnic table looking out at the town. It was one thoroughfare, about a half-dozen concrete buildings on either side. To our left, children of various ages stared thoughtfully at a truck with a flat tire. Nearby, a rooster scratched and pecked at the shrubbery. Across the street, a lamb was tied to a bush. It was wearing a yellow cardigan made of what I could only assume was its own wool.

Being so far from anything familiar, while trying to comprehend a language I could barely speak, was overwhelming. I was glad to have my husband on my team. And I was also relieved that he volunteered to drive. When we passed into vanilla country, our car careened around mountainous switchbacks so severe that the GPS route looked as bunched and twisty as a small intestine. Only then did it occur to me that perhaps this journey was ill advised. We continued down roads that lacked guardrails; roads that dropped down sheer cliffs to rapids far below; roads washed out by waterfalls; and roads narrowed by the jungle, which pressed in on the boundaries of the two asphalt lanes. The jungle chipped away at the edges of civilization here: air plants crept out over telephone wires, where nest-weaving birds hung their teardrop-shaped homes.

As we turned a bend, I glimpsed a vine dangling down from the trees. I immediately recognized the bright green, spear-shaped leaves, climbing like a ladder up its stem. It was a vanilla orchid. After traveling so many hazardous miles to find it, it took my breath away.

Vanilla is a very, very old plant. There are at least 110 members of the orchid genus *Vanilloidae* native to four continents, indicating that the plant evolved before the continents divided. Only the twenty species native to Central America produce large, fragrant fruits that can be used to flavor food. Only two species are commercially cultivated: *Vanilla planifolia*, which is now grown all over the planet; and *Vanilla tahitensis*, a hybrid of two other vanilla species, which was exported from Central America to Tahiti in the mid-nineteenth century. A third, *Vanilla pompona*, a fat vanilla bean grown in Mexico, might come to market one day soon. These three species are hearty, vigorous growers and do well in cultivation. Each tastes dramatically different: *planifolia* has the classic vanilla flavor, warm and woody with hints of fruit or spice, depending on the plant's terroir—the environmental factors where the plant is grown. *Tahitensis* is extremely floral, with notes of honey and hay. *Pompona* has a pleasant butterscotch flavor. The other seventeen species of edible vanilla are largely unexplored, each with its own unique flavor.

When I saw that vanilla vine dangling over the road, I wondered who thought to pick the first vanilla bean. They must have followed the gentle scent to discover a withered vanilla fruit, dried and black from the sun. Whoever that first vanilla forager was, they existed before modern memory. In pre-Columbian America, the Mayas were the first to intentionally grow vanilla. A Mesoamerican civilization, the Mayan Empire peaked between AD 250 and AD 900, and the land they controlled covered the Yucatan Peninsula and stretched south through the Guatemalan highlands to the Pacific Coast. They collected wild vanilla vines from lush jungles and transported them to the arid Yucatan. The vines were planted in cenotes, or sinkholes where the limestone had collapsed to reveal underground rivers. Cenotes tend to be humid, tropical microclimates in the otherwise dry Yucatan. The Mayas took advantage of these unique conditions and planted luxury gardens, cultivating cacao trees alongside vanilla vines.

The Mayas used vanilla to flavor their favorite drink of hot chocolate. Though many think of vanilla and chocolate as opposites, these flavors rose to popularity in tandem.

The Aztecs, another Mesoamerican people, also loved to drink chocolate spiked with vanilla—preferably cold. The Aztecs came into power in central Mexico five hundred years later, in the fifteenth century; their capital city of Tenochtitlán is now buried beneath Mexico City. The Aztec's conquered territories stretched from coast-to-coast. It was this civilization that produced the first written account of the use of vanilla. Two Aztec students described it in a 1552 herbal tome, written in their native language of Nahuatl. They gave instructions for a mixture of herbs to be worn in a talisman around the neck, to protect a traveler. The accompanying illustration depicts the most important ingredient, *tlilxochitl*, a vine with pale yellow flowers and black seedpods. It's the first known depiction of vanilla, its tendrils stretching across time.

The Aztecs required tributes from all their conquered lands, and vanilla was the price the nearby Totonac people paid. The Totonacs' historical home was located in what we now know as northern Veracruz—where I went on my vanilla pilgrimage. At the time, the Totonacs did not use vanilla in their own culture, but they became the Aztecs' suppliers because they were the region geographically closest to Tenochtitlán where wild vanilla grew. The region has remained the heart of Mexico's vanilla production ever since.

The Spanish arrived in Mesoamerica in 1520 and conquered, then colonized, the Totonac and Aztec homelands. The conquistadores became partial to the local chocolate drink. Along with chocolate, vanilla was carried home to Europe. Chocolate was the first caffeinated beverage Europeans had ever tried; its introduction predated tea and coffee. It became wildly popular by the end of the seventeenth century.

To meet demand, in about 1750, Totonacs started planting vanilla farms. The Totonacs took cuttings from forest plants, planted them in neat rows, and trained them up posts. Plantations proliferated by 1760, and they produced larger, healthier fruit than their wild sisters did. The farmers would harvest the beans while they were still green and deliver them to a central curing house that would dry the fruit, another innovation that produced a higher quality product. By the end of the eighteenth century, Totonacs around the Gulf Coast produced about one million beans for export to Europe.

And then came ice cream.

In the mid-sixteenth century, European scientists figured out that adding salt to ice lowered the freezing temperature of water. Shortly after this discovery, chefs began to use the technique to freeze fruit drinks and flavored custards. A little anonymous pamphlet called *A New And Brief Way to Make with Ease Every Kind of Sorbet* was published in Naples, Italy, in the 1690s—and it's the earliest set of ice cream recipes known. It contained one recipe for "vanilla ice," the first for what would become the world's favorite ice cream flavor. But because the Spanish had a monopoly on the sale of vanilla beans, the beans were rare and expensive. In the eighteenth century, Europeans were far more likely to chow down on more common flavors such as violet, orange, or rye bread ice cream than vanilla.

But vanilla ice cream made an impression on Thomas Jefferson, the American minister to France in the 1780s. I've got a soft spot for Jefferson. Like all of the Founding Fathers, he was a complex human being whom I both love and hate in hindsight. Jefferson was a fierce opponent of slavery, but he was also a slaveholder. He wrote some of the most beautiful, resonant text of our country's early government, such as the Declaration of Independence, when he was my age, thirty-three. He was a strong believer in the importance of the separation of church and state. He was possessed with curiosity about the world around him, and wrote to one of his daughters: "Determine never to be idle. No person will have occasion to complain of the want of time who never loses any. It is wonderful how much may be done if we are always doing." Like me, he was always busy; but also like me, he was a migraine sufferer. When I'm bedridden with inconsolable pain and feeling sorry for myself, I think of Jefferson and everything he accomplished despite the malady we share. Because I know these details about his life, he is in my mind the most vivid of our Founding Fathers—and the most human.

And he loved ice cream.

After the death of his beloved wife, Martha, in 1782, Jefferson served as a representative of the new republic of America to France—perhaps he fled to France to escape his grief. He brought with him his slave and personal chef, James Hemings, brother to the more well-known Sally. While in France, James Hemings learned the French language and apprenticed under cooks, chefs, and a pastry chef before officially becoming Jefferson's *chef de cuisine.*

Jefferson laboriously transcribed detailed French recipes: *boeuf à la mode,* blancmange, and *nouilly à macaroni.* Between Hemings's training and these recipes, I think Jefferson hoped he could re-create the taste of cosmopolitan France when he returned to backwoods America. Each dish he selected would eventually become popular in American cooking, especially after he served them at the White House during his terms as president. But none of these recipes became more popular than his vanilla ice cream.

Written in Jefferson's hand on a long, thin strip of yellowing paper, the recipe is titled simply "Ice cream." The instructions that follow are thorough, accurate, and nearly identical to modern directions for a custard-based ice cream—what we now call "French vanilla":

2. bottles of good cream.
6. yolks of eggs.
1/2 lb. sugar

mix the yolks & sugar

put the cream on a fire in a casserole, first putting in a stick of Vanilla.

when near boiling take it off & pour it gently into the mixture of eggs & sugar.

stir it well.

put it on the fire again stirring it thoroughly with a spoon to prevent it's sticking to the casserole.

when near boiling take it off and strain it thro' a towel.

put it in the Sabottiere

then set it in ice an hour before it is to be served. put into the ice a handful of salt.

put salt on the coverlid of the Sabotiere & cover the whole with ice.

leave it still half a quarter of an hour.

then turn the Sabottiere in the ice 10 minutes

open it to loosen with a spatula the ice from the inner sides of the Sabotiere.

shut it & replace it in the ice

open it from time to time to detach the ice from the sides

when well taken (prise) stir it well with the Spatula.

put it in moulds, justling it well down on the knee.

then put the mould into the same bucket of ice.

leave it there to the moment of serving it.

to withdraw it, immerse the mould in warm water, turning it well till it will come out & turn it into a plate.

When Jefferson returned from France, he didn't bring back just the ice cream recipe but also the chef who gave it to him. The recipe has been credited to Adrien Petit, Jefferson's maître d'hôtel while he was in residence in Paris. In this role, Petit managed staff, purchased provisions, and oversaw the presentation of dessert. Jefferson convinced Petit to return with him to the States in 1791. He also bought the equipment necessary to make ice cream: a *sabotiere* (two nesting tin pails lined with ice to freeze the ice cream) and two molds to shape the hardening cream. But Jefferson's best-laid plans for churning vanilla ice cream stateside were soon foiled. In a letter from Philadelphia to an acquaintance in France in 1791, Jefferson writes: "Petit informs me he has been all over the town in quest of Vanilla, and it is unknown here. I must pray you to send me a packet of 50. pods (batons) which may come very well in the middle of a packet of newspapers. It costs about 24s. a baton when sold by the single baton."

Jefferson eventually received his vanilla beans, because ice cream appeared on his dinner table during his term as president several years later. His vanilla beans would have come from Mexico, traveled first to Spain, and then to France, and then finally to America. In 1802 one dinner guest, Manesseh Cutler, a clergyman and congressman from Massachusetts, described his night at the presidential dinner table as "inelegant," despite the fact that he was served two dishes that would become American classics. One, "a pie called macaroni," is one of the earliest mentions of macaroni and cheese, another dish that Jefferson recorded in his recipe collection. Cutler says it "appeared to be a rich crust filled with the strillions of onions, or shallots, which I took it to be, tasted very strong, and not agreeable." Whatever, dude.

Another dish impressed him more: "Ice cream, very good, crust wholly dried, crumbled into thin flakes, a dish somewhat like pudding—inside white as milk or curd, very porous and light, covered with cream sauce— very fine." Later descriptions of this dessert at Jefferson's table describe the ice cream served inside a pastry shell, which might be the "crust" Cutler mentioned.

Jefferson's French Vanilla Ice Cream

I've updated Jefferson's recipe for the modern kitchen and I have made it many times since. Rich and satisfying, it's my go-to for a basic recipe and infinitely adaptable for other flavors and mix-ins, like the Garam Masala Ice Cream on page 116.

Yield: makes approximately 1 quart

1 vanilla bean
2 cups heavy whipping cream
1 cup whole milk
6 large egg yolks
3/4 cup sugar
1/4 teaspoon coarse salt

1. Hold the tip of the vanilla bean down with two fingers. Using a paring knife, split the bean along the seam. With the blunt edge of the knife, scrape out the vanilla seeds. Add the vanilla bean and seeds to cream and milk in a saucepan. Bring to a boil.

2. In a heat-proof bowl, whisk together the egg yolks, sugar, and salt until combined. After cream mixture comes to a boil, pour it *slowly* into the egg mixture, whisking constantly. Remove the vanilla bean.

3. Return to saucepan and cook over low heat, stirring constantly with a wooden spoon or spatula until the custard thickens and evenly coats back of spoon. (It should hold a line drawn by your finger.)

4. Place custard in refrigerator, until chilled—overnight is preferable. Churn in an ice-cream maker until it has "soft serve" consistency, 20 to 30 minutes. Transfer to a resealable plastic container and freeze until firm, at least 2 hours.

The president's dinner table set trends. By the time Mary Randolph, a relative of Jefferson's, wrote her influential cookbook, *The Virginia House-wife*, in 1824, it featured no less than twenty ice cream recipes—the first examples ever published in America. The book contained instructions for making vanilla ice cream as well as "cocoa nut," "oyster cream" (frozen from oyster soup), and "chocolate cream," which she recommended making with a stick of vanilla.

Jefferson and Randolph started a trend for ice cream in America that increased the demand for vanilla beans, but Spain maintained its monopoly on the trade. Vanilla cuttings were transported out of Mexico, through trade or clandestine operations, in an effort to cultivate the plant outside of Central America. By 1820, vines grew in greenhouses in Belgium and England, and were propagated outdoors in tropical climates. A plantation owner on an island in the Indian Ocean near Madagascar—Île de Bourbon, later called Réunion—managed to keep a vanilla vine alive for twenty years. But whenever the orchids bloomed, the flowers dried up and died after only a day. Only on extremely rare occasions did they mature into vanilla pods.

Why did vanilla vines outside of Mexico fail to produce fruit? I was on my way to find out as my car careened around those mountain roads in Mexico. My ultimate destination was a vanilla plantation in the same region the Totonacs had farmed for hundreds of years. There I would finally learn how vanilla was cultivated—and the problem it presented for farmers in the nineteenth century.

The Gaya Vanilla Plantation, outside of Papantla, Veracruz, is the largest vanilla farm in the Totonacapan area (the region is named after the Totonac people, who still live there). The Gaya plantation was founded in 1873 by an Italian immigrant with a knack for fussy agriculture: he had raised silkworms back home. The plantation is now run by the family's fourth generation.

When I arrived, I explained to a group of perplexed workers, in broken Spanish, that I had indeed come all the way from New York City for a meeting. Norma Gaya, great-granddaughter of the plantation's founder, swept out of an office building. She navigated her plantation in a studded tank top, white pants, and wedge heels without breaking a sweat. I, on the other hand, tracked black mud through her office, was covered in weeping mosquito bites, and could not stop the sweat from fire-hosing off my forehead. I apologized for being a general mess. "It's plantation life!" she said merrily.

Cultivating vanilla is an intricate and laborious process from start to finish. That's the reason it's the second most expensive spice in the world, right after saffron. Accompanied by her floppity-eared basset hound, Scooby, Norma took me around the plantation to show me why it's so costly.

On the plantation, the chartreuse-green vanilla vines were given wood posts to ascend, but they didn't discriminate: they climbed anything that got near them. They liked life shady, wet, and hot, and the Gayas used individual greenhouses to test different combinations of the three conditions. They also worked with local and international universities to examine the effects of fertilizers, water, and air pollution on the health of the plants. From the time the vanilla vines are planted, it takes two years to bear fruit if they're in a greenhouse, or four if they're outdoors.

All the vanilla orchids bloom in the month of March, with pale yellow, white, or green blossoms that smell faintly spicy, like cinnamon. The flowers only last a few hours, opening in the morning and shriveling by noon. Although vanilla orchids contain both male parts (the anther, which creates pollen) and female parts (the stigma, which receives pollen), these organs are separated by a thin membrane that seems to prevent the plant from self-pollinating. Botanists believe the plant is pollinated by native animals but are uncertain which ones. For many years, a tiny insect known as the Melipona bee was thought to be the flower's pollinator. But recent research—performed by a team of graduate students who sat on platforms in the jungle canopy to watch wild vanilla orchids bloom—saw many different types of bees, ants, hummingbirds and bats visit the flowers. But none of them showed signs of pollinating. In all likelihood, it might be several of these visitors that guarantee the plant's fertilization.

In the nineteenth century, when the plant was taken outside of Mexico, it lacked the native pollinators necessary for natural fertilization. It was a Belgian botanist named Charles Morren, working with a greenhouse specimen, who first made this link in 1839. He noted "the absence of the species of insect which nature has doubtless given to the climate of Mexico to effect in this latter region a fecundation." To fertilize a vanilla plant, he wrote, you needed to do it by hand: "It is thus necessary to raise the velamen or to cut it when the plant is to be fecundated, and to place in direct contact the pollen and the stigmatic surface." He went on to note: "The fecundation never fails."

If you're confused by Morren's instructions, don't worry, you're not the only one. The single line he wrote about this extremely delicate process baffled botanists around the world. When they attempted to follow his instructions, they had spotty results at best. It's actually not Morren's method that's used to hand pollinate vanilla today. We use the method of the unlikely hero of nineteenth-century botany, Edmond Albius.

Edmond was born in about 1829, a slave on Île de Bourbon. His mother, Mélise, died in childbirth, and he never met his father, Pamphile, who passed away when Edmond was nineteen. When he was old enough, Edmond was sent by his mistress to work at the estate of her brother, Ferréol Bellier-Beaumont, who was known around the island for his skills in botany and horticulture. Bellier-Beaumont was the plantation owner who had kept a vanilla vine growing on his property for twenty years.

Somebody recognized that Edmond was bright, although it is unclear whether it was his former mistress or his new master. Bellier-Beaumont soon invited Edmond to accompany him on his rounds of his plantation. Of Edmond, he wrote, "[T]his young black boy became my constant companion." It was said he instilled a passion for botany in Edmond.

Edmond spent hours studying the botanical samples on the plantation. One day, or over the course of several days, Edmond tinkered with the vanilla blossoms that would not pollinate. They had become a source of concern for his master. Perhaps he sought out this challenge on his own; perhaps he was tasked with it. We'll probably never know. What we do know is that, in the rising heat of a Réunion morning in 1841, Edmond developed the technique to pollinate vanilla that is still used today: he used a thin stick, a bit larger than a toothpick, to split the tubelike side of the flower, exposing the anther sac and the stigma, as well as the thin membrane that separated them. He lifted the membrane up and back, both exposing the stigma and causing the anther sac to shift upward. The anther sac touched the stigma, but just to make sure they connected, Edmond smushed them together with his thumb and forefinger.

The procedure of smashing together the male and female parts of the orchid is known today as "the marriage." If the marriage is successful, the thick green base of the flower swells almost immediately. The swollen base matures into a green fingerlike seedpod—a fruit—that ripens yellow and eventually splits at the end. It would be ready to harvest nine months later, much like a human baby. The entire process is filled with all sorts of bizarre sexual imagery that gives you the heebie-jeebies because it reminds you that your parents had to have sex at least once. Maybe it's just me.

Bellier-Beaumont was strolling through his plantation with Edmond one day when he noticed with astonishment two vanilla pods ripening on the vine. Edmond piped up and said he did it. I bet the boy was proud; perhaps Bellier-Beaumont was, too. Edmond, only twelve years old, would change the world's vanilla industry forever.

Rather than keep Edmond's hand pollination method secret, Bellier-Beaumont invited the heads of other local plantations over for a demonstration. Bellier-Beaumont made no attempt to claim the idea as his own. Edmond was celebrated in his time for his discovery: one source praised him as "ingenious." His technique spread all over the island, and then to the neighboring islands of the Seychelles and Madagascar. The vanilla beans that grow in this region, thanks to Edmond's efforts, are often called Bourbon vanilla—named after the Île de Bourbon.

An 1847 daguerreotype—the earliest commercial photographic process—shows Edmond at eighteen, snappily if simply dressed in light,

Edmond Albius

tight-fitting trousers and a boxy, slightly darker coat. He stares into the camera wide eyed, looking more lanky teen than revolutionary botanist. Shortly after this photo was taken, Edmond would be freed. All slaves in the colony were emancipated at the end of 1848, but Bellier-Beaumont granted Edmond his freedom six months earlier. Edmond—who soon after took or was given the last name Albius—moved from the isolated plantation to the city of Saint-Denis, but life in the racially charged atmosphere of post-emancipation Réunion proved difficult. He desperately looked for work, with little success. Albius, after all, lacked a formal education—and it seemed that Bellier-Beaumont's tutelage accounted for nothing in the minds of potential employers. Eventually Albius took a job doing manual labor, the only sort of work deemed fit for a former slave. Imagine how frustrated Albius must have been, and his situation would only get worse. Albius was involved in a robbery, the details of which have been lost to history, but it seemed that he was either desperate for money or naïve enough to be taken advantage of. He served more than two years' hard labor before petitions from his old master secured his release.

Bellier-Beaumont actively championed for Albius, and did all he could to ensure that Albius would be recognized as the father of the vanilla industry in Réunion—which became the island's major cash crop within Albius's lifetime. Bellier-Beaumont wrote impassioned letters to guarantee that Albius was included in the seminal historical encyclopedia *L'Album de l'Île de la Réunion*. He defended Albius's honor as the original inventor of the hand pollination method when his credibility was doubted: some claimed that Edmond had previous knowledge of Morren's workings in Belgium, while Bellier-Beaumont maintained that Albius came to his realization independently.

There was talk that wealthy planters, rich from the now-abundant vanilla crop, would provide a yearly salary for Albius. It never came to pass. After prison, for lack of other opportunities, he lived the rest of his life by Bellier-Beaumont's charity, on a plot of land on his plantation. I wonder if Bellier-Beaumont thought that Albius would use it to grow food or to continue his botanical work. But the hand pollination method was Albius's first and last known accomplishment. Edmond Albius died on August 26, 1880, at the age of fifty-one; his obituary read: "It was a destitute and miserable end."

Albius's miserable end seems sadly common among freed slaves, particularly those who were gifted. When James Hemings worked in France for Jefferson, he was considered a free man by French law and therefore earned wages. He hesitated to return to America, when he could stay in Europe and stay free. He agreed to return and train a successor as a French cook at Monticello, Jefferson's plantation in Charlottesville, Virginia, on the condition that Jefferson would free him—and he did, in 1796, when Hemings was thirty-one. It seems that after he left Jefferson, Hemings had trouble building a life for himself. When Jefferson was elected president in 1801, Hemings was working as a tavern cook in Baltimore—despite being a highly trained French chef. Jefferson asked him, through a friend, to come work as *chef de cuisine* in the White House. Hemings at first refused, feeling it was "more of a summons than an invitation." Jefferson almost immediately hired another cook, without making an effort to contact Hemings personally. A few months later, it seems they came to a peace: Hemings was running the kitchens at Monticello over Jefferson's summer break, and received a salary. He left the position in September, and less than a month later, Hemings was dead. According to a letter from a William Evans to Jefferson, Hemings had been drinking heavily leading up to his death, and had committed suicide. Hemings was only thirty-six. Jefferson called it a "tragical end."

It is important to remember Hemings and Albius, both for their achievements and the indignities they suffered, especially when so many other black Americans' stories are forgotten. Albius's discovery changed the economics of his home island and would change the flavor of American food—yet today, every American knows vanilla, but few have heard of Albius.

The technique that he developed spread over the islands so quickly that by the 1860s, the French colonies surpassed Mexico in vanilla production. When the technique skipped over the ocean, back to vanilla's homeland, it increased production in Veracruz fivefold. Mexican vanilla was imported largely to America, while the French islands served Europe. With increased availability, prices dropped; more Americans began experimenting with the flavor in new ways. They replaced rose water with vanilla in baked goods. Rose water, in fact, soon became considered old-fashioned.

Albius's technique for vanilla pollination is used on the Gaya plantation. It requires an army of seasonal employees, working seven days a week, to pollinate every flower on the plantation. Each blossom is too valuable to go to waste; each flower represents just one future vanilla bean.

Green vanilla beans have no scent; they must be cured to develop their flavor. The day of our meeting, Norma Gaya rolled open the doors of her plantation's enormous curing building and shooed her dog Scooby out. He wasn't allowed in this important structure. It is behind these walls that vanillin, the single most important chemical component of vanilla's flavor, is carefully developed.

After the beans are harvested, they are sorted: long, straight beans that are slightly underripe are prized for their appearance; these grade A beans will look the most beautiful once the curing process is done. They will end up with the best chefs and cost two for $12 at specialty food stores. Grades B and C beans look less pretty after curing. Beans that were very ripe when they were harvested are split at the end and are sorted into grade B, while grade C beans are short or broken. The latter two grades are simply labeled "*zocata*" on the Gaya plantation, meaning overripe, and are used for making vanilla extract.

The harvested vanilla beans are packed into cedar boxes, which are placed in a massive oven and covered in wet blankets. A steamy heat stops the maturation of the beans, a process developed by Norma's great-grandfather. When the harvested vanilla beans are exposed to heat, their cell walls break down, and hydrolysis occurs, allowing chemicals from all over the vanilla bean to move around, meet up, and react. Most important, glucovanillin, stored in the green bean's center, is diffused and comes into contact with enzymes stored in the vanilla bean's outer regions. When these chemicals come together, they create vanillin.

After heating, the beans are transferred to another set of boxes wrapped in blankets and "sweat" for a day. Then the beans are spread on woven mats and laid out on Gaya's massive cement patio to dry in the sun for three to five months.

"Our secret ingredient is the sun," Norma told me, pointing to the sky. "From November to March, sometimes it's cold or raining. If we have a lot of bad weather, we have to have more time for the curing." More flavor chemicals develop as a result of oxidation. The beans are turned over constantly to prevent moisture from causing rot or fungus growth. Eventually the vanilla beans shrivel into black-brown sheaths, glistening with oil, and are extremely odorous. "The aroma is around everywhere," Norma said. "Everywhere. The cars most of the time stop, to see what is that smelling."

When the curing process is complete, a single vanilla bean contains 1 to 3 percent vanillin and about 30 percent water, as well as about 250 additional chemicals, including sugars, volatile compounds, and essential oils. When the Gayas' beans finish curing, they go to a lab to test the vanillin content before they can be exported. Beans must contain a minimum of 2 percent vanillin to be sold.

Here's one of the biggest secrets I'm going to divulge in this book: the grade B, or zocata, beans are more desirable to the consumer. The grade A beans look pretty: long, straight, and plump. But they contain more water, which is not the key to its flavor. Grade B beans tend to be drier, but since they are often riper when they were picked, they are higher in vanillin. Both of these qualities make them more desirable for cooking and baking. And because they are not as attractive looking, they are cheap. You can usually hunt them down online and buy 10 to 15 grade B beans for $8 to $10.

Norma showed me a real treasure in her office: a box of beans that were missed during harvesting, which ripened and cured on the vine for three months. They were discovered during the next season's pollinating. When she lifted the lid, the smell of vanilla enveloped me. It was so strong, it was easy to imagine the discovery of the first wild vanilla vine; the smell would have called out to passersby until someone stopped to pluck the source. These beans, frosted in crystallized vanillin, were the ultimate vanilla bean. They should be idolized as incredible culinary ingredients, but they're mostly unknown, if not ignored.

Norma shrugged and said she couldn't understand why chefs wouldn't want the *zocata* beans. The Gayas cure them with the rest of their beans and use them to make their extracts, as well as an incredible vanilla liqueur called Xanath, the Totonac word for vanilla. Norma served it to me in glasses set on a silver tray, mixed with sweetened condensed milk over ice. Scooby ran circles around our feet as we stood at the top of the plantation and looked out over the low mountains covered in thick, green jungle where vanilla has been grown for thousands of years. After, I felt a little tipsy and took a nap as soon as I got back to the hotel.

Vanilla Liqueur

Xanath liqueur is not available in the United States, and may never be, so I figured out my own recipe. I've since mixed this vanilla liqueur with Coca-Cola or hot chocolate, poured it over ice cream, and used it as a mixer for rum. If you'd like to try it with sweetened condensed milk, I'd recommend mixing it half-and-half, poured over ice.

Yield: about 16 ounces of liqueur

1 cup water

1 cup white sugar

1 cup vanilla extract (35 to 40 percent alcohol)

1. Make a simple syrup by combining the water and sugar in a medium saucepan. Over high heat, bring to a boil without stirring. When all the sugar has dissolved, remove from heat. Allow to cool to room temperature.

2. Add vanilla extract and stir until mixed. Bottle (or store in a resealable plastic container, mason jar, etc.) and store in the refrigerator for one week to allow the flavor to mellow.

Jefferson wouldn't have been familiar with vanilla extract. It was developed after Albius mastered vanilla fertilization. As more vanilla was produced, extracts became a way to use the less salable short and broken beans. In 1847—the same year that Albius sat for his daguerreotype— Eliza Leslie suggested in *The Lady's Receipt-book: A Useful Companion for Large or Small Families* that home cooks flavor desserts with rose water "or else two table-spoonfuls of Oliver's extract of vanilla." Oliver's, like any brand of vanilla extract, had a major advantage over a vanilla bean: as a liquid extract, it could be used just like rose water. Whereas a vanilla bean needed to be infused, as when heated in cream to make custard ice cream, vanilla extract can be poured into anything for instant flavor, including cakes and cookies.

Though it wasn't always the case, today there are strict government standards for making vanilla extract. Vanilla extract must be made with 13.35 ounces of vanilla beans, with a water content of no more than 25 percent, for every gallon of liquid. The liquid is 35 to 40 percent alcohol and about 55 to 60 percent water. First, the beans are chopped, and then the alcohol is percolated through them like making coffee. The resulting vanilla extract is about 70 to 80 proof (or 35 to 40 percent alcohol) and is called "single fold." Double the beans to the same amount of liquid is called "double fold," which I love to use in my baking. Concentrations up to tenfold are available, but generally only in bulk for commercial applications.

The nature of vanilla changed again with the invention of artificial vanilla extract. Humanity's desire for vanilla cannot be met by the world's capacity to grow it: approximately 95 percent of the world's supply of vanillin is artificially produced. Although vanilla extract was cheaper than buying beans in the nineteenth century, it was still prohibitively expensive for many cooks. Flavor scientists wondered if vanillin, the primary chemical we recognize as vanilla flavor, could be harvested from other, cheaper sources.

The internet is filled with shocking blog posts that declare artificial vanilla is made from crude oil and beaver butts. I want to clear up that misconception. Artificial vanilla is vanillin; when crystallized, it is a white, glittery powder with the sweet scent of vanilla and an extremely bitter taste. Vanillin crystallizes on the outside of some vanilla beans, like the ones I saw in Norma's office. It's important to remember that vanillin is the same chemical, whether it's sourced from a vanilla bean or synthesized in a lab. Vanillin is a very simple compound, $C_8H_8O_3$ (a chemical bond of carbon, hydrogen, and oxygen), which means it's easy to find similar compounds in nature. Vanillin was first synthesized in 1874 from eugenol, a chemical found in cloves. The formula for eugenol is $C_{10}H_{12}O_2$, so to become vanillin, all it had to do was lose 2 carbon atoms, 4 hydrogen, and gain 1 oxygen—which it does by first being exposed to an alkaline solution and then being oxidized. For most of the twentieth century, vanillin was synthesized from lignin, $C_9H_{10}O_2$, which is found in wood. If you've ever tasted vanilla notes in an aged whiskey, that's vanillin. It's water soluble, so it seeps from the wood barrels over time. Additionally, the pages of old books often smell like vanillin, from oxidizing lignin. And probably most strangely, male beavers will smell of vanilla because they spend their days consuming trees. The beavers mark their territory using musk glands on their butts, which are milked for their vanilla-scented castoreum, traditionally used in the fragrance industry. Castoreum was also at one time used as a "natural flavoring" in foods, but little, if any, is used in comestibles today.

Today vanillin is synthesized most commonly from guaiacol, $C_7H_8O_2$, a chemical that naturally occurs in many places, including the tummies of locusts, wood smoke, and some by-products of crude oil production. And regardless of where the original compound comes from, the atoms don't remember their history—the synthesized vanillin has no relation to its source.

There are pros and cons to imitation vanilla extract. A major plus: it's significantly cheaper to produce compared with the laborious growing and curing process of a vanilla bean. If I used one teaspoon of vanilla a week in my kitchen, I'd spend $30 more per year if I used natural vanilla extract as opposed to imitation. However, many cooks feel that imitation vanilla lacks complexity. Although vanillin is the primary flavor component of a vanilla bean, it makes up only about a third of our sensory experience. As I've noted, a vanilla bean has hundreds of other chemicals, including twenty-six important odor constituents.

But I believe there is a time and place to use every version of vanilla in your kitchen: bean, natural extract, and imitation extract. I was first introduced to the potential of imitation vanilla extract in *Cook's Country* magazine, beloved for its thorough taste tests of everyday ingredients. They tested natural vanilla extracts against imitation extracts in blind taste tests, adding them to puddings, cakes, and cookies. Each of these three vanilla-heavy dishes cook at different temperatures: low, medium, and high heats, respectively. Although cakes and cookies bake at the same temperature, around 350 degrees, cakes reach internal temperatures of only around 210 degrees. But cookies, which are small and thin, will exceed temperatures of 280 to 300 degrees. At high heats, all the hundreds of wonderful flavor chemicals of natural vanilla burn off. The result is that your vanilla sugar cookies, baked with natural vanilla extract, end up virtually tasteless. But imitation vanilla, which contains pure vanillin, delivers a much more potent dose of flavor that survives the oven's heat. While real vanilla extract won the low-heat competition for pudding, it tied with an imitation extract for cakes, and lost the cookie battle.

Skeptical? Well, I decided to do an informal taste test of my own. A year before I set foot on Norma's plantation, I gave a lecture on artificial and natural flavors. There were more than a hundred people in attendance. I had baked two batches of snickerdoodle cookies, using identical ingredients except for the vanilla: one had high-quality, expensive, natural vanilla; the other, cheap-as-dirt imitation. The taste test was double-blind—the cookies were labeled so that neither the participants nor I knew which cookies were which when they were distributed. The crowd voted on their favorite.

The imitation vanilla cookies won 2 to 1.

As I announced the results, the audience gasped. This was Brooklyn, ground zero of farm-to-table, slow-food culture. I think the crowd was a little embarrassed they had picked the "unnatural" flavor. But the results started an active debate amongst the attendees. Some participants guessed that consuming artificial vanilla is so common in America, we have a nostalgic attachment to it. Others felt that Americans have always loved strong flavors, and the purity and intensity of the vanillin appealed to us.

I think the main reason we don't use imitation vanilla extract is simply a prejudice against the idea of "chemicals." The use of imitation extract has always been controversial: in 1906 a debate raged concerning whether synthetically derived flavors should be labeled differently than naturally derived flavors. An ice cream trade journal asked: "Do you think the American public could be educated sufficiently to understand all this? And if they cannot be educated up to this point, do you think it is essential to mention on the label something which they do not understand?"

These questions persisted well into the middle of the century. In the 1960s, the US government declared that artificial flavors had to be labeled—which meant that 85 percent of ice creams on the market had to change their labels. But recently, the idea of artificial versus natural has gotten complicated. Scientists are working on a bacterium that poops vanillin—they've created bacteria that poop all kinds of things, such as gold and gasoline. Much like yeast eats sugars and produces alcohol, a newly engineered strain of lactobacillus is given ferulic acid and converts it to vanillin. Although the technology is not yet a cost-effective way to produce vanillin, this bacterium is considered a "natural" source for vanilla. Even though the vanillin didn't come from a vanilla bean, it will be labeled as a natural flavoring on food packaging.

I keep three forms of vanilla on hand in my kitchen: natural extract, imitation extract, and whole vanilla beans. Much like the whole black peppercorns that Martha Washington would have ground by hand, vanilla beans have also experienced a revival—just as Jefferson would have used vanilla two hundred years ago. The trend can be traced back to the popularity of a seventeenth-century English dessert called "burnt cream," an egg custard flavored with a vanilla bean and then topped with a layer of burnt sugar. We know this dessert better by its French name: crème brûlée.

Crème brûlée doesn't work well with vanilla extract. The custard cooks at such a low temperature that it leaves behind the boozy bite of the natural extract or the bitter taste of imitation extract. It's very similar to the custard base of Jefferson's ice cream and needs the gentle infusion of a vanilla bean to deliver the best flavor.

When crème brûlée began to appear in New York's best French restaurants in the 1970s, chefs were pulling from their culinary training and using vanilla beans, not extract. The dessert became a smash hit in the city; in 1985 the *Times* wrote: "If there were a New York dessert of the year award, the 1985 ribbon would go to *crème brûlée*, or burnt cream, which has appeared on countless menus in both French and American restaurants. I am not sure how a dish that has been consumed for centuries in Europe without great fanfare . . . has suddenly achieved such fame in America, but it has."

At first, cooks and consumers thought the black specks of vanilla bean seeds marred the look of white desserts. But ever since the mid-1990s, the telltale dots of vanilla bean seeds have become synonymous with quality, and have cast their constellations through a myriad of high-end sweets. The dots are now so de rigueur that commercial operations will add spent vanilla bean seeds from extract companies to their products, even though there's no flavor left in them after the extraction process. It's purely cosmetic. Perhaps this is one of the reasons a flavor like vanilla has become such an integral part of American cuisine: it is continually rediscovered and reinterpreted.

But as with black pepper, humans also have a biological preference for vanilla. Humans and other primates can detect vanillin at extremely low levels, and our ability to smell the fragrance has been called "extraordinary," particularly considering that humans aren't the best sniffers. But most scents that we can detect at low levels are conversely unpleasant at high levels. That never happens with vanilla: humans find it as pleasant at high levels as we do at low. Why this exceptional preference exists, however, is unknown.

America is the world's largest importer of vanilla—the result of a combination of our biological preference, cultural history, but most importantly our buying power. Since we're a rich country, we can (and do) buy up more than half of the world's supply. Every American consumes about 5.4 grams of vanilla annually—a little over 2 vanilla beans every year. It doesn't seem like much per person, but it adds up to over 638 million beans consumed in the United States each year.

All that vanilla is produced in some of the poorest countries of the world to be consumed by some of the wealthiest. About 60 percent of the vanilla consumed in America today is grown in Madagascar; but despite the thriving vanilla economy, the country remains trapped in poverty. About 70 percent of the population lives on less than a dollar a day. Much like the Totonacs of centuries ago, Madagascar's vanilla farmers sell their produce to central curing houses. The "bean collectors," or middle men between the growers and the curing houses, offer a price well below market rate. With no standardized price set, growers have little option but to accept the price that is offered: the harvest will go bad within a week if the beans are not cured.

Today only about 10 percent of America's vanilla is currently produced in Mexico—compared with 80 percent in 1900. The Gayas want to restore vanilla growing to its native home of Mexico, and in so doing, increase opportunity in an impoverished part of the country. Four hundred local farmers work for the Gayas, growing beans on small plantations. They are paid a living wage and are given plants, organic products, and an agronomist to supervise the process at no cost. The farmers then give their beans to the Gayas' processing facility to have them cured; there's no middleman and no changing market price. If the grower had a bad season, the Gayas take the hit.

From Mexico to Madagascar and back again: to cook with vanilla has always been a privilege; to grow it, a struggle. I went to Mexico to uncover the secrets of vanilla; by the time I had left, I had gained an appreciation for this flavor. I now know that every bottle of vanilla is the result of many hands, starting with the ancient people who first cultivated it, to Albius who pollinated it, to the army of workers that bring it to my kitchen today. Once distinctly exotic, now comfortingly familiar, American cuisine would not be the same without it.

Warm Vanilla Cakes

The popularity of crème brûlée opened the floodgates for vanilla bean desserts by the late 1990s. With vanilla beans fashionable again, pastry chefs incorporated the flavor in new and exciting ways. This recipe for an intense vanilla cake with a soft, creamy center was adapted from one created by Bill Yosses in the early 2000s for the Citarella restaurant in Manhattan's Rockefeller Center. It was later published in the *New York Times*.

Yield: serves 10

7 tablespoons butter; more for baking dishes or ramekins
10 ounces top-quality white chocolate, divided into 7 ounces and 3 ounces

5 eggs at room temperature, yolks and whites separated

3 vanilla beans, split in half lengthwise and seeds scraped

$1/4$ cup plus 2 tablespoons all-purpose flour, sifted

Pinch cream of tartar

$1/4$ cup plus 2 tablespoons sugar

Vanilla ice cream

1. Preheat oven to 375 degrees. Melt butter and 7 ounces of white chocolate in a double boiler over near-boiling water. When the chocolate has melted, remove it from the heat and stir it until no lumps remain. Slowly whisk $1/4$ cup of the butter-chocolate mixture into the egg yolks and then fold the yolks into the chocolate. Add half the vanilla bean seeds. Sift the flour over the mixture and whisk until smooth.

2. In an electric mixer with a whisk attachment, beat egg whites and cream of tartar until fluffy. Slowly sprinkle in sugar and continue beating until peaks form. Fold a heaping spoonful of the chocolate mixture into the meringue and then fold the meringue into the remaining chocolate mixture. Allow to cool to room temperature.

3. Butter ten 5-ounce ramekins. Using a spatula, spoon batter into the ramekins until each is $1/3$ full. Break the remaining chocolate into pieces about 1 inch square. Drop a piece into each ramekin. Cover the chocolate with more batter so the molds are $2/3$ full. Sprinkle vanilla seeds on top and swirl the batter with a knife.

4. Bake 12 to 14 minutes, until slightly golden but still with a jiggle in the center. Serve warm with vanilla ice cream.

Chili powder

Three

Chili Powder

WHEN I VISIT Texas, it feels like the foreign country it once was: the Republic of Texas. There is still a sense of wild independence, of state pride, and of a unique culinary culture born from all the people who choose to call this place home. It is a part of the United States where the lines between Mexico and the United States are blurred, but fences are erected to make certain no one gets too confused. It's the people of Texas we have to thank for chili powder—and chili con carne, the dish that begat it. The story behind chili powder features a group of entrepreneurial women called the Chili Queens and a German immigrant looking for a culinary shortcut.

I stopped in Texas on my way home from the Gaya plantation in Mexico. My then-husband and I had a twelve-hour layover in San Antonio, so I crammed in the sights. I ordered a Texas-brewed Shiner Bock beer at the stately Menger Hotel, built in 1859, where Teddy Roosevelt later drank with his Rough Riders in its wood-paneled barroom. I visited the Alamo Drafthouse Cinema, a movie theater that served food and craft beer, and drank a thick peanut butter milkshake while I scared myself silly watching *World War Z*. And, of course, I made the obligatory pilgrimage to the Alamo.

The Alamo is such an indefatigable tourist destination that the area around it is akin to Times Square: afterward you can head across the street to Ripley's Believe It or Not Odditorium. The sun was beginning to set as I approached one of the oldest and most renowned sites in American history. A swarm of khaki-shorted, neon-T-shirted tourists roiled about me, posing and smiling in front of the 250-year-old mission. We had all come here because it was our responsibility as Americans to do so. To *remember*! . . . something.

In the wide plaza in front of the Alamo, there was a lone vendor selling sno-cones. I asked for blue coconut and chatted with her while she shaved a brick of ice by hand. I told her I was visiting from New York City; she told me she was a Texan, and her family was from Mexico. She smiled and held out my shaved ice. As I took the paper cup, I realized we were both part of a legacy. In this very spot in the nineteenth century, tourists like me lined up at food stalls like hers; but 150 years ago, visitors were in search of the fiery, hot taste of authentic chili. This vendor was an heir to a long line of women who have always used this plaza to earn their livelihood.

I walked, sno-cone in hand, to Main Plaza in front of the San Fernando Cathedral; in the nineteenth century, it was a market and another place where chili vendors set up. The night I visited the plaza, there was an outdoor movie playing, projected for an audience of about two hundred San Antonians. As I approached, I realized the feature that night was *Pee-wee's Big Adventure*. It just happened to be the part when Pee-wee calls Dottie, his friend back home, from a phone booth in San Antonio.

"Hello, Dottie! It's me, Pee-wee!"

"Well, where are you calling from? . . . Where?" Dottie asked with disbelief.

"Honest! I'll prove it!" Pee-wee replied, and he stepped out of the phone booth to sing, *"The stars at night are big and bright!"*

As though it were their civic duty, the movie audience and any passerby within earshot stopped and clapped four times in unison:

"Deep in the heart of Texas!"

My jaw dropped. I learned that night that Texans have a lot of state pride. One of the things they are proudest of is being the birthplace of chili.

The chili I make at home is different from the traditional chili cooked up in Texas. I always use chili powder, dumping heaping tablespoons of scarlet spice on sizzling ground beef. There's such a wide variety of chili powders on the market today, I did a little poking around to figure out what they contained. There is no single recipe for chili powder; each brand's ingredients are considered a trade secret. A typical blend includes garlic, cumin, and oregano, but can also include salt, onion powder, paprika, cinnamon, allspice, coriander, cloves, parsley, black pepper, lemon peel, or even chocolate. But the primary ingredient is always dried chili peppers of one or more varieties, which account for 77 percent to 82 percent of the final product's weight. The more types of chili peppers used in a blend, the greater the depth of flavor.

There's biology behind Americans' love of chili powder: we're addicted to heat. When black pepper was first being consumed in large quantities in the early nineteenth century, it was considered hot, due to its piperine content. Chili peppers contain a structurally similar chemical called capsaicin—both are considered chemical irritants.

Capsaicin bonds to nerve cells in our mouth and nose; specifically to receptors called TRPV1. This receptor is designed to warn us about dangerous sensations such as acid, abrasions, and heat. Capsaicin triggers a "hot" response, which is why we feel warm when we eat it: our body interprets capsaicin as thermally warm, hence the use of the word *heat* when we refer to this particular type of spice. The brain, to help us through what it perceives as a dangerous experience, releases chemicals known as endorphins. These have calming and pain-relieving properties similar to opiates. We like to feel full of endorphins, and they're addictive. Chili powder gets us a little bit high every time we eat it, and the addiction makes us crave spicier foods.

Addictive chili peppers have always been a part of a bowl of chili, but the meaty stew predates chili powder. Chili has its roots in traditional Mexican cuisine. According to Mexican American culture writer Gustavo Arellano, its ancestor could be one of several dishes: *picadillo*, which comes from the Spanish word for "to mince," is a beef hash mixed with peppers and tomatoes often served over rice or beans. There is also *guisado*, a slow-cooked meat stew that today is prepared with chili powder. The first-known English-language cookbook to print Mexican recipes also contained the first printed chili recipe. *The Landmarks Club Cook Book: A California Collection of the Choicest Recipes from Everywhere,* published in 1903, gives the same basic recipe that's been used in Texas for hundreds of years:

> For ordinary sauces, toast lightly your red chiles, dry or fresh, in the oven. Soak in water a few minutes, and grind on a milling-stone or in a mortar, to a wet pulp. Strain in a colander to remove bits of skin. The "hotness" can be graduated by leaving or removing the seeds, which contain most of the fire. Add a little salt and a tablespoonful of vinegar, and fry all together with a little butter. CHILE CON CARNE (MEXICO). Is made by frying beefsteak or other meat, cut in cubes, in this sauce.

Chili was mentioned in American writings long before the first cookbook recipe appeared. It was described by Joseph Chambers Clopper in 1828, who emigrated from Cincinnati to the Mexican state of Coahuila y Tejas, the area that would eventually become Texas. Spain encouraged "Anglo" immigration to Texas starting in 1820. Spain had difficulty convincing the central American residents of New Spain to colonize the dry and barren frontier. Cheap land drew families like the Cloppers—$0.04 cents an acre compared with $1.25 in American territories. While living in San Antonio, Clopper wrote in his journal about the Mexican families that lived around him and what was on their dinner tables: "When they have to pay for their meat in market, a very little is made to suffice a family; it is generally cut into a kind of hash with nearly as many peppers as there are pieces of meat—this is all stewed together." Although Clopper didn't yet know the name for it, this "hash" prepared by Mexican women was chili.

The first time this dish was named in writing—as chili con carne—wasn't until after Texas became a state. Chili and Texas history have always been closely intertwined. By 1830—two years after the time of Clopper's writing—the Mexican government passed the Law of April 6. Americans had been flooding to Tejas, and the law tried to stem the tide by banning further emigration from the States. Yes—at one time a law was passed to stop Americans from immigrating to Mexico. Though the decree was overturned after protests from the Texians, as the Anglo colonists were known, the political climate had changed permanently. In 1836 a convention of Texas's leaders voted for independence.

Now comes the Alamo, a pivotal battle of the Texas Revolution. Jim Bowie, Davy Crockett, and William B. Travis (or as I call him, "the other guy") forced a Mexican garrison out of a secularized mission turned fort known as—wait for it—the Alamo. Antonio López de Santa Anna, president of Mexico as well as general of its army, had decided to march up through Tejas with his troops and make an example out of the rebels. After a thirteen-day siege, he slaughtered everyone in the fort except civilians, and "Remember the Alamo!" became the rallying cry for Texian Revolutionaries out for revenge.

The war was over less than a month later: the Mexican army was destroyed in a clash with Texians at the battle of San Jacinto, around the river bend from where Clopper and his family had landed eight years earlier. And now Tejas was its own country: the Republic of Texas. But it was an unsettled republic. Borderland skirmishes with Mexico were everyday occurrences, the result of a desire for revenge, adventure, or plunder on both sides.

In 1845, after much debate, Texas was annexed to America and became the twenty-eighth state. But the border skirmishes continued. In 1846, under the trumped-up excuse of defending Texas, the United States invaded Mexico. American president James K. Polk wanted to fulfill what he believed was the Manifest Destiny of the United States: for America to reach from coast to coast. Polk was tired of negotiating with Santa Anna to sell Mexico's northern territories—so he decided to seize them instead. The resulting Mexican-American War would lead to the acquisition of California, Nevada, Utah, Arizona, and parts of Wyoming, Colorado, and New Mexico.

War is a great propagator for new culinary movements: in this case, soldiers from America invaded Mexico and then lived there, sampling the local food. They returned home with a taste for spicy Mexican cuisine, including chili. S. Compton Smith, a surgeon in General Zachary Taylor's invading army, published an anecdotal book about his time in the Mexican War from 1846 to 1848. The title of the book, *Chili con Carne; or, the Camp and the Field*, is the first time that chili is named in an American text. Smith said of America's involvement in the war: "Whether the war were a righteous one or not. That was our country's affair—not ours. And with light hearts and bounding pulses we left our homes to test the novelties of a first campaign, and embark in quest of wild adventures in that far-famed land."

Smith took time to describe the local vendors who would come to camp and "display their stock in trade, consisting usually of *carne seco* and *carne fresco, leche de cabro* [which translates to *male* goat's milk, so let's hope that Compton's Spanish was just not very good], *chile con carne, tamales, frijoles, tortillas, pan de maiz* and other eatables." He described chili con carne as "a popular Mexican dish—literally red pepper and meat."

After the war ended in 1848, tourism boomed in the newly acquired state of Texas, facilitated by the rapid construction of railroads. By 1880, if I were a traveler departing from New York, I could board "the cars" in New York City and travel by rail all the way to San Antonio.

The 1881 *San Antonio City Guide* helped tourists navigate the city. It described San Antonio as a sophisticated city full of first-class hotels—like the Menger, where I had that Shiner Bock. After an obligatory visit to the Alamo to celebrate Texas independence, the guide recommended having dinner at the vendors set up on the Alamo Plaza. These mobile food vendors had originally popped up to feed the soldiers in Texas and now thrived on the tourist trade. They set up just before sunset, and whole restaurants unloaded from the backs of wagons: benches and tables with tablecloths, lanterns for light and ambiance, "cheap but gorgeous glassware," and chili con carne that had been carefully prepared at home and set over a fire to stew all night. The proprietresses were young Mexican women; their parents often made the food while younger siblings played nearby until they fell asleep. Customers sat in the open air of the plaza sipping hot coffee, chocolate, or *atole*, a chocolate- or vanilla-flavored drink made with corn flour. One could order a meal of chili con carne, tamales, and enchiladas, all for around 10 or 15 cents. The tourists called these women "Chili Queens"—although the Queens themselves used that title only for the woman who sold the most chili in a night.

In 1894 the *San Antonio Daily Express* printed a drawing of one of these Queens: a young woman, head covered in a shawl and ears pierced, perfect Cupid's bow lips pursed around a cigarette, casting a sultry glance back over her shoulder. The depiction gave the Chili Queens a sensual if dangerous air, and the newspaper description characterized them as flirty, confident women who "put themselves to much trouble to please their too often rowdy customers." For American men, the encounters with the Chili Queens were thrilling. The April 1894 issue of *Forest and Stream* ran a feature on the Queens and described them as follows: "Lazy, soft of voice, slow of motion, feline perhaps, and perhaps really attractive, your *chile* queen would answer you with speech peppery as her wares, but smile at you so kindly you could not take offense, and the next minute teach you were there to eat *chile* and not to be hunting smiles nor expecting them."

The Chili Queens played into their legend to sell their food. The women came from conservative, patriarchal Catholic families, with little opportunity for young women to act independently. But at the chili stands, under the watchful eyes of their parents, they were the center of attention, chatting and flirting with customers all night long.

Although there are many images of Chili Queens' stands from the nineteenth century, there are very few images of the Chili Queens themselves. I've seen a handful of photographs I'd date to the 1890s, based on how the male customers are dressed. In one shot, I picked out a Chili Queen's mother, leaning over the table, serving customers. Her arms were thick and strong, her dress plain, and her two long braids fell down her back. In another, I saw a Chili Queen standing at the center of her stand, in the middle of the crowd and the excitement. She was slender in a white dress trimmed with lace, and her head was wrapped in a vast, dark scarf. Although I could see her figure, she had turned her back to the camera. Was it intentional? If so, was she preserving her mystery, or her propriety? Whatever the reason, she, and the many women like her, remained largely anonymous.

We know the names and stories of very few of the Queens. Martha Garcia was the reigning queen in the 1880s; one account claimed that she went on to pursue a career in the theater. Another, more likely story stated that Garcia married around 1890 and left the plaza to tend to her new home and family.

Sadie Thornhill ascended Martha's throne and ruled the plaza throughout the 1890s. As a teenager, Thornhill sold chili on the plazas, and by her twenties, she had saved enough money to open up her own little café. Unlike the other Chili Queens, Thornhill was not Texan-Mexican, but a white woman. Her father, John, had migrated from Kentucky and married a woman named Susan Smith in Texas. The 1880 census showed six-year-old Sadie (listed as Sarah) living with her family in Live Oak, a town just outside of San Antonio. Sadie had two older sisters and a younger brother. Her mother was listed as a farm laborer. Her father is nowhere to be found in the record. It could be that as Thornhill grew older, the burden to support her family fell largely on her shoulders.

Forest and Stream wrote that Sadie was "dark and adorably Spanish looking, 18 or 20, with fine figure, fine eyes, fine dark hair, and an air which is a mixture of tenderest solicitude, or coquetry and of cold-blooded indifference to you, any of your family or any of your relatives." Thornhill smoked cigarettes as she called orders back to the kitchen in Spanish, and passed out cartes-de-visite to flirtatious customers. These business cards featured a soft-focus glamour shot. Thornhill, round faced and doe eyed, looked straight at the camera, curls balancing on the top of her head. The card read:

"Compliments of

SADIE THORNHILL

The Chili Queen

SAN ANTONIO, TEXAS"

When she closed her shop is unknown, but she passed away in 1952, a grandmother. That is all we have about one of the most famous Chili Queens: a census record, a few newspaper articles, a business card, and a death certificate. Thornhill, like Garcia, and many who came after her, didn't leave many historical documents behind.

Although often left nameless by history, the Chili Queens introduced

Sadie Thornhill

Americans to their namesake dish. But it would be a German immigrant, William Gebhardt, who gave Americans the means to make chili at home. In 1892, at the same time that Martha Garcia and Sadie Thornhill were trading places as the reigning Chili Queens, Gebhardt was serving chili in a nearby beer hall.

Although Texas isn't remembered as a hotbed for German immigration, from 1850 to 1877 German speakers outnumbered Spanish speakers. The German community was established there in the 1830s, when a single family skipped like a stone from Germany, to New York's Kleindeutschland (Little Germany) neighborhood, to a land grant near modern-day Houston. Letters written home, praising the Texas countryside, started a chain of immigration directly to Texas. Later, German nobleman founded a colony in Texas, with the hopes of channeling thousands of unemployed peasants to the new country to alleviate overpopulation in Germany. Seven thousand immigrants from central Germany funneled into Texas, primarily into the area around San Antonio. The foods the Germans brought with them can still be seen in Texas cuisine today: beer, pickles, and even chicken-fried steak—a descendant of schnitzel, the traditional German dish of veal pounded flat and breaded lightly.

The center of German immigration was New Braunfels, just outside of San Antonio, which is still considered the heart of German culture in Texas. I've listened to the Texan-German radio show *German Music–Texas Style* online, broadcast from downtown New Braunfels. It's given both in English, and in a drawling, informal German for the geriatric, self-identifying German American population, a generation that spoke its distinct Texan-German exclusively until entering public school. It's a slangy middle dialect developed to speak across linguistic divides, since immigrants from all over the loosely affiliated city-states that today make up modern-day Germany spoke multiple dialects. It expanded to incorporate Americanese words such as "*wassever*."

German lager beer breweries were established by these German immigrants by the 1850s. Beer is central to German culture, and convivial outdoor beer gardens, serving lager beer and German food, dotted the Texas landscape by the middle of the nineteenth century. In 1875 a man named Edward King wrote a book called *The Great South: A Record of Journeys*, an account of his travels from Maryland to Texas. He described these beer halls: "There, in the long Sunday afternoons, hundreds of families gather, drinking beer, listening to music and singing." An accompanying illustration shows a Texas-German family, seated at a picnic table: bearded and bowler-hatted Papa, elegantly coiffed Mama, son, and daughter all enjoying the fine weather and the fine beer. The scene could be a depiction of any beer garden in Germany, or German saloon in New York—except that the boy in this picture is holding a baby deer on a leash. Texas is always a little more outrageous.

A saloon and beer garden in New Braunfels advertised not only deer to pet and feed but also allegedly had an alligator pit, a badger fight, and a parrot that said, "Have you paid your bill?" in Texan-German. This particular beer saloon opened in 1872 with a bar, billiards, and a brewery in the basement. It changed hands over a dozen times in the following twenty-five years, and it still stands today, retaining the name of its last nineteenth-century incarnation, the Phoenix Saloon. In 1892 William Gebhardt opened a café connected to the Phoenix to serve the saloon's patrons. It was in this building, in downtown New Braunfels, that chili powder was invented.

Gebhardt emigrated from Germany with his family in 1883, when he was eight years old. He opened the café at the tender age of seventeen. He served traditional German fare such as sausages but also sold his own chili, inspired by the Chili Queens' wares he had tasted on trips to San Antonio—or so the story goes. At the café, he laboriously sliced pounds of chili peppers and garlic daily to replicate that taste of the Chili Queens' chili con carne. Gebhardt experimented with dried chilies, but found their flavor lacking: he dreamed of creating a dried powder that contained all the necessary flavors to make chili, but that had the same impact as fresh ingredients.

His experiments resulted in the invention of chili powder. Gebhardt left the Phoenix Saloon in 1896 to found his own chili powder company in San Antonio. He filed a patent for his method of manufacturing chili powder in 1897 and called it Eagle Brand. According to his patent application, he took black pepper and oregano and mixed them with a solution of alcohol and water to create an extract. Then fresh chili peppers, with stems and seeds removed, were added to the mixture. Gerhardt, in his patent, calls these peppers simply *"Capsicum annuum,"* the generic Latin name for any chili pepper; but he became famous for using poblano peppers, also known as ancho chilies when they're dried. Fresh garlic was added, and then the solution steeped for an hour. Finally, it was run through an "Enterprise Meat-Chopper," a hulking, metal hand-cranked meat grinder. From the machine emerged long noodles of chili paste. The chili paste ropes were looped on drying racks and exposed to heat, and then pulverized into a powder. Finally, Gebhardt added ground cumin, as well as additional ground oregano.

In the early twentieth century, it would have been impossible to find the ingredients to cook a proper chili outside of the Southwest. The brilliance of Gebhardt's chili powder was that all the essential flavors of chili were bottled and could be kept nearly indefinitely. Tourists visiting the Chili Queens in nearby San Antonio could now take a little bit of Texas home with them.

He first sold chili powder only in Texas, and the brand soon expanded to include a line of canned chilies and tamales. But when he attempted to market his products nationally, Gebhardt encountered a problem: housewives outside of the Southwest hadn't the slightest inkling of how to cook with chili peppers, let alone how to use this entirely new product, chili powder. So Gebhardt took a page from the marketers of Jell-O, a contemporary product that had surmounted a similar problem, and published a cookbook to teach consumers how to use chili powder.

"What shall I have for dinner?" read a line in the introduction of Gebhardt Chili Powder Company's 1908 cookbook. The answer: *Mexican Cooking*, the name of the cookbook. The cookbook suggested menus of Southwest food using Gebhardt's products, all of which promised to alleviate the boredom of tedious, repetitive meals. The menus were given in both Spanish and English, to add an air of authenticity.

Comida Mexicana	Mexican Dinner
Cocktail de Ostras Con Salsa de Tabasco "Aguila"	Eagle Tabasco Oyster Cocktail
Caldo de Arroz y Veduras	Rice and Vegetable Soup
Fajada de Holibut Con Salsa	Halibut Steak with Sauce
Ensalada Mexicana	Mexican Relish
Gallina Frita Con Chile y Arroz	Fried Chicken with Chili and Rice
Chili Con Carne, Gebhardt's "Aguila"	Gebhardt's Eagle Chili Con Carne
Tomatoes Rellenos	Stuffed Tomatoes
Berenjena Frita	Fried Egg-Plant
Macarrón Con Salsa de Hongo	Macaroni with Mushroom Sauce
Tortillas	
Ensalada de Combinación	Combination Salad
Nieve	Ice Cream
Café	Coffee, Chocolate, and Nueces Descortezadas—Shelled Pecans

The cookbook boasted five recipes for chili con carne, the first of which stayed mostly true to the traditional dish that the Chili Queens would have served on the Alamo Plaza—except that fresh or dried ground peppers were replaced with Gebhardt's Eagle Brand chili powder. The cookbook recommended that the dish be served, as it was traditionally, with corn tortillas and a side of pinto beans.

Gebhardt's Eagle Chili Con Carne

Gebhardt's Eagle Brand chili powder is still made to this day and is considered one of the essential flavors of Tex-Mex cooking. *Mexican Cooking*'s "standard" chili recipe is cooked slow and low, and results in a thick and flavorful dish, redolent with caramelized meat.

Yield: serves 4 to 6

2 pounds of beef (brisket, chuck roast, or short ribs) cut into ¹/₂-inch squares

2 ounces beef tallow, chopped*

Salt

2 tablespoons lard

I small onion, chopped

3 tablespoons Gebhardt Eagle Brand chili powder (can be ordered online)

3 cloves garlic, chopped

1. Mix beef and tallow. Sprinkle with I teaspoon salt.
2. Heat lard in a Dutch oven over medium-high heat until melted. Add onion and cook 3 minutes, or until onion is slightly tender; then add meat.

* This ingredient can be obtained at a butcher, or you can substitute an equal amount of lard.

3. Stir constantly until meat is separated and white. Turn burner to high, and with the cover off, let all the juices steam off until meat has begun to fry in the remaining oil, about 10 to 15 minutes.

4. Add 1½ pints of hot water, chili powder, and garlic. Simmer on medium-low for 3 hours or until meat is tender and falls apart. Salt to taste, and serve with pinto beans and corn tortillas.

I cooked a batch of Gebhardt's chili for two lectures I gave on chili history; first, for a group of New Yorkers at the Brooklyn Brainery, and then in Austin for some "real Texans" (although frankly, most of the Austinites had migrated from New York). I was wary of the cooking directions, which seemed like they would sizzle the meat to inedible toughness. But the meat turned out tender, and the chili thick. However, both groups of test subjects found it shockingly *mild*! It was flavorful and full of aromatics from the spices, but not at all hot.

Which made me wonder if Gebhardt's chili was as hot as the Chili Queens' version. In *The Great South*, King wrote about eating at the Chili Queens' stands; he described the fare as "various savory compounds, swimming in fiery pepper, which biteth like a serpent." The famous novelist Stephen Crane visited San Antonio in 1889 and described his dining experience as follows: "Mexican vendors with open-air stands sell food that tastes exactly like pounded fire-brick from Hades—chile con carne, tamales, enchiladas, chili verde, frijoles." From their descriptions, this food sounds *hot*. Perhaps King's and Crane's Northern palates couldn't handle the heat of real Texan-Mexican food and Gebhardt, to accommodate, manufactured a mild chili powder to appeal to a broader audience.

But the true success of Gebhardt's Eagle Brand chili powder might have had less to do with its flavor and more to do with the austere cleanliness of the Gebhardt factory. In 1906 a new national law, the Pure Food and Drug Act, prohibited the adulteration of food with dangerous additives and required companies to list ingredients on their packaging.

One result of this law was a new public awareness of sanitation and a growing aversion to handmade foods that could have been produced in unregulated conditions—like fare sold by the Chili Queens. *Modern* and *hygienic* were buzzwords that sold food, much like *all natural* and *organic* are today. Just as McCormick advertised its ground black pepper at the turn of the twentieth century as being "absolutely pure," *Mexican Cooking* emphasized that Gebhardt's chili powder was "clean and wholesome."

The Gebhardt factory was everything the Chili Queens' stalls were not: its white walls housed rows of shining metal vats and lines of starchy-aproned employees. By the turn of the twentieth century, the Chili Queens' food was being targeted as unsanitary and potentially dangerous. The situation would come to a head in 1936: after a group of protesting San Antonians claimed the presence of chili stands affected the health and well-being of their neighborhood, the Queens were subjected to increasingly costly health regulations. They had to set up their stands in screened-in tents as an extra sanitary measure. Another law banned cooking chili at home and required that all foods for sale be cooked at a central commissary under tightly monitored conditions. New laws required hot water and sewage connections present at every stand, and demanded that dishes be sanitized in a regulated market kitchen—all of which cost money. By the 1940s, vendors also needed to purchase a costly license. Although the Queens often fought these laws—or operated illicitly—many vendors could not afford to keep up with the changing times.

Consuela Vasquez was the most popular Chili Queen in the late 1930s and early 1940s, at the height of the sanitation controversy. In 1941 she was described as "18 and beautiful" by the *San Antonio Light*. Vasquez worked in the stand with her sister, Gladys, and her sister-in-law, Mary. Wearing a yellow dress, a gold crucifix, and a broad smile, Vasquez served chili con carne and tamales each night to a variety of customers, including city health inspectors. She insisted that her chili was sanitary: "Of course is clean," she told the *San Antonio Light* reporter. "We cook at home and home is clean. Nobody she has been poison here yet," she added sassily.

The money the Vasquezes made supported nine family members, not including the proprietresses themselves. Many of the women working the stands had no education past grade school, so they had limited access to well-paying jobs. But that changed at the start of World War II, when the economy boomed and many men left to fight. Factories searched for new workers, and these jobs were opened to women. A former Chili Queen could even nab a job working on the line at the Gebhardt packing plant, making canned chilies and tamales. Less glamorous than being a Chili Queen, perhaps—but the work was reliable and profitable. With this economic shift, the last of the Chili Queens soon disappeared from the plazas.

In 1967, more than twenty years after the last Chili Queens closed up shop, a reader of the *San Antonio Light*'s Action Line, a sort of user-driven Q&A column, wrote in to suggest bringing back the Chili Queens for the HemisFair '68, a World's Fair hosted in San Antonio. The Action Line editor's response echoed the concerns of an earlier generation: "This is the age of go-go girls and not of chili queens," he wrote. "But mainly, the chili queens and their stands are unable to meet the sanitary standards imposed by the city and its health authorities."

For all the news coverage I read about the alleged lack of sanitation at the Chili Queens' stands, I never came across one account of food poisoning. Consuela Vasquez's claim holds up.

I returned to Texas two years after that first trip. I got up at four in the morning to catch my flight, and was sleepy and dazed as I stepped out of the sliding doors of the Austin airport and into the relentless Texan heat. My friend Ed pulled up to the curb, skinny as a beanpole and all smiles, and swept me away with hugs into his un-air-conditioned car. "I don't care much for AC," he told me with a Texas twang that had somehow thickened in the three years since he had moved away from New York City.

In the car, Ed turned to me and said, "I need your help." He had started his own food truck less than a month before my arrival, an homage to the original Chili Queens—with a twist. He had come across their story while researching chili recipes after he moved back to Texas, and decided to become not just a Chili Queen but a drag queen.

When Ed first started out, he made all his chilies with fresh ingredients, slicing and processing enumerable chilies and garlic cloves—like Gebhardt. Until one day, he'd had enough. "There's got to be an easier way to do this," he said, which I imagined was what William Gebhardt thought when he invented his chili powder. Now Ed uses dried herbs, garlic powder, dried chilies, and heaping cupfuls of chili powder. But his "Texas Red," as the Chili Queens' traditional chili con carne is known today, remains true to its origins. Seared beef is simmered with dried chili peppers that have been soaked in water and pureed, giving the chili a deep scarlet hue.

When we arrived at Ed's food truck, I cooked the chilis while Ed got dressed. He talked me through setting up the toppings, as he topped himself with a chestnut bouffant wig. As soon as his eyelashes were applied and he smoothed his brown gingham apron, Ed jumped in the driver's seat, and we sped off to a local brewery, where we would be serving that afternoon.

It was my first time working in a food truck. I was more Chili Princess than Chili Queen as I toiled and sweated over the enormous stockpots bubbling over gas burners in the back of his stainless steel–lined mobile kitchen. Ed—now Edie—elegantly flirted and bantered with customers like a true Chili Queen. As I ladled the fiftieth-odd bowl of hot chili over Fritos, topped with sour cream, pickled jalapeños, and chopped onions, I felt a kinship with the Queens of the nineteenth century. As Ed put it, "I now know what it was like to cook food all day and serve it to an endless line of drunk people—it's grueling."

The menu also included a tomato-based chili with beans; a white chili made with pork, turkey, and green jalapeños; and a fiery vegetarian chili made with lentils. These are just a few types of chili cooked across America today. As Gebhardt's chili powder spread across the country in the early twentieth century, it inspired not only countless knockoff brands but also many different variations of chili.

Edie's chili with beans reminded me of my mother's chili. My mother and I made our first batch together when I was nine or ten. I remember sitting on the beige carpet in our living room surrounded by stacks of recipe cards and torn-out magazine pages. She had asked me to help her pick some new recipes to try. We were both tired of a repetitive routine of family weeknight dinners. ("What shall we have for dinner?") It was time to shake it up a little. I remember choosing a recipe for a mild chili, made with browned ground beef, simmered for hours with tomatoes and onions. Canned kidney beans were added at the end. It was more savory than spicy, using only a tablespoon or two of chili powder—one of the endless chili blends on the market inspired by Gebhardt's invention. I don't know why I chose it; I don't think I had ever tried chili before. But when we stewed the ingredients together, it became a family favorite. To this day, when I visit home and stumble through the door, ravenous after the harrowing journey from LaGuardia Airport back to that cornfield in Akron, there's usually a plastic Tupperware of this chili in the refrigerator. It's waiting to be topped with shredded cheese and warmed up in the microwave.

That was the first chili I ever made, but I have other favorites. When I was a college student in Cleveland, my roommate Jeff and I made a special trip up Mayfield Road to Skyline Chili. This chili parlor chain was originally founded in Cincinnati in 1949 by a Greek immigrant from Kastoria. Skyline chili was served over spaghetti, hot dogs, or baked potatoes, and topped with beans, electric-yellow shredded cheese, onions, or even a crumble of oyster crackers. I remembered the foreign taste of chili, tangy and sweet, with holiday spices like cinnamon. Served over spaghetti (Jeff insisted), this wasn't the dish I had grown up with. But Jeff had been there so many times, the restaurant had a Polaroid photo of him smiling triumphantly in a book of best customers.

Then there's Ben's Chili Bowl in Washington, DC. Five years or so after my trip to Skyline Chili, I was visiting my friends Bryan and Matt, whom I had known since college, in their new home. One memorable night, after an evening of heavy drinking, we swept into Ben's Chili Bowl. The chili parlor opened in 1958 and to this day draws an infamously long line that stretches out the door and down the block, particularly late at night when the bars shut down. But Matt knew somebody, or pretended to know somebody, and led us straight past the line and through the front door. He waved to the crew behind the counter, and they cheered back. We were seated at a table, and someone came over to take our order—at a restaurant where there was no table service. I bit into a chili-covered half-smoke: a sausage so fat that juice spurted on the table with my first bite. The chili tasted like a hearty meat gravy; deep reddish brown with a heat that made my tongue tingle. Staring down blearily at my chili-covered French fries and chili half-smoke, I felt like royalty.

Skyline Chili and Ben's Chili Bowl are typical of the chili parlors that had been established all over the country by the 1930s. Although Ben's still calls its bowl chili con carne, by the middle of the twentieth century, most people had shortened the dish's name to simply "chili." By that time, chili powder was no longer seen as a Mexican ingredient, or even a Texan one: it was now an essential component to an American dish, one replete with regional variations.

Americans have a lot of strong opinions about the right way to make chili—whether it's with tomatoes and beans, cinnamon or other spices, or simply pureed chili peppers and meat. From these differences arose competitions to determine the best chilis around the country. In 1952 the Texas State Fair hosted the first modern chili competition for housewives to square off with their best recipes. The winner, a Mrs. F. G. Ventura, cooked a pretty traditional chili of ground beef seared in fat and then simmered in water, chili powder, garlic, black pepper, and cumin.

For over a century, and up until Mrs. Ventura's win, chili making was associated with women, and chili consumption with men. But modern chili cook-offs are a mostly male affair, with teams of men serving chili to panels of male judges. For example, in nearly fifty years of the World's Championship Chili Cookoff in Terlingua, Texas, only a third of the winners have been women.

This strange role reversal began in 1967, when two food writers staged a cross-country chili rivalry as part of an elaborate publicity stunt to promote their work—and real estate in a remote Texas town called Terlingua. H. Allen Smith, a well-known author and New Yorker by way of the Midwest, had written an article called "Nobody Knows More About Chili Than I Do." Texans, of course, lost their shit when a Northerner dared to claim chili knowledge. Texans Frank X. Tolbert (known as the Godfather of Chili) and reporter Homer "Wick" Fowler challenged Smith to a chili cook-off to see whose chili reigned supreme: traditional Texas chili or the slop of some New Yorker.

Everyone made a big to-do about the chili challenge in the papers, and quick-witted tongue lashings passed back and forth between the contestants. In the *Corpus Christi Caller-Times*, Fowler called Smith's chili "a soupy, inedible potion," while Smith scoffed that Fowler's chili "would make anyone but a Texan gag." Everyone got so worked up Smith later called the event "the decade's most impassioned culinary embroilment." The cook-off was geared toward a male audience; "And I understand women are going to come crashing in," Smith said to a reporter at the *San Antonio Express*. "It was a stag affair at first."

On October 21, 1967, the big day, hundreds turned up at the "Great Chili Cook-Off at Terlingua." Terlingua was a former mercury-mining settlement and, for all practical purposes, a ghost town. Smith called the area "both bleak and majestic." The chili competition organizers thought the event would bring positive attention to the area, the actual goal being to sell real estate in the town.

While cooking, Fowler wore a sombrero and a colorful striped serape—just imagine a really stereotypical "Mexican" outfit—and Smith wore a sport shirt. Three male judges presided over the competition, and upon sampling the chilis, one voted for Smith, the other for Fowler, and the third faked gustatory distress and abstained from voting. There was no winner. I would have rioted. But it seemed that the proceedings were, more than anything, an excuse for the country to celebrate what had become a beloved national dish. As the *Corpus Christi Caller-Times* noted in its coverage, "If anyone was taking the chili championships seriously, it wasn't evident here."

H. Allen Smith's New York Chili

Smith's original recipe is more of a suggestion than a strict set of rules. He includes kidney beans and a dash of MSG—two decidedly un-Texan ingredients. Here's what he had to say about chili making: "Texans consider it bloody sacrilege to cook beans with their chili. I say they're all daft. They also scream bloody murder at the idea of any sweet pepper being included. You'll have to make up your own mind—just don't let their raucous way of talking overpower you."

Yield: serves 4 to 6

3 pounds beef chuck, coarsely ground

1 can tomato paste

2 medium onions, diced

1/2 bell pepper, diced

2 to 4 garlic cloves, crushed and then minced

1/2 teaspoon dried oregano

1/4 teaspoon dried basil

1/4 teaspoon cumin

2 tablespoons Chimayo ground chile powder* (or another New
   Mexican chile powder)

$^1/_2$ teaspoon MSG

1 can pinto or kidney beans

1 teaspoon salt

1. Sear meat in a cast-iron kettle over medium-high heat. If you do not
   have a cast-iron skillet, any heavy-bottomed skillet or pot will do.

2. Add the tomato paste. Cook until tomato paste is nicely browned,
   about 2 minutes, stirring constantly.

3. Add in onions, bell pepper, garlic, and 4 cups of water. Cover pot and
   cook about 5 minutes, stirring occasionally.

4. Add the oregano, basil, cumin, and chili powder and simmer chili over
   medium low for 90 minutes, covered. Add MSG and beans and simmer about 10 more minutes. Taste and adjust the seasonings.

5. Let the chili set at least 1 hour to allow the aromatics to blend. In
   Smith's words, "It will taste better the second day, still better the third,
   and absolutely superb the fourth."

Wick Fowler's 2 Alarm Texas Chili

Fowler, like Gebhardt, was a canned chili maker in Texas. His prepackaged
2 Alarm Chili spice kit, still available online, is a beloved fast food for many
Texans. Although the 1967 competition was a draw, the International Chili
Society has held an annual chili competition in Terlingua ever since. This
recipe is from Fowler's 1970 cook-off win; he was famous for insisting that
chili should include tomato sauce, a break from Texas tradition.

Yield: serves 4 to 6

* Chimayo chile powder can be purchased online.

2 pounds beef stew meat, cut in 1-inch cubes

8 ounces tomato sauce

1 package of Wick Fowler's 2 Alarm Chili or substitute:

7 tablespoons ancho chili powder

2 1/2 teaspoons cumin

1 1/2 teaspoons cayenne pepper

1 1/2 teaspoons onion powder

1 1/2 teaspoons garlic flakes (or dehydrated garlic)

1 1/2 teaspoons paprika

1 1/4 teaspoons salt

1/2 teaspoon oregano

5 teaspoons masa harina (corn flour)

1. Add meat to dry skillet or heavy-bottomed pot and cook over medium heat. Cook about 5 minutes until meat begins to give up its juices, stirring occasionally.

2. Add in tomato sauce, 3 cups water, and all the ingredients from the 2 Alarm Chili kit.

3. Cover and simmer about 90 minutes, stirring occasionally until meat is tender and chili sauce is thickened.

Arguably, the best bowl of chili in America today can be found where it has always been found: in San Antonio, made by a woman.

Ed and I embarked on a chili tour a few days after my stint as his Chili Princess. By then, I was used to his AC-less car and took in the landscape out my rolled-down window. So much space, so much sky. The immigrants and migrants who came here in Texas's early days must have felt so far from home, staring at this landscape that was so different from where they came.

Our first stop was New Braunfels. The streets were quiet in the afternoon heat, and we parked around a village green surrounded by nineteenth-century storefronts. We visited the Phoenix Saloon, the site of William Gebhardt's first experiments with chili powder. I would have loved this bar even if it wasn't so important to chili history. The large barroom had high, painted pressed-tin ceilings and was filled with long communal tables and benches. The dark wood vintage bar featured taps with beer from local breweries, and a few folks had escaped the heat to sit on bar stools and sip pints. I walked up to the bar and ordered a bowl of its "Double Shot" spicy chili, topped with sour cream, cheddar cheese, green onions, and roasted garlic cloves. It arrived moments later, chunks of tender sirloin swimming in a thick gravy, the spicing so hot, my eyes watered with every bite. But I kept shoveling that delicious chili in my mouth.

After lunch, we rolled out of New Braunfels to nearby San Antonio, first to visit Ed's ninety-six-year-old grandmother, Helen. (She asked if I wanted a glass of wine and then if I wanted to see her recipe collection. Yes and yes.) Then it was back in the car to scope out a local park. We were hunting the Institute of Chili food truck; I had an appointment to meet its founder, Ana Fernandez.

Ana's chili was named the best in America by *Food & Wine* magazine in 2013. But she served it only in season. In the summer, she scooped out heaps of shaved ice slathered in Technicolor sugar syrups, pickled fruits called chamoy, cucumber pickles, and sweet and sour candies. When we found her, she passed one of these massive—and rapidly melting—creations to me through the service window of her big black food truck.

A few minutes later, Ed and I sat on the curb, munching and slurping our sno-cones on steroids. Ana hopped down from her truck to chat with us in the shade of a tree. Sensibly dressed for food truck life, she was in a black T-shirt imprinted with the visage of a Mexican sugar skull, her dark brown hair tied back out of her face.

Ana was a San Antonio native and an art school graduate. Her dad's side had been around since Texas was Mexico, and her mother was three when her family immigrated to Texas from Guerrero, Mexico. As a result, Texan-Mexican cooking had always been a huge part of Ana's life.

Ana had a revelation when she and a friend kvetched about the lack of good chili in the city. When they ordered chili con carne in a restaurant, it was slopped onto their plates straight out of a can. Industrial chili makers like Gebhardt had created a new standard for chili that had lasted into the twenty-first century—and it came from a can. Ana decided it was time for a change; she wanted to return to the past and cook the chili that was originally served on San Antonio's plazas by the Chili Queens.

She went into the archives of the University of Texas at San Antonio Institute of Texan Cultures and began to research the city's original Chili Queens. The more she learned, the more she was reminded of her own grandmother. "My grandmother used to make tamales and sell them," she told me. "It's a tradition; it's a kind of a cultural thing where you've got the grandma in the family who makes tamales, and you'll sell them to your friends and neighbors." Ana was inspired by her grandmother's enterprising spirit, so similar to that of the original Chili Queens.

In 2012 San Antonio passed a law allowing food trucks into the downtown area. Ana opened her truck, the Institute of Chili, and she served a chili made from a mix of ground chuck and brisket, along with salt, pepper, garlic, fresh green chilies, and her own homemade chili paste. She roasted ancho, arbol, and guajillo chilies on a grill, and then blended them in a food processor and pressed them through a strainer. The deep red hue of her chili comes not from tomatoes but from the generous amount of chili paste she cooks with—just like the traditional chili con carne the Chili Queens served.

She's a self-described Chili Queen—the history makes her feel connected to her own cultural heritage, and she wants her food truck to remind people of the Queens, whom she calls "the original mobile street vendors of San Antonio." But she also feels like the Chili Queens never left. Mexican American families still operate food trucks and trailers in San Antonio and all around Texas. It's still a way for many people—particularly women—to provide for their families.

"I don't call myself *the* Chili Queen or my workers *the* Chili Queens. We're just Chili Queens, meaning anybody who makes a living through selling food on the street. Anyone can be a part of that culture and is a Chili Queen, you know?"

I think it's important to remember that chili, and the people who first cooked it, were both Mexican and American. While reading up on the 1967 Chili Cook-Off, I stumbled across an article published the same day as the competition in the *Corpus Christi Caller-Times* about a Republican state senator named Henry Grover. With November elections just around the corner, Grover outlined several issues he thought the Republicans should emphasize in their campaigns. Grover felt that schools with a sizable enrollment of Mexican students should offer courses in Spanish and Mexican history. "The people in New England are tremendously proud of Plymouth Rock in 1621 [*sic*]," he said. "Mexicans also have a 'tremendous heritage in which they can feel proud.'"

When the article was published, Americans were not just thinking about the coming elections, but about Thanksgiving, too. When I consider this holiday, it's easy to see why American culture often focuses on the Colonial hearths of New England: Pilgrims and Plymouth Rock, cranberry sauce and pumpkin pie. But while the English immigrants celebrated the end of their first year in Plymouth, Spanish immigrants were establishing missions in what is today the American Southwest. When Texas became part of the United States, the people that lived there had a culture that became a part of the American story, just like the *Mayflower*. A bowl of chili, drawn from Mexican heritage, influenced by the Germans, and made famous in the state of Texas, is a true American dish.

El Diablito

Although Ana offers her chili only in season, you can get this chili-themed dessert from her truck anytime. Shaved ice is topped with sweet and sour pineapple and jalapeño syrups, spicy pickled fruit, and a dusting of chili powder. This recipe is my pick to fix a chili craving on a hot day.

Yield: enough syrup and chamoy for 8 servings

Shaved ice
Pickled Pineapple Syrup (recipe below)
Pickled Jalapeño Syrup (recipe below)
Green Chamoy (recipe below)
Chili powder
Sour gummi candy

Pickled Pineapple Syrup

1 cup fresh pineapple chunks
1/2 cup white sugar
1/2 cup white vinegar
Dash of cayenne pepper or chili powder
3 tablespoons lemon juice

1. In a saucepan cook pineapple, sugar, and vinegar over medium-high heat for 15 minutes until sugar is dissolved and pineapple is tender. Add dash of cayenne pepper and lemon juice.
2. Pour mixture in a nonreactive bowl (ceramic or glass) and keep in the refrigerator until chilled thoroughly.
3. Strain and chill syrup; reserve pineapple chunks.

Pickled Jalapeño Syrup

4 jalapeño peppers, seeds and stem removed, sliced
$^1/_2$ cup white sugar
$^1/_2$ cup white vinegar

1. In a saucepan, cook jalapeños, sugar, and vinegar over medium-high heat for 15 minutes until sugar is dissolved and jalapeños are tender.
2. Pour mixture in a nonreactive bowl (ceramic or glass) and keep in the refrigerator until chilled thoroughly.
3. Strain and chill syrup and reserve $^1/_2$ cup jalapeño slices.

Green Chamoy

$^1/_2$ cup reserved jalapeños
$^1/_2$ large sour cucumber pickle
1 skinned plum or 3 prunes
2 tablespoons apple cider vinegar
$^1/_4$ cup raw cane sugar (demerara sugar)
$^1/_4$ cup cornstarch
$^1/_4$ cup lime juice
1 teaspoon salt
1 teaspoon citric acid
$^1/_2$ cup reserved pineapple

1. In a food processor, blend jalapeños, pickle, and plum until smooth. You might need to add a little water and scrape down the sides of the food processor bowl to achieve a smooth consistency.
2. Add vinegar and sugar to a heavy pot and heat on low, without stirring, until sugar is dissolved. Turn off heat.
3. Add cornstarch to lime juice and stir until dissolved and there are no lumps. Add cornstarch-lime mixture, salt, and citric acid to the pot.

Add reserved pineapple and blended jalapeño mixture. Stir until just combined.

To assemble the shaved ice:

1. Make shaved ice with a shaved-ice machine or use finely crushed ice made in a food processor or blender. Two cups of ice makes about 1 cup of shaved ice, enough for 2 servings.
2. Pack shaved ice into a cup or bowl, using your clean hands to mound it.
3. Top each serving with 3 tablespoons of pineapple syrup, 2 tablespoons of jalapeño syrup, and 1 tablespoon of chamoy. Sprinkle with chili powder and top with sour gummi candy. Serve immediately.

Curry powder

Four

Curry Powder

THE WINTER AFTER my first trip to Texas, I journeyed to a destination much closer to home: Jackson Heights, Queens, one of around two dozen "Little Indias" in the New York City metropolitan area. Queens is one of the most ethnically diverse places on the planet: over 130 languages are spoken in the borough. On my ride east from Manhattan on the 7 train, I passed neighborhoods of Irish, Korean, Mexican, Thai, and Nepalese immigrants. At Eighty-second Street, I descended the steps from the elevated track to the street and headed down Broadway toward Queens Boulevard to meet the rest of my posse. It was time for our "curry crawl": an orchestrated attempt to taste as many dishes from as many regions of India as possible, all in one afternoon.

The inclusion of curry in this book sparked more debate than any other chapter. Whenever I talked about my research, I was always asked to list the flavors I picked: black pepper, vanilla, chili powder, curry powder . . . "Wait, curry?" someone would say. "That's not American!" I disagree.

Currently, around two million Indian immigrants live in the United States, and nearly three million Americans claim Asian Indian ethnicity, now the third largest immigrant group in the country behind people from Mexico and China.

Furthermore, curry powder has been used in American cooking for well over two hundred years, long before the first Indian immigrants arrived, and a century before a celebrity chef named Ranji Smile made it trendy. Curry powder is a flavor that has been a part of the American culinary landscape for centuries, but has yet to be recognized as an American flavor.

I organized a curry crawl because I wanted to find out what distinguished American curries. My guides were friends: Nina, born in New Jersey to parents who emigrated from Uttar Pradesh in northern India; and Raj, himself an immigrant from New Zealand, whose parents came from Rajasthan and New Delhi. I also invited Jen and Soma, founders of the Brooklyn Brainery—Soma is a casual expert in Thai curries, and Jen is smart and cool. In any case, more people meant more perspectives: we would try to unravel the mystery of American curry together.

The day started warm and rainy, but the temperature slid slowly toward snow. The damp sidewalks shimmered with the reflected light, red and gold, from the fashions in the shop windows. The silk saris on display were saturated pinks, greens, and blues; the jewelry stores exhibited necklaces and bracelets worked in intricate designs from the brightest gold. Barkers stood out front, shouting for us to come inside to see what was for sale. This was a neighborhood where traditions had been transported from India to become a part of New York. It's a mash-up of grit and glamour, hot dogs and hot chai.

"It's been so many years since I've walked down this street; it's even more opulent than I remember," Raj said, as awestruck as I was.

Our rowdy group began at Tangra Masala, which featured "Indian Style Chinese Cuisine." It's named after the Kolkata neighborhood of Tangra, known for its Chinese immigrant population. Nina picked the dishes; they came out quick and were served family style. We ate crispy and slightly sweet chili chicken, dry rubbed with chilies and topped with garlic. We followed it with Manchurian curry with vegetables, drowning in a deep red spicy sauce. Then we paid our bill and stopped for Thai curries at Ayada Thai. Thai and Indian food are blending in Queens because of the physical proximity of the immigrant communities and the shared spices in their cuisine—Indian restaurants have even begun to add "Thai curry" to their menus. At Ayada Thai, we sampled fish swimming in a searing orange-colored coconut curry and buried in chopped chili peppers; then a prawn curry, redolent of coriander, that tested our tolerance for heat.

After a quick stop for some bites of fried South Indian street food, we dropped into my favorite place in Jackson Heights: Rajbhog Sweets, a tiny café that offered a daily selection of Punjabi curries as well as the best chai, *chaat* (chickpeas, spicily sauced and covered in broken pastries called Samosas), and an array of sweets as brightly colored as the saris on the street.

We ordered a dish of turmeric-yellow curried lentils known as dal, as well as eggplants and okra in a tomato-based curry, and paneer—fresh white cheese—in a curry sauce. We hungrily scooped up the curry with roti: soft whole wheat flatbreads made fresh by hand, and slurped down milky-sweet chai tea. It tasted of home for Raj, like a typical meal his mother would have made when he was growing up.

Although these dishes have individual names within their own culture, in English there is one name for all of them: curry.

American curry powder is based on several Indian spice blends. The most well known of these blends is garam masala, used in the north of India— *garam* means "warming," and *masala* means "a blend of aromatic spices." It's the basic model for what's known in the United States as a "mild" or "sweet" curry powder, and it's aromatic without being hot. It contains cardamom, cinnamon, cloves, black pepper, and sometimes coriander and cumin. Many of the spices have antimicrobial properties, as with black pepper, so curry powder keeps food fresher for longer in the hot Indian climate.

There's also *Sambar podi*, a spice blend from South India; American "hot" or "madras" curry powder is a derivative of this spice mix. It's much hotter than garam masala, thanks to a good quantity of chili peppers; their spicy heat is addictive, like chili powder's. The chilies are blended with other spices, including turmeric, a yellow-orange rhizome (an edible, underground stem). Turmeric contains an important chemical called curcumin. A powerful topical antioxidant (it inhibits oxidation that may damage cells) and anti-inflammatory, curcumin inserts itself into cell membranes, making them more resistant to infection. Additionally, it might help to prevent one of the causes of Alzheimer's disease.

The word *curry* is not as old as the various spice blends it describes. Former chef and cookbook author Julie Sahni offers the most plausible explanation in her book *Classic Indian Cooking*. She explained that the term likely came from *kari*, a fragrant leaf used in a spice blend in South Indian cooking. The sauce made from *kari* and other spices was called *kari podi*; this phrase made the linguistic leap in English to "curry powder." Today curry is a catch-all for a variety of powders, pastes, sauces, and dishes; and *kari* leaves are often called curry leaves.

Curry powder made the jump to America through our Anglo roots: the British East India Company had been trading with India since the seventeenth century; England officially made India a colony in 1858. British soldiers, merchants, and government officials stationed in India would write home with recipes for Indian dishes, in part to satisfy their families' curiosity about their exotic lives abroad. When they returned to England, they brought with them a taste for Indian cuisine. In some cases, they brought back their Indian servants and cooks too; in others, they hired British cooks who were trained in India. As early as the mid-eighteenth century, curries could be ordered at local coffeehouses, which meant that even those who had never been to India could taste and enjoy curries.

The British love of curries traveled with English immigrants to America. In 1747 Hannah Glasse published *The Art of Cookery Made Plain and Easy*, an English cookbook that was popular among American colonists. It contained a basic recipe for Anglo-Indian curry. Glasse suggested that home cooks stew up a chicken with finely ground turmeric, black pepper, and ginger, blended into a cream sauce. It was a recipe similar to the simplified Indian dishes the British were consuming in India.

The first curry recipes published in an American cookbook appeared nearly eighty years later in Mary Randolph's *The Virginia Housewife*, the very same cookbook that included the first published ice cream recipes in 1824. "Curry powder is used as a fine flavoured seasoning for fish, fowls, steaks, chops, veal cutlets, hashes, minces, alamodes, turtle soup, and in all rich dishes, gravies, sauce &c &c," Randolph wrote. Her book included a half-dozen curry recipes, a number that suggested that curry was already a popular dish. She described how to make curried catfish, curried veal fillets, and curried baked leg of mutton, as well as homemade curry powder.

Curry Powder

One ounce turmeric, one ounce coriander seed, one ounce cummin [*sic*] seed, one ounce white ginger, one of nutmeg, one of mace, and one of Cayenne pepper; pound all together and pass them through a fine sieve; bottle and cork it well—one tea-spoonful is sufficient to season any made dish.

Her recipe is spicy—both flavorful and hot—and might have been based on South Indian *Sambar podi*, although Randolph probably wouldn't have known that. Randolph's curry powder was used a lot like

Emeril's Essence, the secret spice blend popularized by chef and Food Network star Emeril Lagasse. I imagine Randolph adding a dash to her cooking while shouting some nineteenth-century version of "Bam!" Probably "Huzzah!"

Country Captain Chicken with Mary Randolph's Curry Powder

Country Captain Chicken is a common American curry dish that first showed up in Eliza Leslie's 1857 cookbook *Miss Leslie's New Cookery Book*. It was a popular dish in port cities of the South, where Americans who had sailed to India would have lived and traded. It is still popular in these places—if considered a little old-fashioned. Leslie's technique calls for chicken rubbed with curry powder and fried in butter; the results are crispy and spicy. Recipe adapted by Jill Paradiso.

Yield: serves 4

For the curry powder:
1 teaspoon powdered turmeric
1 teaspoon powdered coriander
1 teaspoon powdered cumin
1 teaspoon powdered ginger
1 teaspoon powdered nutmeg
1 teaspoon powdered mace
1 teaspoon powdered cayenne pepper

For the chicken:
Salt
1 whole chicken, cut into 8 pieces (2 breasts, 2 thighs, 2 drumsticks, 2 wings)

2 large onions, peeled

1 stick butter

Curry powder

$^1/_2$ cup unsweetened coconut, shredded

1. Make curry powder by combining the spices. Grind fresh from whole spices for the best flavor.

2. Bring a large pot of well-salted water to boil. Once water has reached full boil, add chicken breasts and onions and cook for 4 minutes. Then add thighs, drumsticks, and wings, and continue cooking another 6 minutes.

3. Remove the chicken from pot and drain well. Leave onion in boiling water to continue cooking.

4. Melt butter in large sauté pan over medium-high heat. Toss chicken in curry powder until well coated.

5. When butter begins to foam, add chicken to pan and cook about 3 to 4 minutes until well browned. Turn chicken pieces over and cook another 3 to 4 minutes. Turn heat down to low and remove chicken from pan. Season chicken with salt and set aside.

6. Remove onions from water. Slice onions in half lengthwise and then cut into half-moon strips. Add onions and $^1/_2$ teaspoon of salt to pan and cook in curry butter mixture over low heat about 8 minutes or until onions are lightly browned, stirring occasionally.

7. Garnish chicken with sautéed onions and coconut. Serve immediately over any kind of rice you like.

Glasse and Randolph both instructed home cooks to grind their spices fresh, by hand, as it would have been done in India. In the second half of the nineteenth century, groceries that carried the spices needed to make curry powder began to sell spice blends ground in-house. This convenience made curry powder's use even more common, although the results would be less flavorful: ground spices fall victim to oxidation and evaporation, losing the chemicals that give them their taste and aroma. But the pre-ground curry powder became a quick fix, perfect for jazzing up leftovers. Got some of yesterday's chicken or beef? Cookbooks from the period advised home cooks to mince it up, throw some curry powder on it, add some stock or cream, and it was a whole new meal.

Up until the 1880s, the curries available in America were interpretations of the dish that came to the United States either with British immigrants or with American sailors who had traveled to India on merchant ships. But in the last decades of the nineteenth century, small groups of Indian merchants, primarily from Bengal, began arriving in American port cities. They headed toward summer tourist destinations such as Atlantic City, New Jersey, where they sold hand-embroidered silks and other goods made in their hometowns. At the time, Americans were in the grip of a mania for all things Indian, following the trend of the English—who in 1877 crowned Queen Victoria "Empress of India." This fad pervaded all aspects of American culture: even the horse that won the 1881 Kentucky Derby was named Hindoo.

When the Bengalese came to the United States to sell their silks, they might have tried to cook the foods they were familiar with from home. But their influence on American food at the time was minimal, if at all. The trend for an "authentic" Indian experience wouldn't extend to food until the arrival of a singular man, who would arguably become America's first celebrity chef: Prince Ranji Smile.

On May 11, 1879, just two years after Queen Victoria was crowned Empress of India, Ranji Smile was born near Karachi, India, possibly in the province of Balochistan. Today it is a majority Muslim city in modern-day Pakistan: one of the last acts of the British Crown before India gained its independence in 1947 was to partition the Muslim-majority provinces of Bangladesh and Pakistan from India.

Smile's real name might have been Ranji Ismaili, pronounced

"Iss-*smile*-ee." His last name indicated that he belonged to a branch of Shia Islam, one of two major branches of Islam, called Ismaili Muslims. His early life remains a mystery. Smile later claimed to be the son of a wealthy merchant but also boasted of being the fifth son of the emir, or ruler, of Balochistan. But a marriage certificate simply lists his parents' names as Emil Smile and Sara Kididja; he could have just as well grown up herding sheep in the Kirthar Mountains. As a young man, he most likely moved to nearby Karachi to look for work. It was a cosmopolitan port city, then controlled by the British. It might have been there that he began his career as a chef. Smile must have had a natural talent for cooking, because before he was twenty years old, he had moved to London to work in the city's finest hotel restaurants.

Smile first made a name for himself cooking at the Savoy. Nathaniel Newnham-Davis, a retired lieutenant colonel turned food writer, took note of Smile's curries. When he poked his head into the Savoy's kitchen, "Smiler, the curry cook, appeared instantly," he wrote. "Because I talk a little bad Hindustani, Smiler has taken me under his protection, and thinks that I should not go to the Savoy for any other purpose than to eat his curries."

Soon Smile moved to the Cecil, an enormous luxury hotel that opened in 1896. The largest in Europe at the time, the hotel contained accommodations for over eight hundred guests. It touted itself as the choice of foreign dignitaries, particularly for Americans. There was a "First class American bar" (Americans did love a cocktail) as well as "American chairs." It advertised that "American requirements are understood and catered for." Which seems very wink-wink, but I can't imagine what it means.

It wasn't long before Smile was poached from the kitchens of the Cecil to work at Sherry's in America, one of New York City's finest restaurants. Restaurateur Louis Sherry opened the establishment in 1898 at Forty-fourth Street and Fifth Avenue, right across the street from Delmonico's.

Ranji Smile

It remained a popular destination for the city's wealthiest and fashionable residents for decades; Sherry had a knack for bringing the exotic to New York City, much to the delight of his clientele.

During a trip to London, Sherry stayed at the Cecil, likely because of its reputation as a comfortable home abroad for Americans, with its first-class American bar and American chairs. But after sampling Smile's curries, Sherry offered the cook the opportunity to create an exclusive curry menu at his restaurant in New York. Smile agreed. Lieutenant Colonel Newnham-Davis noted later, "Smiler has now, I am told, gone to America to make his fortune."

Smile and his English wife traveled to New York City in 1899. His arrival generated interest throughout the city. The *New York Letter* described him as possessing "clear dark skin, brilliant black eyes, smooth black hair, and the whitest of teeth." Though the reporter noted that Smile was short of stature, he was also thought of as very handsome—his beard was closely shaved and his clothing immaculate. It was said he spoke perfect English with a soft, lilting accent. He asked the patrons at Sherry's to call him simply "Joe."

Smile was a novelty in New York. Although hotels, restaurants, and homes in Britain employed Indian cooks, Smile was America's first Indian chef. He had his own station in Sherry's kitchen, and the French chef was told to mind his own business and stay out of the newcomer's way.

Sherry wanted to provide his clients with the exotic taste of the Orient. Smile, on the other hand, wanted to introduce his patrons to authentic Indian food, a cuisine that he knew was as complicated as anything the French chef cooked.

When Smile's curries hit the tables, they earned headlines. "A Chef from India, Women Go Wild over Him" read the *New York Letter* in 1899. The article made the rounds, Associated Press style, in newspapers across the country and was republished as far away as Oklahoma.

"You take a seat at one of the dainty tables," the journalist wrote, "look over the India menu with a sort of fear and trembling of what's to come, with a delightful uncertainty pervading your soul."

He continued:

Soon "Joe" arrives immaculately arrayed in a heavy white linen India costume, with a gorgeous turban of white all outlined in gold braid with a broad smile which shows you all his gleaming teeth, and with the little seductive manner that pleases the public so much, he lays before you a silver dish. As he removes the cover, you feel that life is not all a weary dream and you become less skeptical on Indian dishes in general. "Joe" makes a cunning little circle on your plate with the deftness of long practice of the whitest, flakiest, curried rice, in the center of which he places a bit of chicken. All this time he is telling you in his gentle sort of way that his one hope is that this may be only the first of many dinners he is to serve you.

The journalist's description of the experience was sensual, surely devised to titillate the *Letter*'s female readers. I mean, after I read this article, I had a crush on Ranji Smile.

The journalist went on to explain that Sherry's menu cost "a lot of money." Little wonder: Sherry's always strove to serve the finest ingredients available. And Smile made all his own curry powders and pastes from scratch, investing time and labor to create a superior product that would have tasted vastly different from a store-bought curry powder.

Guests at Sherry's could order from the Indian menu á la carte or select a multicourse dinner:

Kalooh Sherry

Murghi Rain

Muskee Sindh

Curry of Chicken Madras

Indian Bhagi Topur, Bombay Duck

Lettuce Ceylon

Khurbooja Handari

Coffee Karabsee

When I found this menu, I longed to experience the taste of these dishes served more than a century ago. So I invited a batch of adventurous friends over to my apartment as I attempted to prepare an authentic nineteenth-century American curry feast.

But figuring out the recipes behind Smile's menus was a difficult task. Transliteration of Indian languages into English was not standardized at the time, so the dishes appeared in multiple menus spelled different ways. It's also likely that Smile simply made up some of the exotic-sounding names for the food he served. One example was Kalooh Sherry, which could be a potato curry (from the Hindi word *aloo*) but was also likely named after the restaurant for which he worked. Another is Murghi Rain, which was either a misreported or mistranslated version of Murghi Ranji, a self-named dish listed on another of Smile's menus. I knew that *Murghi* translates to "chicken," but I couldn't guess what it meant to prepare it in the "Ranji" style. Smile liked to christen dishes after himself—probably some he invented; perhaps others he altered to appeal to the tastes of an American clientele.

I deciphered other items on the menu after searching through both historic American cookbooks and contemporary Indian American blogs. Muskee Sindh is a fish curry prepared in the traditional way of the Sindh Province, where Karachi is located, and where Smile first trained as a cook. In this preparation, white fish is gently poached in a cooked mixture of onions, tomatoes, ginger, chilies, and cilantro mixed with turmeric. On Smile's menu, this authentic dish is followed by Curry of Chicken Madras, an Anglicized curry from India's south. It was similar to the recipe in Randolph's cookbook: a whole chicken was jointed, fried with onions, and sprinkled with hot Madras curry powder, and then stewed with stock or coconut milk and served over rice.

Indian Bhagi Topur with Bombay Duck was the result of a similar blending of East and West: *topur* is slang for local fishermen; *bhaji* is a fried vegetable, often potatoes. My guess was that Bhagi Topur was the name for what is now called *bhaji batata bombil*, a dish hailing from the coastal state of Maharashtra. In this preparation, a pot of fried potatoes is paired with Bombay Duck, a lizardfish that is traditionally smoked, salted, and then fried—it was a favorite condiment of the occupying British in the nineteenth century. The fish and potatoes are rubbed with a mixture of chili powder, turmeric, garlic, green chilies, and cilantro, and then coated in oil and fried in layers like a gratin.

Salads as an individual course don't exist in Indian cuisine. So I figured that Lettuce Ceylon was added to comfort diners used to stylish French menus, which always featured a salad course. It's difficult to know whether Lettuce Ceylon was a wedge of iceberg lettuce with some dressing drizzled on top, as was the fashion of the time, or if it was Ceylon Lettuce, otherwise known as Malabar spinach or *pooi*, a climbing vine with tender leaves. A mouthful of this green tastes both citrusy and savory, with a fresh, grassy bite due to the plant's high chlorophyll content. Dinner ended with slices of Khurbooja, or cantaloupe, a melon native to India.

As I assembled my recipes, my stovetop became crowded with pans, all filled with multicolored bubbling sauces. Everything had to come off the stove at once, served steaming with sides of basmati rice. My guests and I scooped and shared from communal platters while discussing the dishes, much like when I had curry crawled in Jackson Heights. We were shocked by how much we liked the Anglicized Curry of Chicken Madras; but the evening's real winner was the beautiful blend of acid and spicy flavors in the authentic Muskee Sindh.

Muskee Sindh

A dish served on Smile's menu at Sherry's, this version comes from Indian blogger Nitu Didi. Make this one only if you love spicy food. The fresh chilies pack a kick, but it's offset nicely by citrusy cilantro and the floral flavor of turmeric. Adapted from her website at www.nitudidi.com and reprinted with permission.

Yield: serves 4 to 6

5 tablespoons vegetable oil

2 medium onions, finely chopped

2-inch piece of ginger, finely chopped

1 teaspoon salt

2 medium tomatoes, chopped

1/2 teaspoon ground turmeric

1 cup cilantro, finely chopped

6 Indian green chilies, chopped

2 muskie fillets, or another white fish such as perch, pike, walleye, grouper

1/4 cup of water

1. In a large skillet, heat the oil on medium-low heat. Add the onions, ginger, and salt. Cover the pan and cook until onions are soft (about 10 minutes), stirring occasionally.

2. Add in tomatoes, turmeric, half the cilantro, and half the chilies. Cover the skillet and cook until tomatoes are soft, about 3 to 4 minutes.

3. Lay the fish fillets on top, making sure they do not overlap. Add water. Cover, and shake pan so the fillets are gently covered by the tomato-onion mixture.

4. Gently poach fish for about 6 to 8 minutes over medium-low heat. The thicker the fish, the longer it will take to cook. Turn off the heat, but keep the pan covered and let it sit another 2 to 3 minutes. The fish will continue to cook with the heat off. Serve topped with remaining cilantro and chilies.

Smile's menu showed influence from all over India, as well as a strong connection to his hometown. It abided by French dining standards but also pulled from established American curry recipes. And it featured dishes created by Smile himself, perhaps designed with an American palate in mind. These were all techniques Smile used to slowly introduce Americans to Indian cuisine. As modern-day Indian American chef Floyd Cardoz told me when we discussed his views on Indian food in America, "I believe if you want people to eat what you make, whatever your culture is, until they embrace it, you have to use things they are familiar with."

Smile told the reporter at the *Letter* that he would like to publish a cookbook someday, so that Americans could prepare Indian cuisine at home. "So many ladies are fearful of my preparations, thinking that everything must be very hot and peppery," he said. "This is not so of India cooking. All things must be so nicely even, and such care as to smoothness, that it will be of so pleasant a taste they can but ask for more."

When Smile arrived in the United States, he was seen as an exotic curiosity by Americans who had never traveled to India. But he was not the only Indian immigrant living in the States at the time. The same year that Smile arrived on the East Coast, four Sikh laborers arrived in San Francisco. They came from Punjab, in the north of India, where Sikhism was founded. Their hair was long and wrapped under turbans, and their beards were unshorn—both important signifiers of their religion. The *San Francisco Chronicle* said of the immigrant Sikhs: "The quartet formed the most picturesque group that has been seen on the Pacific Mail dock for many a day. . . . They are all fine-looking men."

These men, and the nearly seven thousand that would follow them by 1914, lived a very different life than Smile did. Some came to the West Coast to work in lumber yards and on railroads; others to work in the fields, migrating with every harvest. Cheap labor from Asia was integral to food production in California. Many of these laborers aspired to own farms themselves. They were often married but had come without their families, with the intention of sending money home to support them and perhaps one day pay their way to the United States.

Smile himself strived to bring more Indian immigrants to America. He worked at Sherry's for two years, until 1901. The story of what happened next varies from source to source. An English paper said his curries were so successful that Louis Sherry sent him back to England to recruit more Indian cooks. But Smile told other reporters that his father, allegedly a wealthy merchant, had passed away, and he was returning to India to collect his large inheritance. In any case, Smile left his English wife behind in New York and boarded a steamer to cross the ocean.

A few months later, Smile turned up at a hotel in London, perhaps one of the establishments that had employed him previously. He checked in as "Prince" Ranji Smile. With him was a party of twenty-six "personal attendants." He wore at least one silver bracelet around his wrist, and "instead of salaaming to patrons who ate his curries, he was bowed to by obsequious white men." He had come a long way from "Smiler," the hotel curry chef who had first arrived in England.

This incident was the first time Smile adopted the title of Prince, a character he played on and off the rest of his life. His act was made more convincing by the fact he seemed to be in possession of a large fortune. Was it a commission from Sherry to find more workers? Had he really inherited it from his father in India? Or did he save a considerable sum of money during his time as a chef, serving the richest families in New York?

In the end, the persona—and the title—might have been taken on for practical reason: Smile needed a way to get his band of twenty-six Indian immigrants into the United States. After his steamship left England and arrived in Montreal, Smile and his party boarded a train to upstate New York. "The Hindus were allowed to cross the border at Plattsburg on the assumption that they were the personal attendants of a traveling potentate," wrote the *New York Times* in 1901. But as soon as he returned to New York, he was recognized instantly as the famous chef Ranji Smile—not a prince. A steward from Sherry's met the party when it arrived at Grand Central Station, but the restaurant was quick to distance itself from what soon developed into a troubling legal situation.

"I never claimed to be a prince," Smile shrugged to the press. Prince was his first name, he explained. "The Indians who came with me are simply tourists," he added. He mentioned a restaurant that he planned to open in New York, where some of his tourist friends "might" be employed in the future. But they certainly hadn't arrived with that intent. "I determined to come back and go into business in America, because I like America and the Americans," Smile said, likely with a smile.

"Now that the latter [Smile] has turned out to be a restaurant servant importing cheap Indian labor into this country as alleged, it is regarded as a violation of the contract labor law," the *Times* added ominously.

The Contract Labor Law, put into place in 1885, made it illegal for any individual or company to prepay passage for an immigrant or otherwise encourage immigration with the promise of a job. It had the dual purpose of trying to reduce immigration to the United States—particularly of unskilled laborers—and to encourage wealthier immigrants who could afford to pay their own passage. If Sherry's had indeed sent Smile looking for new Indian employees, it had violated the law and could be sued by the US government for up to $26,000 dollars—$1,000 for every employee imported. Smile tried to cover by saying they *might* come work in a restaurant he was opening.

While the US Immigration Bureau pursued the case, Smile gave demonstrations for home cooks in a New York department store.

Advertisements said that Smile, with "his suite of East Indian attendants, will entertain the ladies with instruction and demonstrations of his famous dishes." He also drummed up investors for New York's first Indian restaurant and supposedly opened it, as he had alluded to upon his return, on Fifth Avenue between Thirty-third and Thirty-fourth Streets in Manhattan. It was to be staffed by his immigrant friends. However, most of his party was deported by 1903, and Smile's plans for the restaurant collapsed.

The next year, Smile petitioned for citizenship—whether out of a true feeling of patriotism or fear of deportation, we'll never know. His citizenship request was one of about nine thousand filed under a peculiar heading in the New York City Department of Records and Information Services: "Neither this record nor any of the others with which it is filed contains an order of admission or any notation of memo from which it may be inferred that this person or any of the others was admitted to citizenship . . . it appears clear that either these applications were abandoned by the respective applicants or they were dismissed or denied by the court."

When a man of East Indian heritage, such as Smile or the Sikhs on the West Coast, applied for citizenship in the United States, there was a possibility, but no guarantee, that he would get it. At the time, citizenship policy was still guided by the first citizenship act put into place in 1790, where only a "free white person" was eligible for citizenship. In 1870, after the Civil War, the law was amended to include "aliens of African nativity and to persons of African descent." But if you were "Hindu," as immigrants from India were classified regardless of their actual religion, a judge would decide whether he thought you were white, and thus eligible for citizenship. It appears that Smile might have been denied based on the color of his skin.

Despite this setback, Smile left New York and went on tour. He spent summers cooking in Atlantic City. In 1904 the Hotel Flanders in Philadelphia announced "the engagement of the East Indian Culinary Artist." A headshot of Smile adorned the front of the menu; Indian dishes were offered every day, as well as Ladies' Teas, which were served by "Prince

Ranji and retinue of servants." In 1907 Smile gave demonstrations in Washington, DC, serving *dak bungalow*, a chicken-and-potato curry popularized by the English, to spectators who might have tried to re-create the dish at home.

The *Washington Post* reported that Smile was soon to be joined on tour by his young bride, "Princess Ranjit Smile," formerly Miss Rose Schlueter of Philadelphia. His former English wife was not mentioned—although a few years later, Smile said that she'd passed away. Stranger still: Miss Schlueter and Mr. Smile were never officially wed. Just twenty years old when the article was published, Miss Schlueter was waiting in Atlantic City and, according to the story, planned to meet up with Prince Smile in a few days. It's unclear if she ever arrived at his side; the 1910 census listed her as living with her parents in Camden, New Jersey, still single. In 1923 she was recorded as a lace maker in a business directory, working at her father's tailoring business in Camden. And that was where she stayed for the rest of her life: forty years of city directories show her making lace, first for her father, and then for her brother when he took over the business. Making lace and unmarried.

Smile's romance with Rose didn't slow him down. He became a celebrity chef, orchestrating demonstrations at halls and department stores, just like a Food Network star. In October 1907 he traveled to Indianapolis, performing with a troupe of jugglers, sword swallowers, and disappearing acts. In Pittsburgh, he served a six-course dinner "to the ladies of the Pennsylvania State Hotel Association," starting with a "Prince Cocktail" and including a chicken curry named after a historical Persian mathematician.

Different cities, different ladies. In 1910 he applied for a marriage license with Anna Marie Davidson but seems to have never gone through with the vows. In 1912 he bagged aspiring Broadway star Violet Ethel Rochlitz. He was thirty, she was twenty—he kept getting older, but the girls stayed the same age. Rochlitz was called "undeniably pretty," and a ravishing portrait of her appeared in the newspaper when they toured together in Boston. "Boston is entertaining a real Prince of India," a Utah newspaper reported. "He is Ranji Smile, a dapper little Oriental, with American clothes of the latest cut, and an American wife, who was formerly Miss Violet Ethel Rochlitz of New York City." In the photograph, she peered out from under an enormous hat with sleepy, sultry eyes; she clearly had a flair for the dramatic, much like her husband. Rochlitz credited her husband's cooking for making her more beautiful, and she even "espoused the Mahomedan faith," suggesting she had converted to Islam.

Rochlitz was not just Smile's arm candy; she had her own career. In 1914 she was cast on Broadway in the chorus of *Dancing Around* starring Al Jolson. The show's hit, "When the Grown Up Ladies Act Like Babies (I've Got to Love 'Em That's All)" is a bizarre little ditty: "When they walk like babies, talk like babies / That's the time I fall / And though they may be forty-three / Oh, how I want to bounce them on my knee . . ." I wonder what Smile thought of the song and if he came to watch her perform.

I found Smile and Rochlitz's wedding certificate on file in the New York City archives; New York was one of the few states that did not have antimiscegenation laws criminalizing interracial marriage. And as I studied their relationship, I wondered how they were received as they traveled across the country. Did their celebrity status exempt them from the growing racism toward immigrants of the period, or did some Americans react unfavorably to an Indian man married to an American woman? Whatever Smile and Rochlitz's relationship was like, it was over by 1916. Rochlitz contracted an infection—one that would spread to her heart and kill her. Her death certificate lists her as "single"; there is no mention of Smile.

Shortly after Rochlitz's death, Congress passed a new law that would have been important to Smile: the Immigration Act of 1917.

Sikh immigration on the West Coast was a trickle until 1910. In January 1910 ninety-seven "Hindoos" were admitted to the United States. By

April, eighty to a hundred Indian immigrants were entering the country every week. Local papers began wailing about the "Hindu Horde." Those who wanted to exclude Indians argued that these immigrants were "racially unassimilable laborers who competed unfairly with white workers and sent their money home."

In response to the public outcry, on February 5 the Immigration Act of 1917 was signed into law. It officially excluded South Asians from immigration to the United States, with a few exceptions, including tourists and highly skilled workers such as doctors. The Indian men who already lived in California could stay, but they would not be allowed to bring over their wives and children. Ironically, one of the big music hits that year was "Down in Bom-Bombay." "Where the girls are nice," the record sang, "They eat curried rice / Full of red hot spice in India far away."

Just two months after the new immigration restrictions were enacted, America entered World War I, and Smile, along with every other man of age in America, had to fill out a draft card. Despite the fact that America had banned immigration from India, South Asians living in the United States were expected to fight for their adopted country. The draft card listed his race as "Oriental." It also noted that he was living with a woman named May Smile. She was not his wife at the time, but they would get married in 1918. It is his fifth documented relationship.

Smile did not fight in the war but returned to New York from touring, where he got a job cooking in a hotel kitchen. In 1920 the census recorded a Ranjit Smile living at a new address in Harlem and with a new woman: Rebecca Smile. There is no legal record of their marriage, and no mention of May Smile, either. Rebecca, it turned out, came from Pennsylvania; she was listed as "black." Ranji, too, was listed as coming from Pennsylvania, and also as "black." They hosted a lodger, a recent immigrant from the West Indies. Smile's community was quite diverse; although many families listed in the census were categorized as black, some were Hispanic, others Asian. His neighbor Annie Uyesugi was a black woman married to a Japanese man, Willie Uyesugi. Their daughter, Belva, was listed as mulatto.

Some of Smile's neighbors were Indian, too, and belonged to the growing community of Bengali Muslims in New York City. Despite the law banning their immigration, a steady stream of undocumented immigrants found their way into the city. During World War I and afterward, Muslim Indian maritime workers, mostly from the eastern province of Bengal (now Bangladesh) worked the worst and most laborious jobs on British vessels, in the engine rooms and kitchens, earning a fraction of the wages that their British counterparts did. When ships were in port in New York City, some of these men would go ashore and never come back. If they could escape, they found better paying jobs in restaurants and factories onshore. In the 1920s and 1930s, many settled in Harlem. I imagine it might have been a comfort to Smile to live in a community of Indian men, with a shared religion, even if they originally hailed from hundreds of miles across the continent from Smile's hometown.

Smile had found a community, but he still straddled two worlds: one of celebrity and the other of growing oppression. In 1922 he was featured in the *New York Hotel Review*, a prominent trade magazine, in an article entitled "The Chef—The King of the Kitchen." His full-length photo appeared in the middle of the page: handsome at forty, in crisp kitchen whites and a turban. "Prince Ranji Smile, Chef at Breslin Hotel," the caption read. To either side of him were images of prominent French chefs working in New York. "America has given no attention to the development of a school of cookery of its own," wrote the author, Mary Pickett, "but has imported its cooks from all parts of the world and when the American culinary school is finally developed it will have embodied in it the good points of the culinary art of all the world."

Another name that appeared in print that year was Bhagat Singh Thind. A Punjabi Sikh, Thind had studied at the University of California at Berkeley, served in the army during World War I, and afterward applied for and received his citizenship. But the US Bureau of Naturalization appealed the decision "on the ground that the appellee was not a white person and therefore not lawfully entitled to naturalization." His citizenship was revoked. In 1923 the Supreme Court upheld this ruling, which meant that any Indian in America who had gained citizenship in the years leading up to this decision lost it as well. And all future applications by Indian men would be denied.

Smile had lived in America for thirty years, worked here, loved here, and even married here. Now he was being told that he belonged to a class of people unworthy of citizenship. Racial prejudice grew in America, and Prohibition would have made it difficult for Smile to find a job. When the sale of alcohol was banned in 1919, it cut off restaurants' main source of revenue. The loss of income greatly affected the fine-dining industry in New York; in fact, Smile's old employer, Louis Sherry, closed his restaurant in 1919, asserting that the passage of Prohibition was the deciding factor.

This hardship might have led to his decision, as he reached his fiftieth birthday, to leave America. In 1929, just a few months before the stock market crashed, Smile boarded a steamship bound for England. He went alone—no wife or children by his side, despite his many relationships. When he arrived in Southampton, the ship's manifest listed that his destination was the Hotel Cecil, his old employer. He might have returned to a job there, but the ship's manifest also indicated he didn't intend to make his home in the United Kingdom. I wonder if he was just passing through on his way back, finally, to Karachi.

Either way, that's the last known record of Smile; there are no further documents to indicate how he might have lived the rest of his life and how he might have died. I can imagine how difficult it must have been to make the decision to return to the country where he was born. After thirty years in the United States, a country in which he had enjoyed great triumphs and great defeats, Smile left. Interestingly, May Smile, his last official wife in America, filed for an annulment of their marriage in 1937. A notice appeared in the *Brooklyn Eagle* summoning

Ranji to appear in court—but long gone, and possibly deceased, it's unlikely he responded. The notice suggests even May didn't know what happened to Smile in the end.

While in America, Smile attempted to elevate Indian cuisine to the same respected status of French cuisine. He had mixed success: although Americans were fascinated by his cuisine, they did not embrace it outright as a part of the American culinary landscape—despite the growing number of curry recipes and Indian restaurants that appeared in the twentieth century.

In the years after Smile's departure, undocumented Bangladeshi immigrants in New York City began to open restaurants in Midtown Manhattan. They wouldn't have cooked in their home communities—where women oversaw food preparation—but in America, they attempted to re-create the flavors they remembered from home. In 1939 the *New York City Guide*—a reference book for tourists assembled by writers in the Works Project Administration (WPA), the government organization that created work for artists during the Great Depression—lists several Indian restaurants in the city. "Curries, chutneys, copra (dried coconut), tamarind wine" were available for order at four different establishments in Midtown Manhattan, including the Ceylon India Inn at 148 West Forty-ninth Street. There is still an Indian restaurant at this address, although it's now called Bombay Masala. It might be the oldest continually operating Indian restaurant in the country.

At the same time, newspapers and cookbooks abounded with recipes featuring curry powder. Fannie Farmer's 1921 cookbook offered twenty recipes that included curry powder, an impressive number in a book that is otherwise very slim in its use of spice, favoring primarily black pepper. There's Curried Lobster, Chicken Livers with Curry, Curried Eggs, and Crab Meat, Indienne. From the 1920s through the 1940s, the *New York Times* recommended adding curry powder to cold mayonnaise salads, corn chowders, and—like nineteenth-century cookbooks—as a way to dress up leftover chicken, mutton, or turkey—the latter of which was recommended for the day after Christmas. These restaurants and recipes indicate that by the middle of the twentieth century, curry powder was featured prominently in American cuisine.

Smile wouldn't be the last chef to become frustrated by America's reception of Indian food. The first time I traveled to Jackson Heights was nearly a decade before my curry crawl; I met with chef Floyd Cardoz, arguably the most famous Indian American chef working today. At the time, I was working as the head videographer for *New York* magazine. I remember climbing into a car with Josh Ozersky, editor in chief of the popular food blog *Grub Street*, and Floyd, who was then the head chef at Tabla, the celebrated Indian restaurant at Madison Avenue and Twenty-fifth Street in Manhattan. We drove far out into Queens, where Floyd—always kind and soft-spoken—walked us through Indian supermarkets, handling the vegetables gently as he told stories. We ate *jelabi*, fried chickpea funnel cakes soaked in sugar syrup, and it was the first time I had ever heard of *kulfi*, Indian ice cream. As he explained each dish, his excitement in sharing his love of his homeland's cuisine was palpable.

Remembering Floyd's passion for Indian cuisine in America, I reached out to him for an interview as I researched this book. I contacted him through his Twitter handle, and he actually responded. We set up a phone interview for eight in the morning; I sat at my desk at a quarter to eight, sleepy eyed in my jammies and sipping tea, waiting for his call.

I asked Floyd to tell me his story: he grew up in an upper-middle-class family in Mumbai, one of six, hardworking and smart. The family thought he'd become a doctor—because, as he told me, "That's what good Indian kids do."

But even as a child, food was more important to him. Every moment, he thought about what his next meal would be. He would hang out in the kitchen with his family's cook, to taste and to learn. When it came time for college, Floyd went to hospitality school. His family was not pleased, but he followed his interests. He was selected for a chef training program in India and, unsurprisingly, graduated with honors.

Floyd continued his studies at Les Roches International School of Hotel Management in Switzerland, before moving to New York City in 1987. He promised himself that if he didn't find a job in three months, he would leave. The day before his deadline, he got a position in a tiny curry joint called Indian Café, at 108th Street and Broadway in Manhattan. The food there was typical of American curries after Smile's departure: "There was one pot of gravy that they put everything in and made it a curry," Floyd said. One-pot curries, as Floyd called them, were based around a red sauce made with onion, tomatoes, garlic, ginger, turmeric, some chili, and garam masala.

"Then they'd take that to build the different dishes, so you say you want masala, they'd pull that out, they'd add some ginger and chilies and peppers, and they've got some masala. If you wanted korma, they'd take that same sauce out, add some cream, add some cashew paste, and give you korma." To Floyd, this style of service lacked the complexity of good Indian food.

Floyd reworked the menu at Indian Café, striving to create authentic food that he remembered from home. He felt the key to introducing new flavors was to make the menu smaller, so that it was easy to decide on what to order. He kept some ingredients that Americans were familiar with and then introduced diners to new ingredients he thought they would like. His menu was a success.

From Indian Café, Floyd moved to a position as sous-chef (assistant chef) at Raga in Rockefeller Center, which served food prepared by cooks from all over India. In the late nineties, Floyd went to work for the famous restaurateur Danny Meyer, and in 1998 opened Tabla. Floyd described the restaurant as using French technique but with Indian spicing. Like Smile, Floyd invoked the style of French cooking to elevate Indian cuisine in the American mind. But he also continued to innovate. He served the "home-style Indian food" of Indian homes in the United States, where Western ingredients were adapted with Indian spicing. For example, he made a mustard-green pizza, based on a Punjabi corn-flour bread called *makki di roti*, which was topped with a spinach-and-mustard-green curry and goat cheese.

In 1999 *New York Times* food critic Ruth Reichl wrote a three-star review that described eating at Tabla as a transcendental experience. "This is what I have been waiting for," she enthused. "Nothing I have tasted since has changed my mind." She went on to describe the dishes: mushroom soup "electric" with tamarind and ginger; and a roast chicken dusted with black pepper, cinnamon, and other "powerful" spices. The roti and naan—basic Indian breads—were presented "in crazy flavors— horseradish, buckwheat-honey, pumpernickel-caper . . ."

"This is American food, viewed through a kaleidoscope of Indian spices," Reichl wrote. "The flavors are so powerful, original, and unexpected that they evoke intense emotions."

Tabla closed in 2010, after the economic downturn. Floyd went on to cook in American-style fine-dining establishments where he occasionally injected his dishes with Indian spicing. He reached national fame after taking home the grand prize on the TV series *Top Chef Masters* in 2011 and, much like Smile, achieved celebrity status as an Indian chef.

He most recently opened White Street in Tribeca, which features "Indian-accented American fare," such as pumpkin soup spiced with clove, green cardamom, cinnamon, and red pepper. But he admitted that he has always toyed with the idea of opening a "fast, casual Indian" place in the vein of Chipotle, the hugely successful build-your-own-burrito chain. After more than a century of Indian immigration to America, it's tough to understand why Indian food isn't as well represented in American cuisine as Mexican food is.

"The important thing I believe is that no one yet has made [Indian food] user friendly," Floyd said. "Indian food is about flavor, it's not about overspicing; it's about seasonality, it's about freshness, it's about texture."

In the past ten years, the number of Indian restaurants in the United States has increased by 30 percent—and some of those are fast-casual establishments founded by Americans with Indian heritage. Tava Indian Kitchen, a chain in San Francisco known locally as the "Indian Chipotle," offers "burroti." In this Indian burrito, traditional ingredients such as fresh paneer cheese are coated with a choice of Indian sauces and rolled with brown rice in a foil-wrapped roti. In Manhattan, Desi Shack and Goa Taco use flaky *paratha*, another north Indian flatbread, for the same end. Desi Shack, near Union Square, leans Indian in its fillings, offering chicken tikka and curried potatoes with a choice of chutneys that range from mild to hot. On the Lower East Side, Goa Taco favors Mexican fillings such as pork belly with chipotle mayo, or chicken chorizo with herby *chimichurri* sauce, but it also offers a version of a Vietnamese *banh mi* sandwich, stuffed with veggies. Goa is packed at lunch and in the evenings, when the post–happy hour crowd comes to fill their cravings. After a beer or two, I devoured my paneer taco filled with masala spice chickpeas and tomatillos.

What's more, 13 percent of Americans cook Indian food in their homes at least once a month. The last time I ate a home-cooked curry, I was visiting my curry crawl buddy Raj and his wife, Jess, at their home in Brooklyn. Squeezed into their closet-like kitchen (standard for New York), they worked together to make Coconut Chicken Curry from the 2006 edition of the classic American cookbook the *Joy of Cooking*—although curry recipes, including Country Captain Chicken, have been included in this cookbook since at least the 1970s. Raj browned chicken in oil, and then added carrots, peas, onions, ginger, garlic, and cayenne pepper. Finally, a curry sauce was concocted from coconut milk and a tablespoon of golden-yellow curry powder.

For Raj, growing up in New Zealand, cooking has always been a big part of his life. "I'm a real Indian food snob," he told me. "A lot of us born outside India grew up experiencing food through our moms' kitchens." His mother always packed the refrigerator with all the ingredients she needed to cook a delicious Indian meal. When Raj immigrated to the United States, food reminded him of the comfort of home. Jess grew up in

New York, where, in her words, "takeout was just a phone call away." She admitted that she didn't begin to cook until she met Raj.

The chicken curry they prepared for me is one of their favorite recipes. "But I don't think of this as Indian food," Raj said. The bright-yellow curry was unlike anything his mother made. "It's totally an American curry."

Unlike Ranji Smile, Floyd and Raj both gained their American citizenship. Both were able to immigrate thanks to the Immigration and Nationality Act of 1965 (also known as the Hart-Celler Act), which President Lyndon B. Johnson signed into effect. The law abolished the race-based quotas for immigration—including the laws that prohibited Indian immigration. I watched Raj sworn in at his naturalization ceremony on April 9, 2013; it took place in the visitor center of the Lower East Side Tenement Museum, where we both work. The Tenement Museum is an institution dedicated to telling the story of immigrants in America, whether they arrived a hundred years ago or yesterday. The museum emphasizes that immigrants don't just become American; America is also changed by immigrants.

Garam Masala Ice Cream

This is a recipe of my own invention. Garam masala works particularly well in sweet dishes. In this recipe, the pairing with creamy dairy is magical— the result reminded me of spice-rich pumpkin pie. The garam masala gives the ice cream a little texture; if you'd like the ice cream perfectly smooth, use whole spices to infuse the cream while it's heating, then strain them out.

Yield: 1 quart

1 tablespoon garam masala
1 recipe Jefferson's French Vanilla Ice Cream (from chapter 2),
   leaving out the vanilla bean

1. Over medium heat in a dry skillet, gently toast the garam masala until it is fragrant, about 45 seconds.
2. Stir into warm ice cream custard and refrigerate overnight.
3. Freeze in your ice-cream maker until it reaches a soft-serve consistency. Scoop into a resealable storage container and freeze at least 6 hours, preferably overnight.

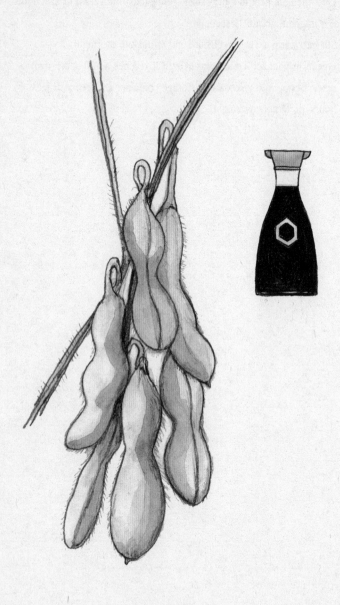

Soy sauce

Five

Soy Sauce

IN MAY 2014 I drove a little over an hour north of New York City, across the Triborough Bridge to the spring-lush Catskill Mountains of upstate New York. I passed through a small town in the Hudson River Valley and then turned down an industrial driveway into a shady parking lot. When I stepped out of my car, the air smelled clean, like trees and fresh water—but with just a touch of the savory scent of soy. I had traveled northward to visit the American division of Wan Ja Shan in Middletown, New York: a Taiwanese company that makes Japanese-style soy sauce.

Soy sauce is the third-best-selling condiment in the United States, behind mayonnaise and ketchup. But it's for more than pork fried rice. The year before my trip to Wan Ja Shan, I hosted Thanksgiving dinner at my apartment in Queens—or should I say Friendsgiving, since it was a gathering of thirtysomethings avoiding holiday travel. In addition to the turkey, I made a classic Green Bean Casserole, straight from the recipe on the Campbell's Soups website. It's my favorite Thanksgiving side: green beans swim in a rich brown gravy, topped with the crunch of salty fried onions. The original recipe was created in 1955 by the wonderfully named Dorcas Reilly, a staff member in the Home Economics Department of the Campbell Soup Company. Her goal was to create a fast, simple recipe with six ingredients that American housewives would always have on hand: green beans, canned cream of mushroom soup, French's Original Crispy Fried Onions, milk, black pepper, and *soy sauce*.

As I stirred together these ingredients, I wondered how on earth a condiment that featured prominently in Chinese and Japanese cuisines had come to be included in this recipe. Soy sauce became popular in the late nineteenth century after the arrival of waves of immigrants from China— and after the advocacy of the first self-proclaimed Chinese American, a man named Wong Chin Foo. But the flavor wouldn't be considered "American" until the twentieth century, as a result of the first Japanese manufacturing plant to open in the United States: a Kikkoman soy sauce factory.

As with all of the other flavors included in this book, I always keep a bottle of soy sauce in my pantry (like Dorcas Reilly). But I never really knew what it was and how it was made. I didn't have to travel far to find out: one of America's few soy sauce breweries was located just a short drive from my home. Wan Ja Shan is one of four soy sauce companies that brew in the United States: the world's largest soy sauce manufacturer, Kikkoman, as well as Yamasa and San-J, which are comparable in size to Wan Ja Shan. There is also one "microbrewed" soy sauce company, inspired by the thousands of small-batch soy sauce companies that are traditional in Japan. It's made in Kentucky, from the same limestone-filtered water of many of the country's finest bourbons, and aged in used bourbon barrels.

Wan Ja Shan was founded in Taiwan in the 1940s and expanded to America in 1977. The company opened its US outpost in the mountains of the Hudson Valley because the owners wanted to be near the large Asian customer base in New York and New Jersey. But additionally, the clean-tasting limestone-filtered water of the region is essential to making Wan Ja Shan's soy sauce.

When I arrived at the factory, company president Michael Wu bounded out from a back office to shake my hand. He had a broad smile and laugh lines to match. He led me to a room where he had set up a flow-chart on how soy sauce was made and handed me a cold mug of lychee-flavored fruit vinegar drink. Welcome to my perfect day.

Michael compared the craft of making a fine soy sauce to the art of making a fine wine. Both industries are very old, and both processes are deceptively simple. "Even though the ingredient is the same, the enzyme, the yeast the same—the result is different," he told me. "We can have a unique flavor compared with the Kikkoman. That's why we survive."

Most of the ingredients for Wan Ja Shan's soy sauce come from New York State: the wheat is purchased from farmers in the Finger Lakes, and the salt is mined in the same area. Only the soybeans are brought in from the Midwest. To make their soy sauce, Michael explained, the wheat is first dry roasted and then crushed. Soybeans are cooked with water, and then the two are mixed. Chinese soy sauce is often made only with soybeans—these are called tamari soy sauces in Japan—while most Japanese soy sauce is made with equal parts wheat and soy. Although Wan Ja Shan is a Chinese company, Michael prefers the flavor the roasted wheat adds. I do find that tamari soy sauce has a thinner flavor; soy sauce with wheat and soy tastes more robust.

To these cooked ingredients, a mold is added: *Aspergillus oryzae*. This fungus is used in many Asian countries for processing food, including fermenting soybeans for miso paste or fermenting rice for sake, the alcoholic beverage. It has been used in China for at least two thousand years, originally to make *jiang*, a salty food fermented from fish, meat, or grain. *Jiang* is the ancestor of miso, fish sauce, and soy sauce.

To make traditional Japanese soy sauce, *Aspergillus oryzae* is cultured on cooked rice; once the mold starts growing on the rice, it's called *koji*. It's then added to the soy-and-wheat mixture. At Wan Ja Shan, the soy sauce is fermented slightly differently: the cooked soybeans and wheat are inoculated directly with *A. oryzae*, which is then cultured for sixty hours. This mixture becomes the *koji*, or in Mandarin Chinese, *ch'ü*. While the mold grows, the grains sit in a trough in a dark room—Michael undid a complicated locking mechanism, like a bank vault, to show it to me. The grains are mixed daily by a friendly looking robot on tracks.

After sixty hours, it's time for salt. A 23 percent saltwater brine is made with that perfect Catskills water and combined with the other ingredients. The salt prevents the growth of any harmful bacteria, while still allowing the *A. oryzae* to do its thing. And its thing is fermentation: it breaks down proteins and starches in the soy and wheat, and converts them into sugars and amino acids such as glutamic acid, the source of soy sauce's earthy, umami flavor.

Humans have a natural preference for glutamic acid's savoriness, and combined with salt, it's irresistible. In the year 2000, scientists identified taste receptors on the tongue that recognized glutamic acid. Umami—or savory—became an official fifth taste, alongside sweet, sour, salty, and bitter. It can also be considered "protein taste," because of its presence in protein-heavy foods. When your glutamate receptors come across this taste, your brain interprets the food as containing protein. Humans need protein to live: it helps us repair old cells and make new ones. When we find it, our brains reward us with feelings of pleasure. Soy sauce is high in protein, at 1.3 grams per tablespoon.

The fermented mixture is sent to enormous aging tanks. Each is the size of a grain silo and holds a hundred tons of maturing soy sauce, which is mixed weekly from bottom to top using high-pressure air valves. "Boom!" Michael used his hands for emphasis as I imagined the soy sauce sloshing around inside the tanks. The soy sauce sits for six months to mature; then the liquid is pressed from the grain, pasteurized, and bottled. One batch of soy sauce at Wan Ja Shan yields eight tons of finished product.

Wan Ja Shan's soy sauce is brewed naturally, which means that it is vastly different from the condiment that comes in packets with Chinese takeout. This type of soy sauce is known as HVP soy sauce, or hydrolyzed vegetable protein. It's made with soybeans that have been defatted for the soy-oil industry. Instead of *koji*, these beans are treated with hydrochloric acid to break down the sugars and proteins. After a few days, the acid is neutralized with sodium carbonate (a base), sweetened with corn syrup, and mixed with salt, water, and caramel coloring. It's a quick and inexpensive product: it takes three days to brew, while soy sauce at Wan Ja Shan takes six months. The HVP method has been used by companies in Asia and America for nearly a century.

Naturally brewed soy sauce has a much older history in the United States than the HVP method does. The first soy sauce manufactured in the Western world was produced in 1767 in Thunderbolt, Georgia, near Savannah, long before the first Chinese and Japanese immigrants arrived. A British immigrant named Samuel Bowen introduced soybeans—today a principal crop in America—for the purpose of making soy sauce.

In the eighteenth century, the same merchants who traveled to the Far East in search of black pepper were also the first Europeans to taste, and import, soy sauce. By 1750, it was available in New York as an English import, just like black pepper. Only affluent Americans could afford to purchase the condiment, which was bottled in small casks or ceramic jugs. Bowen saw an opportunity to make soy sauce more affordable. As a sailor on a British East India Company ship, he had been arrested during a trading trip to China as part of a crew that had violated trade embargos. He was imprisoned for four years. Somehow during his time there, Bowen witnessed how soy sauce was made and got his hands on some soybeans. He brought this knowledge with him when he immigrated to America. By the time of the American Revolution, Bowen was selling his own patented soy sauce up and down the Eastern Seaboard.

Bowen's Patent Soy wasn't satisfying the needs of any ethnic population—which is how other flavors in this book became broadly used in America. Nor was it appeasing the appetites of a seafaring community that had developed adventurous tastes overseas, like curry powder did. By Bowen's time, the flavor of soy sauce was accepted as an essential flavor of English-descended American cooking. In the eighteenth and early nineteenth centuries, recipes for making soy sauce at home appeared in English and American cookbooks. Since soybeans were not widely available, these recipes used local ingredients such as mushrooms, walnuts, and fish—the latter mimicking fish *jiang*, or fish sauce. *The Cook Not Mad, or Rational-Cookery*, published in America in 1830, included a recipe made from anchovies and stale beer that (according to the author) "is by many preferred to the best Indian soy." These soy sauce knockoffs were used as a base in sauces for fish and meat, or could be poured into small glass soy cruets for use at the table alongside other condiments, such as vinegar and mustard.

Tomato was another popular ingredient for making American "soy" sauce. Mary Randolph featured a recipe in her 1824 *The Virginia Housewife*—the same book that featured early recipes for vanilla ice cream and curry recipes. She used the juice of cooked tomatoes, added salt, and then boiled it with onions, mace, and black pepper. Recipes published after Randolph's suggested that the home cook add vinegar to this recipe. The names for these varying sauces were "ketchups," or "catch-ups," or "catsups," derived from the Indonesia word for soy sauce: *ketjap*. I've made a recipe from Eliza Leslie's 1847 cookbook. Leslie directed the home cook to layer mushrooms in a crock with salt and set it in a warm spot. I layered my mushrooms in a stoneware crock and hid them on a back shelf in my Queens apartment, away from the skeptical eyes of my roommates.

Leslie recommended that the mushrooms sit for a day, though other recipes suggested a week or more. Every day, I watched as juice separated from the mushrooms, and eventually I strained the liquid and boiled it, as directed by Leslie. When it was done, I ladled it over slices of roast venison. The result tasted like no condiment in American kitchens today; it was almost medieval in its use of fragrant spices, but also deeply earthy and savory.

Eliza Leslie's Mushroom Catchup

Traditionally, this sauce was used as a dressing for meat; you can use it in all the places that soy sauce is used today. This recipe uses mace, a red, flaky spice that is part of the nutmeg fruit; it can be ordered online or found in Indian spice stores.

Yield: makes about 1 3/4 cups

2 quarts mushrooms, wiped clean
1/4 cup salt
1 1/2 ounces whole black peppercorns
1 1/4 ounces whole allspice
1/2 ounce sliced fresh ginger
3 whole cloves
13 blades of mace
1/2 ounce whole dried cayenne (chili) peppers
1 whole nutmeg

1. Spread a layer of mushrooms in the bottom of an earthenware crock or plastic Tupperware and top with a generous sprinkle of salt. Repeat until you have used all your mushrooms. Cover the crock with a clean kitchen towel. Let the mushroom-and-salt mixture sit for about 6 hours in a warm place; then break up the mushrooms into small pieces with your fingers and mix well. Let sit overnight.

2. Transfer mushrooms and liquid to a medium pot and add in black pepper. Bring mixture slowly to a boil and then add in remaining spices. Simmer over medium heat for 15 minutes, stirring occasionally.

3. Remove from heat and allow to cool. Strain through a cheesecloth-lined colander, pressing and squeezing the mash with your hands or a spatula to ensure that all the juices are released. Bottle and refrigerate.

It was these ketchups and catsups that would end up replacing the more expensive soy sauce in American kitchens. So although soy sauce was made in the United States long before the first Chinese immigrants arrived, it was largely forgotten by the time these immigrants settled in large numbers. The earliest Chinese immigrants came to New York with the Far East trade in the early nineteenth century. Ships often returned to harbor in New York City with Chinese crew members, who settled around the port areas. There was a tiny Chinatown near Mott Street in New York City in 1830, and perhaps fifty Chinese people living in the whole city by 1860. I wonder what some of America's earliest Chinese immigrants thought of Bowen's Patent Soy, if they ever encountered it. Was it a comforting dose of home? Or, like the waffles and maple syrup I ordered while in the middle of a Mexican jungle—did it fall short and become a reminder of how far they were from their birthplace?

Around the same time Chinese immigrants were settling in New York City, the Chinese population boomed on the West Coast during the California Gold Rush of 1848. Many young men came from the province of Canton (modern-day Guangzhou), driven by overpopulation, natural disasters, and wars with Western powers. Regular trade with the United States meant contact with American sailors and the idea of the lucrative opportunities that awaited them in the United States. Families sent sons to work in America; the money they made went back to China to support the family.

The work these Chinese men found was as low-paid laborers in mines, on farms, and on railroads. Many men who didn't go into mining themselves supported mining communities by opening stores or restaurants in the Wild West of California's early years. By the time California became a state in 1850, fifty Chinese merchants were invited to take part in the commemorative festivities. By 1852, there were more than twenty thousand Chinese living in California; by 1870, that number would grow to fifty thousand.

Wong Chin Foo arrived during this first boom in Chinese immigration, but his story was different from those of his fellow immigrants. He was born in the northeastern province of Shandong in 1847. He was from a well-to-do family and spoke Mandarin—unlike the struggling Cantonese laborers that made up the majority of the immigrants to America. But Wong's family lost their money when he was young, and at thirteen years old, his aging, destitute father could no longer take care of him. He was given to the care of American missionaries living nearby.

Wong adapted well to the religious community, though he would later renounce the Christian faith as an adult. He was so successful in his studies that a Baptist missionary named Sallie Little Holmes brought him to the United States in 1867; he enrolled in a university and was set on the path to becoming a preacher. He studied first in Washington, DC, and then in Pennsylvania, mastering English, and lectured to earn money to make ends meet. He spoke in cities along the East Coast, including Salem, Massachusetts, giving talks to church groups. He'd speak on the customs and religion of the Chinese people and how they differed from Americans in their habits, including topics such as courtship, marriage, education, and religion.

Much in the same way that Ranji Smile attracted attention because he was different, Wong was considered exotic and intriguing. A photo of him at this time shows an eager, bright-eyed young man, dressed in fine Chinese silks, with a tremendously long braid, or queue, trailing to the floor. Wong patiently explained aspects of Chinese life in order to humanize the people of his country to Americans who had no firsthand knowledge of China. Later, he used descriptions of Chinese cuisine to serve this same purpose. Audiences were rapt, and Wong eked out a living.

He returned to China in 1870, got married, and fathered a son—before he had to flee to the United States to escape arrest. Wong was involved in revolutionary activities with designs to overthrow the Chinese imperial government. He was also excommunicated from the Baptist Church for extolling the virtues of Buddhism. It was a busy time.

When he returned to the United States, leaving behind his wife and son, he petitioned for citizenship, which was granted in 1874. Wong soon embarked on a multistate, multiyear lecturing tour, which was noted in publications of the period. *Harper's Weekly*, in 1877, described him as an "intelligent, cultured gentleman, speaks English with ease and vivacity, and had the power of interesting his audiences." The article also featured a large lithograph of Wong wearing traditional Chinese garb and in a very casual pose: legs crossed, his left arm draped over the back of a chair. He is broad faced and handsome at thirty, his eyes untroubled, his expression one of calm confidence.

Within a decade, Wong secured recurring features in major American newspapers. He wrote about Chinese life, particularly the daily activities in the Chinatowns of American cities. Food was one of his main topics. He described the dishes found in local restaurants, how they were prepared, and how they tasted. He gave American readers knowledge that, like any good food blog today, made them bold enough to venture into an unfamiliar Chinese restaurant themselves. He explained carefully how the Chinese used condiments such as soy sauce and introduced Americans to the preparations of dumplings, rice, vegetables, fruits, and insects. He even taught Americans his strong opinions on how to brew a proper pot of Chinese tea.

The food that Wong described was different from what he'd grown up with in China. The Chinese men who immigrated to America brought with them a longing for the foods they ate back home, but much like the Bengali men who immigrated to New York at the turn of the twentieth century, these men weren't cooks. They were farmers, raised in communities where food was traditionally prepared by women. So whether these men were cooking for American miners in the California Gold Rush, for tourists in New York, or for their own homesick community, they themselves were learning how to cook. They experimented with local American ingredients—adding ingredients from home such as soy sauce when they could—and blended them with Chinese cooking styles. As a result, their food would evolve into a new, Chinese American cuisine.

These Chinese men would go on to open restaurants, which, in California, were known locally as "chow chows," a slang term for the food they served. According to a *New-York Tribune* reporter visiting San Francisco in 1849: "There are three Chinese houses, denoted by their long three-cornered flags on yellow silk. The latter are much frequented by Americans, on account of their excellent cookery, and the fact that meals are $1 each, without regard to quantity. Kong Sung's house is near the water, Whang-Tong's in Sacramento Street and Tong-Ling's in Jackson Street. There the grave Celestials [Chinese] serve up their chow-chow and curry, besides many genuine English dishes." Curry was one of the few English words Americans had to describe the unfamiliar Chinese dishes of vegetables, sliced meat, and soy sauce cooked quickly together over a hot fire.

Although Chinese immigrants were an integral part of the community in cities such as San Francisco—and also in the diverse and rugged California frontier—as their population increased, so did the prejudice against them. By the second half of the nineteenth century, they were considered the strangest of America's immigrant groups: unassimilable heathens whose different physical appearance, dress, and customs singled them out for harassment. "An American yesterday attacked a Chinaman on Dupont Street, beating him shamefully," reported the *Daily Alta California* in 1853. "The Chinamen in the neighborhood were afraid to interfere, and the Americans, of whom there was a large crowd, stood by and

Wong Chin Foo

saw the poor Chinaman abused. The assailant held the unfortunate Celestial by the queue and kicked and beat him until he was tired, and when the poor fellow got loose and was going off, a policeman came up, saw by his bloody face that he had been in a fight, and arrested him."

Aside from being the targets of violence and racial slurs, Chinese residents in California were also the targets of race-based laws. In 1852, Chinese miners were subjected to special state taxes. In 1863, Chinese children were forbidden from attending public schools; shortly thereafter, men were legally forbidden from testifying in court. California Chief Justice Hugh Murray said of the latter law: "The same rule which would admit them to testify would admit them to all the equal rights of citizenship, and we might soon see them at the polls, in the jury box, upon the bench, and in our legislative halls."

In 1882, the Chinese Exclusion Act was signed into national law. This law banned Chinese from entering the country, with very few exceptions, and prohibited Chinese immigrants already living in the United States from becoming citizens. Although the law would initially stay in effect for only ten years, it was soon made permanent and was largely in place until 1965.

By the time this law was enacted, Wong cut off his long queue and began to dress in American clothing. As an educated former missionary, he would have been one of the few exceptions defined by the Exclusion Act. Nevertheless, he agitated on behalf of all Chinese immigrants: organizing Chinese communities in America, publically debating anti-Chinese spokesmen, and eventually testifying in Congress in opposition to anti-Chinese immigration laws. Wong became an extremely prolific writer, launching the first Chinese-language newspaper in New York City in 1883, which he dubbed the *Chinese American*. It's the first time this term was used in print. It symbolized the blended American identities of Chinese immigrants—a blend that was also reflected in Chinese American food.

In New York, Chinese eating habits were focused on in the newspapers and often negatively stereotyped. An 1883 *New York Times* article asked, "Do the Chinese Eat Rats?" after a nosey neighbor claimed he saw the butchered bodies of rats or small cats in his Chinese neighbor's rear yard. The reporter uncovered no incidences of cat eating—just two frustrated Chinese men making a vegetable stew.

Wong used the American interest in Chinese food to attempt to create empathy for the Chinese Americans themselves. In one series of articles on Chinese cooking, he wrote: "Contrary to the general impression, rats, cats, and puppies are no more commonly eaten by Chinese than by Americans. Poultry and pork are the favorite meats. They are very clean in their cooking."

In 1884 he wrote a lengthy column for the *Brooklyn Daily Eagle* entitled "Chinese Cooking. Wing Chin Foo's [*sic*] Account of His Countrymen's Customs. The Oriental and Occidental Cuisine Compared. Plain Viands and Mysterious Dishes." In it he included a description of a dish called "chop soly," better known as chop suey. This was the first time the dish was mentioned in print.

Wong compared chop suey to a ragout and went on to claim that it "may be justly termed the national dish of China. Each cook has his own recipe." Foo's description of the dish is what is called today a stir-fry. He wrote that it included "a mixture of chicken's livers and gizzards, fungi, bamboo buds, pig's tripe, and bean sprouts stewed with spices," and was served with a gravy made from a version of Worcestershire sauce. He assumed that Americans were unfamiliar with soy sauce, and since Worcestershire is a descendent of soy sauce, it was a good comparison. This dish, Wong emphasized, was a staple of Chinese American cooking.

I've often heard chop suey dismissed as "not real Chinese food." But Renqiu Yu, a history professor at the State University of New York at Purchase, who has extensively researched the origins of chop suey, wrote that when this dish first appeared in America, it was very authentic. "Chop suey" is the Americanization of the Cantonese phrase "*za sui*," meaning, literally, "different pieces." In cooking, *za sui* referred to cooking entrails and giblets; when offal was fried, it was called "chow chop suey." In America, chop suey featured a host of ingredients, some of them Chinese, others American. But it was cooked by Chinese men using Chinese cooking techniques. It was a Chinese dish that evolved as immigrants adapted to their new home. And it was because of this dish that Americans began buying soy sauce again, in order to re-create Chinese cuisine in their own homes.

Shortly after Wong's article was printed, recipes for chop suey appeared in newspapers and cookbooks across the country. Although these recipes were adapted to Americans tastes, featuring familiar ingredients such as peas and asparagus tips, they also included unexpectedly accurate Chinese ingredients, such as chicken gizzards, and ingredients that would require a trip to Chinatown, such as soy sauce.

I made chop suey for the first time in front of a TV camera, as the resident chef on NYC TV's *Appetite City*. The show, hosted by *New York Times* food columnist William Grimes, was based on his book of the same name—a history of food in New York City. For six days, while the show was shooting, a director and two cameramen crammed into my Queens apartment, and my kitchen became a cooking studio set. It was my job to show viewers how to re-create dishes from New York City's past.

As we prepared our episode on Chinatown, I looked for an original recipe for chop suey. I dug one up that had appeared in a 1901 *Times* article designed to bring the exotic taste of New York's Chinatown to the home kitchen. The recipe, the American author promised, "can be made by any intelligent housewife."

For four persons—Two chickens' livers, two chickens' gizzards, one pound young, clean pork, cut into small pieces, half an ounce of green root ginger, two stalks of celery. Sautée this in a frying pan over a hot fire, adding four tablespoonsful of olive oil, one tablespoonful of vinegar, half a cup of boiling water, one teaspoonful of Worcestershire sauce, half a teaspoonful of salt, black and red pepper to taste, dash of cloves and cinnamon. When nearly done, add small can of mushrooms, half a cup of either bean sprouts or French green peas, or string beans chopped fine, or asparagus tips. The See Yu sauce which is eaten with this delectable dish can be procured at any Chinese grocery.

See-Yu sauce is soy sauce—from the Japanese word for it, *shoyu*.

I cooked all of these ingredients in a regular pan, not a wok, just like an intelligent American housewife of the early twentieth century. But then there was the matter of the gizzards. The gizzard, by the way, is an organ in a chicken's digestive tract that grinds food. My Chinese American friends couldn't stop talking about how delicious they were when their moms cooked them. But everyone failed to mention—or didn't know— that gizzards should be parboiled before they're stir-fried, as in chop suey.

With the cameras rolling, I took a few tentative bites of gizzard. It had a texture I can only describe as a meat-apple. Meaty, yet crunchy. I chewed a few times before spitting the gizzard out into a napkin as delicately as possible.

Chop suey in a proper restaurant must have been more delicious than my attempt; or at least its novelty made it popular. By 1903, there were 300 to 400 chop suey houses in New York City, and between 1870 and 1920, the number of Chinese workers employed in restaurants grew from 164 to 11,438. Chop suey was also one of the earliest forms of Chinese takeout in New York. According to the *New-York Tribune* in 1903, "Few Bohemian gatherings are complete without a pail of chop suey, brought, fresh and hot, from Chinatown." I imagine some turn-of-the-century hipster hauling a bucket of steaming chop suey from her favorite spot before a night of partying. Around this time, chow mein also became popular. It was essentially the same dish, loaded with soy sauce and served over noodles, sometimes with a side of rice. Chinese food, and the all-important condiment of soy sauce, was leaving the kitchens of restaurants and coming directly into American homes.

Chow Mein—Latest

My dear friend Kat included this recipe in a cookbook of recipes assembled for me by my colleagues at the Lower East Side Tenement Museum. She added this note: "My Dad has chased the Chinese food of his 1930s New York youth for at least 40 years. He finally took the search into his own kitchen and hit upon this 'latest' 'recipe,' a balance of memory, nostalgia, and dedication. I forced him to write it down—it's the closest I have to a family recipe!" The original recipe was only a list of ingredients, and I added instructions with the help of Henry Low's *Cook at Home in Chinese*, published in 1938.

Yield: serves 4

For the sauce:
1 ½ tablespoons cornstarch
¾ cup chicken broth
2 tablespoons beef broth
1 tablespoon sugar
1 tablespoon sherry
1 tablespoon sesame oil
1 tablespoon hoisin sauce* or ½ tablespoon molasses
4 tablespoons soy sauce
¼ teaspoon ground ginger
¼ teaspoon MSG

* A sweet sauce made from soy beans; look for it in the Asian section at the supermarket.

For the Chow Mein:

1 cup dried chow mein noodles (such as La Choy brand)

2 tablespoons peanut oil

1/2 pound chicken, white or dark meat, cut into long, thin strips

1/2 cup bok choy, stem cut off and sliced thinly

1/2 cup thinly sliced celery

1/2 cup thinly sliced onion

1/4 cup canned mushrooms, sliced thinly

1/2 cup bean sprouts (fresh or canned)

1 scallion, white and green parts sliced thinly and separated

1. Combine the sauce ingredients and whisk until smooth. Place the chow mein noodles in a serving bowl.

2. Add the peanut oil to a skillet or wok and heat over high heat until smoking. Add chicken and cook for 2 minutes, stirring constantly.

3. Add the vegetables (except green parts of scallion) and sauté another 2 minutes, stirring constantly.

4. Add sauce and cook for 2 minutes more. Make sure to incorporate the sauce well, so that it is evenly distributed, and the chicken and vegetables are well coated.

5. Pour the mixture over chow mein noodles. Top with green scallions. Serve immediately, family style.

In 1898, just as chop suey and chow mein were becoming popular in America, Wong Chin Foo decided to return to China. After twenty-five years, he longed to reunite with his wife and son. When he arrived, he experienced severe culture shock. He felt out of place in his homeland. In one letter, he wrote, "I will never be able to live among [the Chinese] anymore." He was no longer Chinese, but Chinese American. He had a foot in both worlds, but perhaps felt at home in neither. Before Wong could return to America, he took ill and died of heart failure, a few miles from the mission where he was raised. He was fifty-one.

Wong's writings left a mark in the memories of many Americans. In 1908, a reporter from the *Brooklyn Daily Eagle* paid tribute to him: "A remarkably clever young Chinaman dwelt in this city. He was a constant contributor to the newspapers," he wrote. "Hundreds of my readers will recall the name of Wong Chin Foo, and I am sure many reporters of the early eighties will remember meeting him out on assignments." Wong's legacy was his writing, which focused on the experience of the Chinese men and women who chose to make the United States their home—in doing so, he tried to normalize their presence for their American neighbors.

By the time Wong left America, soy sauce was used in American kitchens for the preparation of Chinese dishes such as chop suey. Although Americans had been cooking with some form of soy sauce since the eighteenth century, by the late nineteenth century, it had been replaced with condiments like Worcestershire sauce and tomato ketchup. Chinese immigrants made soy sauce popular again in America, but Japanese immigrants would make this flavor American by demonstrating how it could be used in a variety of traditionally American dishes.

Japanese immigrants first arrived in the United States during the last two decades of the nineteenth century, their numbers growing from just 148 people in 1880 to 72,157 in 1910. During that time, Japan was thought of as a rising military power, after an unexpected victory over the Russian Empire in the Russo-Japanese War of 1904–05. Many Japanese men left home to escape compulsory military service, and ended up in California, taking many of the same jobs as Chinese men: miners, farmers, shopkeepers. But whether an immigrant had left from China or Japan, upon arriving on the West Coast his first impression of America was the same: the Angel Island Immigration Station in San Francisco Bay.

There is one dominant immigrant narrative that many students are first taught in grade school: Ellis Island, the huddled masses, the open doors. But New York was not the only port of immigration in the United States. Built nearly twenty years after Ellis Island, in 1910, the immigration station at Angel Island enforced race-based laws such as the Chinese Exclusion Act. It ferreted out those whom Americans believed did not belong on its shores. While Ellis Island detained only 20 percent of all the immigrants who passed through its doors, Angel Island detained 60 percent; and while Ellis Island deported 2 percent of immigrants, Angel Island deported 14 percent.

Angel Island processed an enormous number of Chinese immigrants, but people arrived from many other points of origin—including Sikhs from Punjab, India, and Japanese immigrants. However, the Japanese immigration experience was very different. As the population of Japanese in California increased, many became successful farmers who were seen as competition for white American farmers. Anti-immigrant sentiment gained momentum. In 1906 the San Francisco school board ordered all Japanese students into segregated "Oriental" schools. Japan considered this "an affront to its national honor," and if there's any clearer indication that Japan was regarded as a country not to be messed with, President Teddy Roosevelt interceded personally.

In comparison with Indian and Chinese immigrants, who were being banned outright from entry into the United States, in 1907 Roosevelt sent a delegate to Japan to forge an informal "Gentlemen's Agreement" that would regulate the movement of Japanese immigrants. The Japanese government agreed to deny visas to Japanese laborers, while allowing the emigration of "desirable" classes such as students and merchants. However, Japan insisted that, unlike other excluded immigrant populations, Japanese who already resided in the United States could send for their families to join them, including new brides. Under this exception, another 120,000 Japanese immigrants came into America by 1924 starting the tradition of "picture brides." Most Japanese marriages until the mid-twentieth century were arranged, so if a suitor lived in the United States, the potential couple could exchange photos through a matchmaking intermediary.

Shizu Hayakawa was a picture bride; she left her family's dairy in

Fukuoka in 1919 to meet her husband in America. She remembered the steamship stopped overnight in Hawaii, where she and the other picture brides were allowed to disembark for the evening: "We all dressed in Japanese kimonos and went *shan shan* [walking with pride] to a restaurant where we ate delicious sukiyaki [beef cooked in a soy sauce]," she said. When Shizu arrived at Angel Island and met her new husband, Shuneki Hayakawa, she was pleased to find that he had brought her sushi when he came to the dock. The sushi was likely brushed with *nikiri*, a mixture of soy sauce, dashi (a broth made from a kelp called kombu), sake, and mirin. With Japanese women came Japanese cuisine, and with it, more soy sauce. It is used in some way in every aspect of Japanese cooking, whether as a marinade, a seasoning, a sauce, a pickling base, or a dip.

Japanese immigration dwindled after stricter immigration laws went into place in 1924, and stopped altogether in 1942, after the Japanese surprise attack on the US naval base at Pearl Harbor. President Franklin Roosevelt issued an executive order that forced thousands of Japanese Americans from their homes and businesses and into internment camps. The ten camps were located far from civilization, such as Manzanar in California: tucked in the Sierra Nevada Mountains, about a hundred miles from Death Valley. They were simple barracks that would become the home and the prison of Japanese American citizens for nearly four years. In December 1945, the US Supreme Court found that holding American citizens without charge was unconstitutional, and the families were finally allowed to return to their communities.

In America, Japanese families were the victims of racism bred from fear; on the other side of the ocean, American soldiers stationed in occupied Japan met and married Japanese women. These war brides immigrated to America, which they found often isolating. Since they followed their American husbands—as opposed to joining Japanese husbands like the picture brides—they often ended up in parts of the United States far from Japanese communities. They sought out foods and flavors from home as a source of comfort in their new country, and in turn shared those flavors with their American families. Suddenly there was a new audience for Japanese products—and brands began to take notice.

Hisa Tanaka, who moved to Seattle in 1952 after marrying US Army sergeant Bob Feragen, remembered purchasing Japanese products in the groceries of Seattle's Little Japan.

"Especially Kikkoman soy sauce," Tanaka said. "He [Kikkoman] really appreciate war brides because we invite American people, teach all family, husbands' family . . . how to make Japanese food, all neighbors." She explained, "So they all have sudden need, all business start growing because of Japanese war brides."

In 1949, 251,000 gallons of soy sauce were imported from Japan to America; by 1954, 333,600 gallons were needed to meet demand—and Kikkoman products represented 85 percent of those imports. Kikkoman had established itself as an importer in America as far back as 1885, supplying the Chinese and growing Japanese populations in California. It continued to gain popularity in the twentieth century because Kikkoman products tasted better than other soy sauces for sale in the United States. After World War II, the market was dominated by domestically made HVP soy sauce. Kikkoman soy sauce, on the other hand, was brewed naturally for superior flavor—much the way that Michael Wu makes soy sauce at Wan Ja Shan today.

Kikkoman had a larger goal in mind. It wanted to expand its customer base. The company orchestrated a carefully crafted plan to make soy sauce an indispensable part of the American pantry. After the war, much of Kikkoman's raw material for making soy sauce—soy and wheat—were grown in America and exported to Japan for brewing. In 1972, as business expanded in the United States, the company decided to open a factory close to its raw materials, in Milwaukee, Wisconsin. It was the first Japanese manufacturing plant to open in the United States.

You heard me right. Not cars. Not computers. Soy sauce.

The American men who went to work at Kikkoman were peppered with questions and accusations: "How can you work for those Japanese? Don't you remember World War Two?"

But the Kikkoman takeover could not be stopped. The year after the factory opened, Kikkoman released an eighty-page cookbook called *The Kikkoman Way of Fine Eating: Discover a New World of Flavor with Brewed Soy Sauce*. The cover featured a photograph of a backyard cookout, including a new version of the all-American family: white dad, Japanese mom, and two Japanese American children. And bottles and bottles of Kikkoman soy sauce.

This cookbook boasted a variety of recipes, all of them incorporating soy sauce. It presented authentic Japanese dishes, such as Udon Noodles and *Nigiri* Sushi. It also included tiki recipes, made popular by US servicemen who'd fought in the Pacific during World War II and returned home with a craving for Asian foods—much like the soldiers who craved spicy bowls of chili after fighting in the Mexican-American War in the nineteenth century. These recipes combined culinary traditions from Hawaii, Polynesia, and Japan, such as Menehune Chicken, a recipe for chicken wings pictured on a platter surrounded by a floral lei; and Braised Island Pork, made with brown sugar, cider vinegar, carrots, onions, green peppers, and sweet, soy-based teriyaki sauce.

Most notably, the book included classic American recipes, but added soy sauce. Western Nuts and Eastern Bolts, a Chex Mix–style snack, was tossed with Kikkoman teriyaki sauce. Soy sauce appeared in a Vinaigrette Salad Dressing and a Western Barbecue Sauce. Tuna Casserole, Sloppy Joes, and Teriyaki Meat Loaf all called for healthy doses of soy. And Chicken Confetti asked home cooks to mix chicken with a can of condensed cream of mushroom soup and a package of frozen mixed vegetables, much like the Green Bean Casserole I made for my Friendsgiving.

This cookbook reintroduced soy sauce to Americans as an everyday ingredient—much like it would have been used in the late eighteenth and early nineteenth centuries. Kikkoman succeeded where Wong Chin Foo had failed, because Japanese food, unlike Chinese food, escaped the label of "ethnic." Reporter John Birdsall of the food website Chowhound said it best in his 2012 article titled "The End of 'Ethnic,'" writing: "The problem is that *ethnic* implies other: the food of some shadowy minority that's not quite—us. It demeans, diminishes. A lot of us use *ethnic* as one set in a food duality that sees 'normal'—that is, 'American' food (spaghetti, steaks, and Caesar salad)—in opposition to foreign, i.e., 'ethnic' food (Korean tofu soup, saag paneer, and goat-meat birria)." In that word, he says, there is the implication of a negative value judgment.

Not so for Japanese food, which is considered "foreign" or "international" rather than "ethnic." This perception first started to build as immigrants from these countries arrived in America: the Chinese were seen as impoverished job competitors, tight-knit and unassimilable. The Japanese, as a recognized military power, were more respected, and American laws limiting their freedoms were often overturned. It was also about numbers: the Japanese came here in much smaller groups compared with the Chinese; the smaller communities were perceived as more assimilated, helped by the fact that many Japanese women also immigrated to the United States, as opposed to the male-dominated Chinatowns. For these reasons and others, Japanese restaurants maintained a fine-dining status, comparable to French cuisine. As of 2015, thirteen Japanese restaurants in New York carry Michelin stars, including three-starred Masa at Columbus Circle, allegedly America's most expensive restaurant: dinner for two, sans alcohol, clocks in at around $1,100. Only two Chinese restaurants boast even a single Michelin star, one of which is considered "a steal" because the most expensive dish is $25. Chinese food is often stereotyped as takeout: at best, soy sauce–laden pints of chop suey or General Tso's chicken; and at worst, a mysterious and unidentifiable mix that could include ingredients like organ meats—or rats and cats.

Wong struggled with this negative perception in his writing. This work continues by way of a new generation of Chinese Americans, such as Wilson Tang, who runs Nom Wah Tea Parlor.

Tucked into a crook of Doyers Street, Nom Wah is the oldest continually operating restaurant in New York City's Chinatown. It first opened its doors in 1920, and is known today for its carefully curated collection of teas and its extensive traditional dim sum menu: everything from chicken feet steamed in a black bean sauce, to spare ribs drizzled with sweet soy sauce.

Nom Wah has been owned by one family for many years. Wally Tang, a Chinese immigrant, began working there in 1950 at the age of sixteen. In 1974 he bought the restaurant and operated it until he retired in 2010. Wally's American-born nephew, Wilson, attended Pace University and worked in finance—and was massively unhappy. He kept coming back to the food service industry, although his family discouraged him from pursuing it as a career. Food service is seen as an acceptable job for new immigrants, who know little English and have few other options to make a living—much like the chow chow cooks of 150 years ago. But Wilson decided to do it anyway. He inherited the Tea Parlor and renovated the kitchen, but kept the cook of thirty years along with the vintage 1960s interior.

I took my mom out for lunch at Nom Wah many years before I started writing this book. We slid into red vinyl booths in a dining room that felt like it was from another era. I made the mistake of ordering an embarrassing amount of food. At the time, there was no indication of portion size on the menu, just the names of the dishes and photos. I was too shy to ask our waiter, who spoke hesitant English, how much to order. So the little plates just kept coming: "The Original Egg Roll," perfectly puffy crisp egg crepes wrapped around tender chicken and vegetables, and deep-fried to order; Roast Pork Buns, a soft, sweet bread with a savory filling; and a slightly gelatinous rice noodle folded around a filling of beef, swimming in soy sauce. The soy sauce was the constant companion to these snacks, an inseparable condiment. At Nom Wah, it's like keeping a shaker of salt on the table.

Wilson has made certain changes to the restaurant that have kept it popular both with an American clientele and a younger generation of Chinese Americans. First, there's a menu, which is not often an option at dim sum parlors. The dim sum are made fresh to order as opposed to being delivered premade off a cart. Wilson also keeps Nom Wah open late. Though traditionally a breakfast food, his dim sum are served for lunch, dinner, and evening snacks. Wilson has revitalized and is now expanding Nom Wah: he opened a second location in Philadelphia in 2015. Additionally, he partnered with chef Jonathan Wu to open Fung Tu, a fine-dining establishment in November 2013. After getting off to "a tentative start," it received two stars and a critic's pick recommendation from the *New York Times* in 2015.

"What we do at Fung Tu is authentic in spirit," Wu said at a panel discussion with Wilson at the Museum of Chinese in America (MOCA). "It can't claim to be authentically any sort of regional cuisine. It's not authentically Sichuanese, it's not authentically Taiwanese, etcetera." They start with a Chinese dish and "work the other direction," deconstructing it by taking traditional Chinese ingredients and methods of preparation and using them in new combinations with nontraditional ingredients.

At Fung Tu, three types of soy sauce are used as condiments and are integrated into the dishes. When I sat down to dinner at the restaurant, I ordered an egg roll filled with pork belly and briny olives, and seasoned with soy sauce—a take on Nom Wah's Original Egg Roll. For my main course, I had a pork chop deep-fried in a soy-and-maple glaze and a cheesy potato gratin drizzled with thick soy sauce. For dessert, I ordered a white chocolate mousse that had a slightly salty-savory tang; I suspect it incorporated miso, soy sauce's fermented-bean paste cousin.

Wilson's and Jonathan's food is not fusion cuisine. Instead, it comes from their experience of growing up as New Yorkers. Rather than remaining true to tradition, Fung Tu has decided to pursue a new type of Chinese American cuisine, one that evolves naturally in its new surroundings, as though New York were simply a province next door to Sichuan.

Cuisine brought to the United States by immigrants continues to evolve, but American cuisine also expands to include the influence of immigrants. Over fifty years ago, Kikkoman built a factory in Wisconsin to meet an American demand for soy sauce; today Wan Ja Shan is rapidly expanding its operations, not just because Chinese immigrants continue to arrive in America but also because Whole Foods in the New York metro area carries Wan Ja Shan products. On my visit to Michael Wu's brewery, I gazed at the new warehouses, stacked high with barrels of naturally brewed soy sauce. He had mentioned offhand that 50 percent of his sales were commercial, not retail, because many companies use soy sauce as an ingredient in their recipes. I asked if he sold mostly to businesses that produced Asian foods.

"Oh no!" Wu laughed. "The most popular food, you eat every day! McDonald's!"

Soy sauce, it turns out, is a key ingredient in the barbecue dipping sauce for Chicken McNuggets. McDonald's remains one of Wu's biggest customers.

Soy Sauce Chocolate Mousse with Fruit Compote

This dessert is inspired by a dish I tasted at Fung Tu. The addition of soy sauce makes this deeply chocolatey mousse even more addictive. When I eat it, I feel all kinds of taste receptors tripping: salty meets sweet, blended with fat, and—just barely—an umami sensation. Paired with a tangy berry compote, it's an unusual dessert that's easy to love.

Yield: serves 8

For the compote:

2 cups of in-season fruit*

½ cup white sugar

½ cup water

2 tablespoons lemon juice

For the mousse:

12 ounces semisweet chocolate, chopped

1 tablespoon vanilla extract

1 tablespoon soy sauce

4 tablespoons unsalted butter

1 envelope flavorless gelatin

2 cups (1 pint) heavy whipping cream, cold

1. Refrigerate mixing bowl and beaters.

2. Make the compote: Combine fruit, sugar, water, and lemon juice in a saucepan. Cook over medium-high heat until the fruit is soft, about 10 minutes. Chill.

3. Set up a double boiler: Fill a medium saucepan with several inches of water and set over high heat. In a heat-safe bowl (I use glass), combine chocolate, vanilla, soy sauce, and butter. Bring the water to a boil and then turn burner down to a medium-low heat. Place the bowl over the top of the pan. It should be of the right size so that it sits above the simmering water, heating only from the steam. Stir constantly until the chocolate and butter have just melted. Remove from heat.

4. Sprinkle chocolate with gelatin; stir gently until dissolved. Set aside 15 minutes.

---

* I like blackberries, but I've also made this with blueberries and cranberries. Any slightly tart fruit would work well.

5. With an electric mixer, beat whipping cream until stiff peaks form. Gently fold chocolate into cream in two batches. Fold until just blended; it should have some streaks of white whipped cream.

6. Refrigerate for 1 hour or up to 3 days. Spoon the mousse into serving glasses and top with berry compote.

Garlic

Garlic

THE FALL AFTER my visit to the Gaya Vanilla Plantation in Mexico, I climbed into a car with my friend Val—a scenic artist who is always game for an adventure—and drove from New York City to eastern Pennsylvania. Our destination: the twenty-first annual Halloween Garlic Dinner at the Rosemary House. The witchy herbal gift shop in the small town of Mechanicsburg hosted their dinner in its homey, candle-lit café. Guests crowded around tables, waiting for garlic-laden food. Over the meal, we each consumed three large bulbs of garlic integrated into four courses, including a remarkable dessert of lightly cooked garlic cloves covered in dark chocolate and a garlic carrot cake frosted with garlic cream cheese.

"More garlic!" the table near us cheered, tipsy and raucous.

Val and I spent four hours on the drive home, burping and farting. I got back to my apartment and brushed my teeth to no avail. I still smelled like garlic.

Had it been a century earlier, that stink would have been thought of as un-American: garlic was once strongly associated with Italian immigrants and was symbolic of their resistance to assimilation. But today people throughout the country—including the crowd in Mechanicsburg—celebrate the flavor at annual events. The Gilroy Garlic Festival in California—held in Gilroy, a town known as the Garlic Capital of the World—started in 1978 and today draws over one hundred thousand people over the course of a weekend. Another sign of garlic's omnipresence appeared in the 2013 Lay's potato chips first annual "Do Us a Flavor" competition. It asked the public to submit potato chip flavor ideas and then vote on three semifinalists. Second place was Sriracha, which I'll talk about in chapter eight. The winning flavor was Cheesy Garlic Bread.

Garlic is used more frequently in American food than any other flavor in this book. After my multicourse garlic dinner, I felt driven to discover how a plant that was once so maligned in America was now universally celebrated. Although those Italian immigrants who came at the end of the nineteenth century cooked with large amounts of garlic, it was a revival of French cuisine—and the origins of the farm-to-table movement—in the twentieth century that would make this flavor accepted as American.

Garlic is a potent member of the allium family, which also includes onions, shallots, and leeks. It is believed that all garlic evolved from a variety of wild garlic that still grows on the sunlight-dappled forest floors of Eastern Europe and Central Asia.

A clove of garlic, the part of the plant we cook with most often, is actually a leaf: a storage vessel that packs away energy for the next growing season. The energy stored in the cloves is in the form of sugar—specifically fructose—which is why a clove tastes sweet when it is cooked slowly and caramelizes when roasted. Each clove can sprout its own roots and green shoots, and you can grow your own garlic by sticking individual cloves into the ground. And should green sprouts start poking out of the cloves in your fridge, there's nothing dangerous about them—it's just an indication the clove is less than fresh. But keep in mind that as garlic ages, its flavor becomes more potent.

Garlic cloves are also packed with sulfurous compounds, which are responsible for their strong aroma and flavor. An intact bulb of garlic has no smell: the cloves must be chomped, smashed, or cut to become odorous. When a clove is cut or crushed, a relatively odorless compound called alliin is brought into contact with the enzyme alliinase. The resulting chemical reaction produces allicin, a powerful antioxidant and my prediction for the hottest new name trend for girls. It's similar to the way flavor develops in vanilla beans: the cell walls are broken down, and chemicals from all over the plant combine, producing flavor. But unlike vanilla, the flavor of which matures slowly, in garlic this process happens almost instantly. For the strongest flavor, mash or chop the garlic as much as possible. But allicin also decomposes quickly, and many of these sulfurous chemicals break down or react during the cooking process—which means that garlic also loses its flavor soon after it is cut and changes flavor when it is cooked. A dash of raw garlic, added to a dish at the end of cooking, would add flavor components that are lost otherwise.

The potent flavor of garlic is a defense mechanism: it doesn't want to be eaten. Its repellent properties are apparent from an old New York City expression: a nickel will get you on the subway, but garlic will get you a seat. Neither part of that is true anymore, but regardless, garlic has long been vilified for the pungent smell it leaves behind—and the pungent smells it causes.

There are at least four sulfides that survive the cooking process and hang out even after the garlic is consumed: three in the mouth and one in the gut. It's these lingering compounds that cause garlic breath. These are related to the chemicals in a skunk's spray—a group known as thiols—that can be neutralized by the "browning enzymes in many raw fruits and vegetables."

I performed my own garlic-breath-remedy taste test—again, forced upon hapless students who had signed up for my garlic lecture at the Brooklyn Brainery. Chlorophyll-packed herbs worked the best, including mint, cilantro, and parsley. Cloves were also favored for their ability to hide both the taste and smell of garlic. Historically used as a breath freshener, they have an extremely high concentration of flavor oils, and their eugenol content gives them a cooling, numbing sensation. However, allylmethyl sulfide, the sulfurous gas produced in your gut, is unaffected by these remedies. So good luck with that. Additionally, consuming garlic causes the body to produce hydrogen sulfide, which results in some wicked farts—like the ones Val and I filled the car with on our way home from the Rosemary House's Garlic Dinner.

Different garlic varieties have different concentrations of sulfurous compounds, which affect their pungency. There is only one species of garlic, but there are hundreds of garlic cultivars, varieties produced by selective breeding. In a grocery store, you're most likely to find what is known as "softneck garlic," distinguished by its flaky white skin and soft stem. This very pungent garlic is popular because the bulbs store well, but its flavor is sometimes criticized by cooks for lacking subtlety and depth. In my research, I've found that Americans seem to prefer strong flavors. We like the spiciest black pepper variety, Lampong, and the taste of pure vanillin. And I don't think there's anything wrong with that.

Visit any green market in the North, and you'll find hardneck garlic, which grows better in cooler climates. It's named for the tough, woody stem that runs up the center of the bulb. There are many cultivars of hardneck garlic, each with its own unique flavor. Before visiting the Rosemary House's Garlic Dinner, I taste-tested a dozen of them with curry crawl buddies Jen and Soma, the founders of the Brooklyn Brainery. We also roped in three students who had showed up to the Brainery for a friendship bracelet class that had been canceled. They were game, and (even better) they brought wine.

German White is a common variety. During our taste tests, its potent raw cloves made us cough. Its flavor was retained when roasted, which added incomparable sweetness to its spiciness. Spanish Roja is another popular variety; its raw cloves can border on bitter, but it's mellow and caramelized when roasted. The hardneck known as Music was a personal favorite of mine: I enjoyed its buttery texture when roasted. But Red Rezan was the hands-down winner, with its rosy red skin and warm, rather than hot, taste.

It is no surprise that so many garlic varieties are grown in the United States, since the average American currently consumes about 2 pounds of garlic per year. But it's only recently that garlic became part of the American diet; for most of our history, garlic sat in the medicine cabinet. In 1796, *American Cookery*, the first cookbook published in America, advised: "Garlicks, tho' used by the French, are better adapted to the uses of medicine than cookery."

Although much of medicine begins in the natural world—with a willow leaf or a bread mold—and ends in the lab—as aspirin or penicillin—I wanted to see if garlic's alleged medicinal properties were actually based in fact, and how much of it was an old wives' tale past its expiration date.

I discovered—from nineteenth-century medical guides—that most of the medical advice trickling into American households at that time wasn't very trustworthy. In 1861, *Gunn's New Domestic Physician; Or, Home Book of Health: A Complete Guide for Families* recommended a poultice of roast garlic for ear infections: "An excellent remedy for earache is as follows: Take three or four roasted garlics, and while hot mash, and add a tablespoonul of sweet oil and as much honey and laudanum; press out the juice, and drop of this into the ear, warm, occasionally." I'm no doctor, but I suspect that laudanum, a diluted form of opium, might have done more good than the garlic. *Gardening for the South, or*

How to Grow Vegetables and Fruits, an 1868 botanical guide, claimed that garlic caused the patient to sweat, which, like bloodletting, was believed to leach out disease. It also suggested: "The juice is good cement for broken china." I gave it a try, and it worked remarkably well—until I put my chipped plate in the dishwasher. By the late nineteenth century, doctors also used garlic to treat tuberculosis and hemorrhoids. But America's general aversion to garlic is captured in an 1879 article in the *Brooklyn Daily Eagle*: "Garlic is said to be a sovereign remedy for gout. There is no remedy for garlic."

To this very day, garlic is believed to cure all kinds of maladies, and doctors and scientists perform clinical trials to test its efficacy. In fact, garlic studies have increased in recent years, hitting an all-time high in 2012. The results are varied. Studies have shown that garlic is not an effective treatment for high cholesterol. It *might* have lowered high blood pressure, helped control blood sugar, and reduced the risk of gastric and colon cancers in some patients. It did help prevent arteries from hardening and significantly reduced the rate of heart attacks. And, in a double-blind study, patients who took a daily garlic capsule developed colds two-thirds less often than those who swallowed the placebo, and recovered a day faster when they did get sick.

Cornell University also researched this flavor's antimicrobial properties—along with black pepper and curry spices—and found that garlic was among the most effective of plants tested, killing 99.9 percent of the microbes with which it came in contact. But garlic exhibits this antimicrobial effect only when it is applied topically. Its proven antifungal properties are being rigorously researched; and as I discovered—after talking about garlic in a room full of ladies—it's inevitable that someone has inserted a clove into their vagina to try to combat a yeast infection. Studies have shown it has some beneficial, if temporary, effects. In any case, I've already made a mental plan for surviving the zombie apocalypse that involves planting loads of garlic to replace topical antiseptics.

Although garlic is still being researched as medicine, I wanted to know how Americans shifted from using garlic to treat hemorrhoids to consuming it in enormous quantities. The change had its roots in the early nineteenth century, with an internationally influential French chef named Marie-Antonin Carême, who innovated cuisine through his use of fresh, flavorful ingredients such as garlic.

Carême was born into poverty and came of age in Revolutionary-era France. In 1792 his parents abandoned him right before "la Terreur," the worst of the uprising, when perceived enemies of the revolution were guillotined. Carême was only eight years old. While the details of what happened next are unclear, we do know that the boy was soon taken in by a cook and later apprenticed at a patisserie. He was a quick study. He became well known, at seventeen or eighteen, for his sugar-and-pastry banquet centerpieces: fantastical ruined castles, Egyptian pyramids, and extravagant fountains. Paris's richest families purchased his creations for extravagant dinner parties. A culinary historian himself, Carême recounted spending long hours in the library as a young boy, collecting inspiration for his sugar scenes, as well as researching historical methods of cooking. Later in life, he operated as a sort of freelance chef, accepting high-paying gigs for nobility in Paris and the surrounding area. He cooked for the Bonapartes, as well as for the king of England and the Romanovs of Russia.

Carême was known in his time for his technical ability and complicated edible centerpieces, but his lasting legacy is that of simplicity. His most important innovation, one that would be emulated throughout the world, was to replace the imported spices used in the medieval era through the eighteenth century with fresh herbs and highly flavored plants—such as onions and garlic. Until then, spices versus herbs signified a class distinction between the high and the low: the wealthy flavored their foods with imported spices, while the poor used local herbs and garlic. In his recipes, Carême avoided the heavily spiced foods of a generation before—like Martha Washington's pepper cakes and venison roast. Carême's 1833 cookbook, *L'art de la cuisine française au dix-neuvième siècle* (*The Art of*

French Cooking in the Nineteenth Century), relied heavily on onions, thyme, parsley, bay, basil, and garlic for flavor.

His recipes for fish are particularly emblematic of his style of cooking. Consider Perch in a Garlic Butter Sauce. The fish is first flavored lightly with fresh aromatics and then smothered in melted garlic butter.

Take five large Seine perch; extract the gills, gut them and then tie their heads with several turns of string. Half an hour before serving, put them in a *poissonnière* [an oblong copper pan for simmering fish] containing water to which you add white salt of a sufficient quantity and the flesh of a seeded, sliced lemon, a thinly sliced carrot, onion the same way, and a little parsley in branches, a fragment of thyme and laurel [bay leaf] and a little mace. Bring to a boil over a hot fire, then simmer gently. Just before serving, drain the perch and remove the fins; then put them on a plate and use the tip of a knife to remove the scales from both sides of each perch; and then arrange them on a napkin placed on the platter, placing the biggest in the center; surround the biggest with potatoes cooked in salted water; put the red fins straight in the middle of each perch along the length; supply two saucers of sauce with garlic butter.

Perch in Garlic Butter

I translated this from the original French recipe, published by Carême in 1833, with a great deal of help from my mother, who happens to be a former French teacher. You can make more than one fish, or even a larger fish, without needing to adjust the amount of aromatics. Additionally, you can substitute any mild, medium-fleshed whole fish for perch.

Yield: serves 2 or more, depending on quantity of fish

3 waxy potatoes (such as Yukon Gold or a red-skinned potato)

2 teaspoons salt

1 lemon, sliced thinly

1 medium onion, peeled, halved, and sliced into half moons

1 carrot, peeled and sliced thinly

5 sprigs parsley

2 sprigs thyme

1 bay leaf

1 piece of mace (optional)

1 whole perch, head and tail on, cleaned and gutted

Salt to taste

Garlic Butter (recipe below)

1. Peel potatoes; place in a saucepan and cover with cold water. Add 2 teaspoons salt. With heat on high, bring to a boil, and then reduce heat to medium-low and cook until tender when pierced with a fork. Cool, then slice into half-inch pieces.

2. Add lemon, onion, carrot, parsley, thyme, bay leaf, and mace to a pot or straight-sided sauté pan large enough so that the perch can lay flat. Place the fish on top of the aromatics in the center of the pot. Add enough water so that it just begins to come up over the sides of the fish. Salt well and bring to a boil over high heat.

3. Immediately reduce heat to low, cover, and gently poach until done, about 15 minutes for a 1-pound fish. To check for doneness, push the skin aside with a fork. When the center of the fish turns from opaque to white, it is ready.

4. Transfer the whole fish and the potatoes to a platter. Remove skin from the top of the fish, ladle melted garlic butter on the potatoes and fish, salt to taste, and serve immediately.

Garlic Butter

Carême's recipe for garlic butter is hard to track down, so I consulted another famous source of nineteenth-century French recipes, *The Epicurean* by Charles Ranhofer, published in 1893.

2 large cloves of garlic
$1/4$ cup butter, room temperature
$1/4$ teaspoon paprika
$1/2$ teaspoon salt

1. Peel garlic, remove ends, and blanch for about 2 minutes in briskly boiling, well-salted water. The garlic is done when it is softened slightly and a paring knife can pierce the center easily.
2. Remove garlic from water. Add garlic, butter, paprika, and salt to a food processor and blend until all ingredients are incorporated evenly. You might need to scrape down the side of the food processor bowl from time to time. Melt butter over the stovetop or in a microwave. Transfer butter to a container and refrigerate if not using immediately.

One visitor to the Rothschild household, Carême's clients and one of Europe's wealthiest families, remarked of the food: "Its character was that it was in season . . . no high-spiced sauces, no dark brown gravies. . . . Every meat presented its own natural aroma, every vegetable its own shade of verdure." The diner was struck by the fresh flavor of the unadorned food, unseen on tables of the elite until this time. I was struck by how familiar this praise sounded to me. It felt like a review of modern farm-to-table restaurants that, like Carême, focus on simplicity, freshness, and flavor. Take, for example, the *San Francisco Chronicle*'s review of Chez Panisse, the Berkeley restaurant that is considered the founder of the farm-to-table movement. In 2014 reporter Michael Bauer wrote about a menu inspired by Provence, a warm region in the south of France that borders Italy: "There's always something on the menu that's a revelation of how something should taste. One time it was a pork loin; another visit, grilled asparagus; and yes, on one it was a peach. There's an unsurpassed respect for ingredients and a clarity of style that emerges no matter the menu or who is in the kitchen." But, as Bauer explained, "What seems most simple is often the most difficult to pull off."

Though Carême cooked for some of the finest households in Europe, his life as a chef would not have been an easy one. His work was physically demanding—on his feet, preparing several meals a day—and he performed it under difficult conditions. "The cook too often spends his working life underground, where the false day of artificial light enfeebles his eyesight, where condensation and drafts accelerate rheumatism, and where his life is miserable," he wrote. "If kitchens are on the ground floor, the chef is healthier, but even so, he often only sees the four walls and his own reflection in polished copper and all he breathes is charcoal fumes and steam." Carême died at the age of forty-nine in 1833, from what is now believed to be low-level carbon monoxide poisoning—the result of a life spent underground cooking over charcoal.

Carême's influence on French cuisine was monumental, even after his death. Many French tastes were imported to American soil—including, remember, vanilla ice cream. After Carême introduced a new style of cooking to France's elite, a taste for garlic also traveled across the ocean to America. Good ol' Mary Randolph called for "two heads of garlic chopped with thyme and parsley" in her recipe for Beef a-la-Mode, a pot roast stuffed with aromatics, bread crumbs, and ground meat. The dish had French origins, and her use of garlic and fresh herbs was very Carême.

However, a generation later, garlic had faded from the pages of American cookbooks. Eliza Leslie, the prominent cookbook author of the 1840s, was more hesitant in her use of the herb: she suggested just "two or three drops" of garlic vinegar to flavor a dish. "More will be offensive," she warned. "The cook should be cautioned to use it very sparingly, as to many persons it is extremely disagreeable." By the end of the nineteenth century, garlic appeared only in French recipes. In 1893 François Tanty—who had trained under Carême—published *La Cuisine Française: French Cooking for Every Home. Adapted to American Requirements*. He listed garlic as a necessary ingredient in a dozen recipes, many of which originated in Provence. On the other hand, Fannie Farmer's *The Boston Cooking-School Cookbook* published just three years later used garlic in only a single preparation. She advised the home cook to rub an uncut clove on a piece of French bread and then discard it. Only the faintest scent of garlic was allowed in Farmer's kitchen—and in the kitchens of the many Americans who treated her word as gospel.

That would soon change. A new immigrant group flooded into America, and they believed, like Carême, that garlic was an essential flavor in most every dish. Four million Italians, mainly from southern Italy, came to America between 1880 and 1920; by 1920, they represented 10 percent of the US population. Italian Americans would alter the cultural and culinary makeups of the United States forever.

If you were a southern Italian at the end of the nineteenth century, life was rough back home. Widespread poverty, in addition to blight, volcanic eruptions, and cholera outbreaks made eking out a living in the south nearly impossible. The result, according to one turn-of-the-century study, was "a terrible, permanent lack of food." In these conditions, southern Italians ate what they could grow in their vegetable gardens, what could be foraged from the forests, and what they could get from their animals, such as eggs and goat's milk. Garlic was a valuable ally: it was easy to grow, and its strong flavor made even the simplest food more delicious.

A 1901 study estimated the yearly income of the Italian to be about $45. But the average American laborer in 1901 could hope to make $750 a year. The higher wages enticed many Italians to immigrate to the United States. When Italians first arrived in America, they were maligned—much like Chinese immigrants were. The perception was that Italians in America lived in ethnic enclaves and refused to speak English. Many worked as comparatively low-paid laborers and sent the money back to Italy to support family members and buy land. Some immigrated to this country as seasonal workers, returning home for most of the year; in fact, 40 percent of Italians didn't settle in this country but went to live in houses bought with dollars earned in the United States. Because many Italians came here with no plans to stay, they resisted assimilation—especially when it came to food.

In 1900, during the height of Italian immigration, the *Brooklyn Daily Eagle* reported on an Italian wedding: "Two persons of the opposite sex from the land of glowing sunsets, organ grinders, and garlic have become so infatuated with each other that they have decided to traverse this troubled vale side by side." This condescending article reduced Italy to stereotypes—and one of them included garlic.

Italian immigrants became huge consumers of Italian imports: cured meats, Parmesan cheese, semolina pasta, and olive oil—foods they couldn't afford back home. Whereas life in Italy was all about poverty and austerity, Italian American food became known for abundance. Italian American cuisine also was more garlic heavy. Originally, it might have been to hide the taste of what were considered inferior American ingredients or to freshen up the flavor of Italian imports that had spent weeks traveling across the ocean.

Ironically, many Americans praised the diet of Italians in Italy, while criticizing Italian American cuisine. In 1922 Bertha M. Wood, a social worker as well as a dietitian, wrote a book to help teach cooking classes at social aid organizations known as settlement houses. Built in urban

Italian Immigration

neighborhoods, these institutions provided English classes, health care, leisure activities, and nutritional advice for recent arrivals.

"Often it has been said, 'They should learn to eat American foods if they are to live here,'" Wood wrote in *Foods of the Foreign-Born in Relation to Health*. But she thought—and many agreed—that the American diet had ruined the naturally healthy diet of Italian immigrants. Italians would have to be reeducated, emphasizing the latest innovations in food science: vitamins, minerals, and calories. "In attempting to furnish this instruction," she writes, "native dishes and raw food materials should be recognized and preserved as far as possible." Wood encouraged the use of garlic in instructional classes to make the scientifically balanced diet seem familiar. It appeared in many of her recipes, such as Spaghetti—Italian Style, where pork chops were sizzled in pork fat, and then adorned in a garlic-and-tomato sauce and served over noodles.

Although nutritionists like Wood supported the use of garlic in immigrant cooking classes, it's doubtful that most Americans would have cooked with it in their own homes. Garlic maintained its anti-American connotations well into the twentieth century, long after Italian immigration to America had all but stopped. Even as late as 1939, in a *Life* magazine cover story about Joe DiMaggio, baseball superstar and son of Italian immigrants, the reporter pointed out that even though Italian was the New York Yankees outfielder's first language, Joe "is otherwise well adapted to most US mores." He continued: "He never reeks of garlic and prefers chicken chow mein to spaghetti." That is some first-class casual racism—particularly considering that DiMaggio was born in California. (Also, notice how chow mein is considered American by this time, but not spaghetti.)

Ironically, at the same time the DiMaggio article was written, garlic was being idolized in print for its association with French cuisine. Following the end of World War I, many American artists, writers, bon vivants, and millionaires moved to France. Nearly thirty thousand Americans lived in or around Paris in the 1920s and 1930s—among them food writer M. F. K. Fisher, dancer Josephine Baker, photographer Man Ray, and novelists Gertrude Stein and Ernest Hemingway. Many more expats ended up in Provence. One of these travelers was journalist Waverly Root, who would live most of his life in France, writing about food and culture. He took a particular shine to Provence.

"Unless you know the contrary," Root explained in his most popular book, *The Food of France*, originally published in 1958, "it is fairly safe to assume that any dish appearing on the menu as à la Provençale will be accompanied by cooked tomatoes strongly seasoned with garlic."

Provence's food shared ingredients with northern Italy, not just because of proximity but because of the similar climate. Garlic is a prominent and indispensable part of Provençal cuisine.

On the eve of World War II, when Root returned to the United States after thirteen years abroad, he was startled by the shift in the American food scene. "Garlic has been the vehicle in the United States of a self-reversing snobbery. Before I left America to live in Europe in 1927, you were looked down upon if you ate garlic, a food fit only for ditch diggers," he observed. "When I returned in 1940, you were looked down upon if you *didn't* eat it. It had become the hallmark of gastronomic sophistication, and I was overwhelmed by meals offered by thoughtful friends, who catered to my supposedly acquired dashing Gallic tastes by including garlic in every dish except ice cream." The influence of the important American artists living in France had created a new trend for French food in America, represented by Provençal cuisine laced with garlic.

Garlic Soup

In his book, Root shared a special Provençal soup made almost entirely from garlic: "a testimonial," he wrote, "to the Provençal fondness for this item, for here garlic, usually employed to accompany more substantial ingredients, is pretty much the be-all and the end-all." This soup is simple yet satisfying, the gentle flavor of cooked garlic made heartier with toasted bread and cheese, much like a French onion soup.

Yield: serves 6

24 garlic cloves, peeled
1 sprig thyme
1 sprig sage
1 whole clove
1 ½ teaspoons salt
1 teaspoon fresh ground pepper
6 slices French bread
Olive oil
½ pound Gruyère cheese, grated

1. Preheat oven to 350 degrees.
2. To a large pot, add garlic, herbs, clove, salt, pepper, and 8 cups water. Bring to a boil over medium-high heat and then reduce heat to a simmer. Cook an additional 15 minutes.
3. While the soup is cooking, brush the bread with olive oil and toast in the oven on a baking sheet for 10 minutes.
4. To 6 oven-safe bowls, add 1 cup of soup broth each. Top with bread and allow to soak 5 minutes. Transfer bowls to baking sheet, sprinkle cheese on top of bread, and bake in oven until cheese is melted, 3 to 5 minutes. Serve hot.

During World War II, when American troops were stationed in Provence, the influence of its cuisine—and the use of garlic—would spread even farther. In 1945 James Beard—the future cook, television personality, and author who would one day be anointed the "dean of American cookery" by the *New York Times*—was stationed in Marseille, the largest city in Provence. He delighted in eating like a local: Beard sampled eggplants stuffed with garlic, rosemary, and meat, as well as chicken marinated in lemon, basil, and garlic. These dishes had a long-lasting effect on Beard's cooking, most famously in his now-iconic recipe for Chicken with Forty Cloves of Garlic, a casserole with chicken legs and thighs, covered in olive oil and vermouth, and topped with tarragon, parsley, celery, and forty cloves of garlic. After baking for ninety minutes, the chicken comes out tender and mild—as does the garlic. Sulfurous chemicals bake away, and sugars caramelize and make the garlic cloves sweet. With its simple seasoning, this recipe could have been pulled from one of Carême's cookbooks. And it was the perfect recipe—like a gateway drug—that allowed even the garlic-timid to experience the mild flavor of baked garlic. In 1945, while Beard was serving in Provence, Americans consumed 4.5 million pounds of garlic; by 1956, they were chowing down on over 36 million pounds annually.

In the 1970s, chef Alice Waters picked up the torch that Carême had lit and Beard had carried. In 1971 she founded Chez Panisse in Berkeley. The restaurant's menus emphasized locally produced ingredients, blended with garlic-laden Provençal cooking techniques. In 1976 Waters launched an annual garlic dinner on July 14, the French day of independence, Bastille Day. It came about at the cajoling of one of her former waiters, John Harris, who, after having experienced Chez Panisse's garlicky French cuisine, went on to author a cookbook devoted to garlic.

In 1977, the second year of the Bastille Day Dinner, director Les Blank shot a documentary called *Garlic Is as Good as Ten Mothers*. He featured

Waters's fete prominently in the film. Footage showed a legion of chefs peeling and mincing garlic cloves with amazing skill and alacrity in the Chez Panisse kitchen. Then they shoveled enormous spoonfuls of diced garlic into the bellies of suckling pigs. When Waters came on-screen, she looked as precious as could be, sporting a crown of garlic set atop her feathered hair.

"It's something that can't be ignored," she said of garlic. "You either like it or you don't like it. And it causes you to react in some way. And I love that about food; I like people to make a response to it. Whether it's positive or negative, I want them to say 'That's *garlic*!' . . . I think that's why we use it so much; I don't like people to be indifferent when they eat."

The Bastille Day Dinner at Chez Panisse continues to this day. A few months after my trip to Pennsylvania's garlic dinner at the Rosemary House, I decided to re-create Waters's first garlic feast. A very helpful man at the office of Alice Waters named Roy Button tracked down the original menu for me.

The Garlic Gala—Bastille Day

Wednesday, July 14th

$15.00 (including wine. by reservation only.)

Whole garlic and mushrooms baked with olive oil in grape leaves

Roast garlic pureed and served with baked chicken legs

Garlic mayonnaise served with green beans and little red boiled potatoes

Fresh pasta served with a paste of garlic, basil, pine nuts, olive oil and parmesan cheese

Beef tripe with basil and garlic

Fresh fish poached in a fish stock with tomatoes, with garlic mayonnaise thinned with the broth

Leg of Lamb marinated with garlic and wine, stuffed with prosciutto, and served with a sauce with mint, garlic and wine that's simmered for hours

Potato puree with garlic infused cream

Fresh figs, white cheese, and garlic honey

Garlic whole, roasted, pureed, minced, infused—Waters's menu explored every method of its preparation. My friend Emily—a former pastry chef and assistant of Waters—offered to help re-create the feast, along with my intern Jill, a former chef and recipe tester. Jill, Emily, and I pulled recipes from Waters's many cookbooks, and we figured out other dishes by drawing from our own cooking experience. We decided that our main course would be the roast leg of lamb—handled by Jill, an expert with meats—and I'd make the accompanying potato puree with garlic-infused cream. In a saucepan, I soaked garlic and potatoes for a few hours. I brought this to a boil and then reduced it to a simmer, until the potatoes were tender. Finally, I pureed the mixture without draining any of the liquid. The result made you say, "That's *garlic!*" to use Waters's own words. The garlic was rich and full bodied, infused into the fats of the dairy. They were the best garlic mashed potatoes I had ever eaten.

We added a few intriguing dishes from the 1977 menu, the one featured in Les Blank's documentary. Emily whipped up a cheesy garlic soufflé, which was light and airy, the garlic enhanced by the tanginess of Gruyère. I prepared a sorbet of garlic and apples, cooked together with cinnamon, nutmeg, and white wine.

Waters's menu taught me to love garlic in sweet dishes. While not everyone was sold on the sorbet, the garlic-infused honey I prepared for the last course was a resounding success. I stuffed a jar of honey with a dozen peeled garlic cloves and let it infuse for about a week. When I opened it up the night of the dinner, I was concerned. The odor was so strong, even

I thought it was vile. But when drizzled over fruit (nectarines, sour apples, and crescents of clementines—or figs, like Waters recommends) and crumbles of feta cheese, the combination was craveable. "Oh, that garlic honey!" the guests cried out, whenever we reminisced about that evening. The simplest, freshest dish was the best of the night. Carême would have been proud.

The blend of French and Italian influences in Waters's menu illustrated how Americans were consuming garlic by the 1970s. From France, the influence of Carême and Beard, such as poached fresh fish and garlic mayonnaise, the latter better known as aioli. The prosciutto-stuffed leg of lamb and fresh pasta with pesto—or as Waters called it, "a paste of garlic, basil, pine nuts, olive oil, and Parmesan cheese"—was a nod to the millions of Italian immigrants who had slowly but surely influenced American food.

By the end of the garlic dinner, we all stunk. But when everyone smells like garlic, who is left to notice? And already, by the 1970s, few Americans would have taken note—we were eating more garlic than ever before. Chefs such as Waters were a part of this shift, but so were second- and third-generation Italian Americans. The American-born descendants of Italian immigrants cooked garlic-heavy Italian American food at home. And they celebrated garlic love publicly at events like the Gilroy Garlic Festival, which was founded by the son of Italian immigrants (who got the idea from a similar garlic fest in a town in France).

Today Americans who self-identify as Italian American make up 6 percent of the US population and are the seventh-largest ethnic group. Their presence in the gene pool has increased garlic consumption because the preference for the plant has been found to be passed on biologically. A study in the United Kingdom discovered that about 46 percent of human beings inherit a preference for garlic from their parents. Additionally, the flavor is transmitted in amniotic fluid; fetuses consume several ounces of amniotic fluid daily, which is "flavored" by their mother's food choices.

Some scientists believe it helps a baby to understand which foods are safe to eat even before they are born. But a preference for garlic can also be passed from mother to child when a baby is nursing: breast-feeding infants consumed more milk when their mothers ingested garlic. A large garlic-consuming Italian population meant that their American-born children would have a biological preference for garlic, as would *their* children, and so on. A love of garlic, written into American DNA.

Garlic-themed bacchanals like the one in Gilroy are replicated in towns all over the country. In late September, a month before the Rosemary House dinner, I attended the Hudson Valley Garlic Festival in upstate New York. More than thirty thousand people packed the two-day event, where heirloom garlic from regional farmers and garlic-themed trinkets were available for purchase. But the main attraction was the food, most of which was inspired by Italian American classics. I walked the avenues of stands, tasting everything: garlicky fettuccini Alfredo, greasy garlic bread with hunks of chopped garlic, creamy garlic potato soup in a bread bowl, garlic cupcakes topped with a candied clove, garlic sausages bursting with minced garlic, and sliced red potatoes drowning in potent garlic butter.

As one vendor ladled a bowl of garlic soup, he asked the woman in line—a hip-looking lady about my age—"Do you, uuh . . . want more garlic on top?"

"Oh yeah," she responded. "You can just put as much on there as possible."

Italian American food is now considered mainstream American fare, with Italian American restaurant chains ranking among some of the highest-grossing food businesses in United States. The first Olive Garden location opened its doors in 1982—four years after the first Gilroy Garlic Festival—and by the end of the decade, it was one of the fastest-growing chain restaurants in America. Today there are over eight hundred locations nationwide, and it's the sixteenth-largest chain restaurant, ranking behind another Italian American joint, Domino's Pizza. With the mainstream acceptance of Italian American food has come the mainstream acceptance of garlic.

"Domino's Pizza is absolutely the result of Italian American cuisine," I was told by Mario Carbone, New York City chef and owner of the Italian American restaurants Parm and Carbone, and partner in the now-closed Torrisi Italian Specialties. We were in a classroom at the Lower East Side Tenement Museum Visitor Center. In exchange for a private tour of the museum's historical kitchen spaces, I asked if he would give me some perspective on Italian American cuisine in the twenty-first century.

Italian food in America today is often called inauthentic compared to its Italian heritage. The judgment is frequently reinforced in the media, including this headline on the website Business Insider: "8 Real Italian Dishes You Should Order Instead of the American Knockoffs." Mario observed the same reaction in tourists: "You should watch the Italians come from Italy and go to Little Italy and eat Italian food and complain about it." He said they were his least happy customers at Carbone: "They're like, 'Why do you consider this Italian food?'" On one of my own food tours, an Italian tourist told me how excited she was to come to the United States and try fettuccini Alfredo—which she considered an American dish. After she sampled it, she said she couldn't understand why anyone would like it. Which was baffling to me: it's cream, butter, cheese, and garlic. What's not to love?

Bertha Wood would have been equally unhappy with the evolution of Italian American food. The turn-of-the-century dietitian argued that the US diet had corrupted the immigrant. Mario had a different perspective.

"Italian American is effectively its own regional cuisine," he told me. He explained that in Italy, you cooked the cuisine of your home region, with local ingredients. Wood addressed the same thought: "Naturally they are painstaking, good cooks," she wrote. "The raw food materials of the Italian diet, many of which were easily procured from their own farms, when combined in their home-country ways, furnished a cheap, well-balanced diet."

In the United States, Italians from many different regions came together and shared their culinary heritage. Mario's own family hailed from all over Italy, so he never felt a kinship with one region or another. He always thought of himself as Italian American. Add in the influence of American ingredients—cooking locally, just like back in Italy—and the result was Italian American cuisine. The food doesn't need to be authentic to Italy; it's authentically American.

Mario's restaurants tap into this idea of an Italian regional cuisine here in America. "A Tuscan chef would never bring something to Bologna and serve it," he said. "It's like a crime. So if we're going to do this Italian American thing in New York, let's try to only use American ingredients and make something new to ourselves . . . I'm in New York City; I pull from Ludlow Street and Orchard Street and Canal Street. We find inspiration there, and we make our New York cuisine that way." Mario's focus on the evolution of New York cuisine is much the same idea that drives Wilson Tang and Jonathon Wu of Fung Tu, which is located on Orchard Street.

"As the generations move on, it has no choice but to fade into something else," Mario said of the destiny of Italian American food. "And I don't know what that's going to become, but it won't be as potent. It can't be."

But the garlic will stay potent. Although it was French cuisine that got Americans interested in the plant, it's the full assimilation of Italian culture into America that has made garlic an indispensable part of our cooking. Bertha Wood said of the waves of immigrants arriving at the turn of the century: "Their housing conditions are changed—their style of clothing must be changed; many of their social customs as well as some of their religious ideals, must be given up; the only habit and custom which can be preserved in its entirety is their diet." Food survives when all the other trappings of foreign culture fade away. We don't speak the same language that our immigrant forebearers did, or wear their same clothes—but Grandma's recipes become a guarded part of family tradition. And one day those recipes become American food.

Rosemary House Garlic Carrot Cake

This delicious dessert was the last course of Rosemary House's annual all-garlic dinner. I know what you're thinking—but trust me. If carrots can work in a cake, why not garlic? Reprinted with permission from Susanna Reppert-Brill, manager of the Rosemary House, which was founded by her mother, Bertha, in 1968.

Yield: serves 8 to 12

For the cake:

2 cups unbleached all-purpose flour

1 1/2 cups sugar

2 teaspoons baking soda

1/2 teaspoon salt

2 teaspoons ground cinnamon

1 teaspoon ground ginger

1/2 teaspoon ground cloves

1/2 cup vegetable oil

1/2 cup olive oil

3 eggs, lightly beaten

2 teaspoons vanilla

1 pound carrots, peeled and grated

1 cup crushed pineapple, with juices

1 cup walnuts

2 tablespoons minced fresh garlic

For the frosting:

8 ounces cream cheese

1/2 cup margarine

Juice of 2 lemons

Zest of 1 lemon

1 or 2 cloves garlic, peeled and finely minced*

1 pound (1 box) confectioners sugar

1. Preheat oven to 350 degrees. Grease a 9 × 13-inch baking pan. Set aside.

2. Sift the flour, sugar, baking soda, salt, and other spices together in the bowl of an electric mixer. Add the oils, eggs, and vanilla and beat, starting at a low speed and working up to medium-high, until well mixed and slightly fluffy. With a spatula, fold in the carrots, pineapple, walnuts, and fresh garlic.

3. Pour the batter into the prepared pan. Bake 45 to 60 minutes, until a cake tester inserted in the center comes out clean. Cool in pan for 10 minutes. Invert onto plate and cool completely.

4. Prepare frosting: blend frosting ingredients until creamy. Frost cake. If desired, sprinkle additional walnuts on top.

* One clove yields a subtle flavor, while two is strong but still very pleasant.

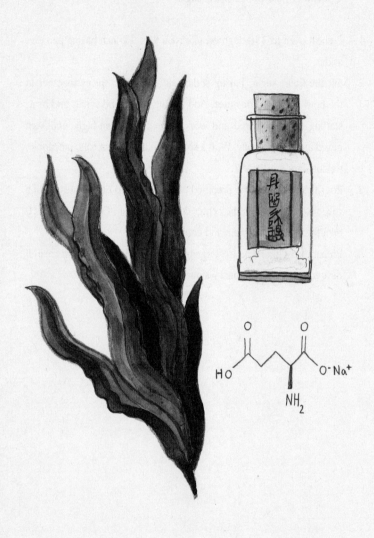

Monosodium glutamate

Seven

Monosodium Glutamate (MSG)

PUBLIC OPINION OF MSG runs directly contrary to proven science. In 2008 the *New York Times* published a piece titled "Yes, MSG, the Secret Behind the Savor." Reporter Julia Moskin wrote: "Even now, after 'Chinese restaurant syndrome' has been thoroughly debunked (virtually all studies . . . confirm that monosodium glutamate in normal concentrations has no effect on the overwhelming majority of people), the ingredient has a stigma that will not go away."

The *Times* published only two of the angry letters it received in response to this article, although I feel certain there were many more.

"Monosodium glutamate, and all of its stealth identities, are known causes of headaches in the vast majority of migraine sufferers," wrote a resident of Brooklyn. Another letter, from a reader in Los Angeles, said, "It is anger-provoking to be told, in essence, that the splitting headaches and uncontrollable restlessness that I get from MSG are all in my head."

In 2014 the *Washington Post* published a similar post on its *Speaking of Science* blog titled bluntly, "No, MSG Isn't Bad for You," written by reporter Rachel Feltman. The comments on this post speak volumes:

"This article is not the 'truth': it's pure, unadulterated BS."

"Rachel, I can't imagine why you would write an article such as this. I get pounding, crippling headaches which bring me to my knees when I eat MSG spiced food."

" 'Double-blind study'. . . that's if you're leaving it to someone else to tell you what's good and bad for you. No thanks, the stuff's *not* good for my body."

When you talk MSG, it hits a certain, sensitive chord with foodies. And at one time, I agreed with the general public: particularly as a migraine sufferer, I thought MSG was bad for me. But after learning the story behind MSG, I changed my mind.

I began to question my beliefs the spring before my visit to Mexico, after a trip to Dead Horse Bay, a section of beach far out in Brooklyn where New York City breaks apart into a patchwork of marshes. The city first started sending garbage to this distant island in the 1860s and didn't stop for the next eighty years. Since then, the ocean has slowly eroded the old landfill.

I adventured out there with a group of treasure-hunting friends. We found the footpath off a main highway and walked through the woods, toward the beach. There, along the dunes, artifacts such as old bottles and ceramic plates blanketed the beach. When the waves shifted the broken glass, the sound was like a thousand tiny wind chimes. I picked hundred-plus-year-old garbage, collecting blue glass bottles, ceramic tiles, and shards of painted plates. A friend handed me a well-preserved bottle, brown and four inches tall, empty except for scraps of seaweed. It was from maybe the 1940s, and the vintage label proclaimed "*Wyler's* MEAT TENDER-IZER *with M.S.G*" in large lettering that took up half the front of the bottle. "Contains: Salt, Mono-sodium Gluta-mate, 99% pure."

I have *never* seen a bottle labeled "with MSG!" in a grocery store aisle—only products proclaiming that they did *not* use MSG. But judging by this little bottle, in the 1940s, using MSG was something to advertise. And not too long ago, someone in New York City bought Wyler's Meat Tenderizer and cooked with it.

I put that little bottle of meat tenderizer on the windowsill above my kitchen sink. It reminded me that beliefs are not static, and that our ideas of what is healthy and what is not change over time. What's happened to MSG's image is the result of what happens when rhetoric gets in the way of fact.

My love for MSG grew as I learned the history and science behind it. MSG, a salt, can be made naturally from boiling kelp. In the chilly waters off the coast of northern Japan, a type of kelp, or kombu, is grown, harvested, dried, and made into a traditional broth. This broth, kombu dashi, has been prepared since at least the eighth century and is the basis for nearly every soup and stock in Japanese cooking.

Depending on the variety, kombu grows as tall as a person or up to thirty feet high. In a grocery store in Chinatown, I found packages of it stocked on the shelves, its enormous grasslike blade folded back on itself into a neat square. I bought a pack, so that I could make dashi from scratch.

I cut the kelp to an appropriate size for my pot. You can also buy it cut and tied into handy knots. I covered the seaweed with water, added some salt, and then brought the water to a boil very slowly over low heat. I removed the kombu just as the water came to a boil; leaving it in can make the stock bitter. I could have added some bonito, thin flakes of preserved, dried fish, or some dried shitake mushrooms. But I wanted to keep this version of kombu dashi as simple and pure as possible. When finished, I sipped the warm, olive-green broth that tasted of the sea. But there was another, more powerful flavor: a mouthful of kombu dashi is as savory as a Sour Patch Kid is sour. That savory taste is MSG.

This broth was prized in Japan, as it made vegetarian dishes taste meaty. For much of Japan's history, meat was seldom eaten: Buddhism

Dr. Kikunæ Ikeda

and Shintoism encouraged a vegetarian diet, and the small, mountainous country also lacked pastureland to graze animals. Instead, kombu dashi, with its powerful flavor, became a cornerstone of Japanese cuisine.

Japanese cooks had been using the power of kombu dashi for a thousand years before chemist Dr. Kikunae Ikeda first discovered, then harnessed, monosodium glutamate. In 2009, in honor of the hundredth anniversary of the first commercial production of MSG, Ajinomoto Co.—the world's largest producer of MSG—released an online comic book that told his story. I was tickled by the illustrated adventures of this Edwardian-era biochemist.

The first panel of the comic introduced its superhero: "In autumn of 1899," it read, "a 35-year-old scientist with a heart full of hope stepped down to the train platform in Leipzig. His name is Kikunae Ikeda." Ikeda, a recent graduate of the Department of Chemistry at Tokyo Imperial University, had traveled to Germany for further study. At the time, the Germans were at the cutting edge of organic chemistry. But Ikeda struggled to fit in. He had trouble with the language, sometimes understanding only half the lectures he attended. Additionally, he felt his physical appearance made him stick out. Although he dressed in Western-style clothing— a three-piece suit, with the high shirt collars popular at the turn of the century—he was short and slight.

"I was abashed by the greatness of this country," Ikeda wrote, "and I realized that the strong physique of the German people was due to their diet. I couldn't help but wonder why the Japanese build was so small and frail in comparison."

While Ikeda studied in Europe, he also ate unfamiliar foods such as tomatoes, cheese, and asparagus. "There's a commonality in taste between these foods," Ikeda explained a few years later. "It is usually so faint and overshadowed by other, stronger tastes that it is often difficult to recognize it unless the attention is specially directed towards it."

When Ikeda returned home to Japan, he realized that the same taste was present in Japanese cuisine: in bonito, dried mushrooms, miso, and soy sauce. He noticed it particularly in a favorite dish from his hometown of Kyoto called *yudofu*: tofu simmered in kombu dashi.

According to Ikeda's papers, in 1907 he began to experiment with kombu dashi to determine the chemical source of its taste. The broth was affordable and easy to make, so it was an ideal material to work with. Ikeda evaporated the kombu dashi down until nothing was left but its solids, which he separated into its major components. The majority, 1 percent weight by volume, was a white powder. When he tasted it, he discovered that it was savory—particularly in combination with the natural sea salt attached to kombu. What Ikeda had discovered was MSG.

Yodufo

Yodufo is a simple, cheap meal of savory broth and tofu. Because it has so few ingredients, it's important to procure the best quality of each. Try to find freshly made tofu—easy to do if you have access to a Chinatown—but grocery store tofu will do.

Yield: serves 4

1 ounce kombu

1 pound silken tofu, cut into 4 even pieces

3 tablespoons soy sauce

1 teaspoon mirin (rice wine)

Grated ginger; scallions (*negi*), sliced thinly; and toasted sesame seeds for garnish

1. Make the kombu dashi: gently wipe the kombu with a damp paper towel. Place the kombu in a pot with 4 cups of water and soak 2 to 3 hours; the longer the kombu soaks, the more intense the flavor—but it maxes out after 3 hours. Turn the burner on to medium-low heat.

Simmer over gentle heat for about 30 minutes, then remove kombu and discard. Scoop out 2 cups of kombu dashi and set aside.

2. Add tofu to remaining 2 cups of dashi. Simmer gently until tofu is heated through. Meanwhile, make the dipping sauce by combining reserved dashi with soy sauce and mirin.

3. Serve: the tofu can be served tableside directly from the cooking vessel. Evenly distribute dipping sauce and tofu into small bowls for each guest. Garnish with ginger, sesame seeds, and scallions to taste.

I wanted to understand what it was, exactly, that Dr. Ikeda had discovered. So I called upon all the experts I knew: I spoke to Soma, amateur food scientist and my buddy from the Brooklyn Brainery; I called up my brother, Greg, a doctor of biochemistry, like Ikeda; and I emailed Ole G. Mouritsen, author of *Umami: Unlocking the Secrets of the Fifth Taste* and a recognized expert on savory taste.

I found out that monosodium glutamate, like table salt, is an ionic bond between two chemicals. Table salt is an ionic compound of sodium and chloride; MSG is an ionic compound of sodium and glutamate. Glutamate is unbounded glutamic acid, one of twenty amino acids on the planet that make up all proteins. Glutamic acid and free glutamate are in our bodies: our muscles are 17 percent glutamic acid, and breast milk is 0.02 percent.

When protein-laden foods such as meat or cheese are cooked, fermented, cured, or ripened, the protein chains break down, and the amino acids are free to move around, unbound. They're sometimes called free glutamates when they're in this state. At any one moment, there are about 12 grams of free glutamate just chugging around our bodies.

The negatively charged glutamate ions are attracted to positively charged ions of sodium—an extremely common element present in much of our food and in our own bodies. Think of the bond between these two ions as like that between two magnets: they can stick together, but they can also be easily pulled apart. When glutamate and sodium bond, they are monosodium glutamate.

Salt is everywhere, and glutamic acid is everywhere, and neither is thought of as dangerous on its own. But there's a general perception that once they're bonded together, they become a health risk. But as with table salt, monosodium glutamate is instantly water soluble. If I add it to water—a broth, or simply the saliva in my mouth—it separates instantly into glutamate and sodium. And if I boiled down that broth until no water was left, I would find recrystallized MSG at the bottom of my pot. The bond can be broken and reformed easily; together or apart, salt and glutamic acid are no more or less dangerous.

When Ikeda evaporated his kombu dashi, he discovered crystallized MSG. A small bottle of the original monosodium glutamate he extracted still exists in the collections of the Department of Chemistry at the University of Tokyo (formerly known as Tokyo Imperial University, where Ikeda both attended and later taught). I've seen a photo of this artifact. It's a clear glass bottle with a wooden cork; a brown label was pasted on the front, with vertical Japanese lettering. It looks like it's from the worn, wooden shelves of a mystical apothecary rather than the much-maligned world of modern science and food additives.

When Dr. Ikeda first tasted monosodium glutamate, he knew he had discovered a previously unrecognized taste. In a speech to the International Congress of Applied Chemistry in 1912, he described it as follows: "Just as honey and sugar gave us so clear a notion of what sweet is, the salts of glutamic acid are destined to give us an equally definite idea of this peculiar taste quality. Anyone who tastes a solution of sodium glutamate will at once recognize its taste to be different from all other well-known qualities."

Ikeda needed a word to capture the qualities of this savory taste sensation. He came up with *umami* from the Japanese word *umai* for "delicious" and *mi*, for "essence, taste, or flavor." In the Western world, we don't have a single word to describe this taste, although it's common in our cuisine. As Ikeda pointed out, the umami flavor is common to many vegetables, cheeses, and meats—all of which naturally contain glutamic acid and MSG. We have since appropriated the word *umami* to describe what has become known as the fifth taste of savory.

In 1908 Ikeda partnered with a successful iodine company—which also manufactured its product from seaweed—to mass-produce monosodium glutamate. Ikeda believed that manufacturing MSG as a flavoring agent was important because it could be used to improve the national diet. If a highly nutritious food tasted bland, all it needed was the generous addition of MSG to make it delicious.

The company Ikeda founded was named Ajinomoto, or "essence of taste." Soon Ikeda and his partners discovered a more efficient method to produce MSG. Instead of evaporating kombu dashi, MSG could be harvested from fermented sugar or grains, which is how it is produced to this day. In Japan, molasses is fermented with *koji*, the same yeast that's used to make miso and soy sauce. In America, MSG is fermented from corn, wheat, beets, or other glucose-rich sources, using *Corynebacterium glutamicum*, a bacterium that eats nutrients such as glucose and produces proteins high in glutamic acid. It's a natural fermentation process, the same that occurs in soy sauce production. The resulting slurry is filtered and centrifuged, and the glutamic acid is crystallized with sodium.

Though Ajinomoto had found an easier way to produce MSG, its marketing efforts stalled. The company encountered the same problem that William Gebhardt had faced when he first started selling chili powder: no one knew how to use it. Ajinomoto partnered with cooking schools in Japan, giving every graduate a free sample bottle of MSG, along with a recipe book. By the mid-1930s, Ajinomoto developed a shaker-style bottle, designed to sit on the dinner table alongside the salt and pepper. MSG had been designed for use in the kitchen, but now it was being applied directly to food as a condiment.

◦　◦　◦

In America, MSG is associated not with Japanese cooking but with Chinese food. So how did this Japanese ingredient get into Chinese cuisine? Ajinomoto expanded advertising and production beyond Japan, and MSG was introduced to mainland China via Taiwan, which was under Japanese control from 1895 to 1945. Monosodium glutamate became popular with street food vendors, who, in addition to cooking with it, would also sell it by weight to home cooks. From there the product spread to mainland China. Because many parts of China were Buddhist, and therefore vegetarian, MSG became popular in Chinese restaurants as a cheap way to make a flavorful vegetarian stock. Some of the Chinese imitation brands even invoked the religion in their names, such as Ve-Tsin, or Buddha's Hand.

Chinese immigrants were among the first to use MSG in their cooking in America. *Cook at Home in Chinese* by Henry Low, published in 1938, is one of the earliest Chinese cookbooks targeted at American readers. Nearly every recipe, including one for a bean-curd-and-mushroom soup, contained a teaspoon or more of "gourmet powder," the direct translation of the Chinese name for MSG. Low called it one of the five "Chinese staples" needed to cook authentic Chinese food.

Bean Curd and Mushroom Soup

From Henry Low's *Cook at Home in Chinese*. Combining the crunchy textures of bamboo shoots and water chestnuts, and topped impressively with a poached egg, this soup looks intriguing and tastes even better. It's hearty enough for a main course.

Yield: serves 4

1/2 cup canned straw mushrooms
1 chicken liver, sliced thinly
1/4 pound lean pork, sliced thinly
1 cup baby bok choy

¼ cup canned bamboo shoots

¼ cup canned water chestnuts, sliced

4 cups chicken stock

½ teaspoon salt

1 teaspoon MSG

Dash of pepper

2 eggs (or more, if desired)

1 pound silken tofu, cut into eight pieces

1. In a large pot, add all ingredients except for eggs and tofu. Bring to a boil over medium heat.

2. Reduce heat to a gentle simmer. Break eggs into soup and simmer for 3 minutes.

3. Turn off heat and add in tofu. Cover pot and allow tofu to heat through, about 5 minutes, and then serve.

MSG was already popular with Chinese Americans by the 1930s, but Ajinomoto wanted all Americans to use MSG in their homes, like Japanese families did. Ajinomoto launched an aggressive campaign to promote the use of MSG in American kitchens. That's where my bottle of Wyler's Meat Tenderizer comes in, with the label emblazoned with its MSG content. Ajinomoto introduced little perfume bottle-style packaging, which it thought would appeal to housewives, while Ac'cent (Ajinomoto's main competitor) tried tabletop shakers. Both brands encountered limited success. Though the *New York Times* occasionally printed a recipe featuring this flavor, in 1950 an article titled "Origin of Aji-no-moto," noted that in America, MSG was used primarily by fruit and vegetable canners, not home cooks. Another *Times* columnist wrote in 1955, "[C]ommercial food manufacturers use it enthusiastically. Condensed and dried soups probably would be unmarketable without it." In America, MSG was not frequently used in the home cook's dishes, but became an essential ingredient in mass-marketed convenience food.

By 1969, fifty-eight million pounds of MSG was being produced in America every year to meet the demands of food manufacturers. MSG's main advantage, from an American perspective, was that it made crappy food taste *better*. The use of MSG in processed food gave it a bad reputation in the second half of the twentieth century. The thought was that if monosodium glutamate was added to bad food, MSG must be bad for you too. It was the opposite of what Ikeda had intended, since he dreamed of using it to improve healthy food.

I used to believe that I had a sensitivity to the MSG found in processed foods. I'm a migraine sufferer, and I thought it triggered my headaches. I came to this belief because I had a fondness for a certain chicken-flavored cracker, made with "cooked chicken for natural flavor" and a healthy dose of MSG. They were so delicious. But every time I ate these crackers, they made me ill. My cheeks flushed, my head ached, my heartbeat raced. Then came a migraine. I blamed the MSG.

I ate these chicken crackers for the last time on a bus ride to visit my brother Greg in Boston. He picked me up, and as I tumbled into his car, head throbbing with a migraine, I moaned about my MSG sensitivity.

"You don't have a sensitivity to MSG," Greg insisted. "They've done a ton of studies that show that's a myth. There are preservatives that are used along with MSG in crappy foods that people with migraines often have sensitivities to. Sulfites and nitrates."

I flipped over the box of chicken crackers and read the list of ingredients. There, next to the MSG: a type of sulfite. I've heard competing science as to whether migraineurs like me are sensitive to these preservatives, and I don't want to just shuffle blame to another hapless chemical. But it planted a seed of doubt. I wanted to know when the fear of MSG originated, and if it was grounded in fact.

In Ikeda's time, science was worshipped. But by the 1960s, some had begun to mistrust its claims to progress. The world had witnessed the tragedy of thalidomide, a routine pregnancy drug prescribed in Europe, Australia, and Japan for morning sickness. Before being banned in

1961, thalidomide had resulted in over ten thousand severe birth defects. Laboratory-created food additives soon came under fire as well. The US Food and Drug Administration (FDA) banned the sugar substitute cyclamate in 1969, after research showed it could cause bladder cancer in rats—never mind that the research was funded by the sugar industry and is considered to be based on shaky evidence.

The next target: MSG. In 1968 the *New England Journal of Medicine* printed a fairly innocent letter under the heading "Chinese Restaurant Syndrome." Dr. Robert Ho Man Kwok of the National Biomedical Research Foundation began: "For several years since I have been in this country, I have experienced a strange syndrome whenever I have eaten out in a Chinese restaurant, especially one that served Northern Chinese food."

> The most prominent symptoms are numbness at the back of the neck, gradually radiating to both arms and the back, general weakness and palpitation.
>
> After some discussion, my colleagues and I at first speculated that it might be caused by some ingredient in the soy sauce, to which quite a few people are allergic . . . Some have suggested that these symptoms may be caused by cooking wine, which is used generously in most Chinese restaurants . . . Others have suggested that it may be caused by the monosodium glutamate seasoning used to a great extent for seasoning in Chinese restaurants . . . Another alternative is that the high sodium content of the Chinese food . . . The Chinese food causes thirst, which would also be due to the high sodium content.

At the end of this letter, he noted that his facility lacked personnel to commit to research in this area and wondered if there might not be another facility interesting in taking on a study.

After Dr. Kwok's letter was published, several other *Journal* subscribers wrote to say that they themselves, family members, or patients experienced similar symptoms after meals at Chinese restaurants. One letter described an attack after eating matzo ball soup in a kosher delicatessen. From the several possible causes that Dr. Kwok listed, MSG was fingered as the villain. Several scientists and research facilities decided to take up Dr. Kwok's call to arms; since his letter was penned, MSG has become the most rigorously studied food additive in history. In twenty years, nineteen different studies explored MSG.

In 1969 a study published in the journal *Science* by Herbert H. Schaumburg, Robert Byck, and two other researchers at the Albert Einstein College of Medicine in the Bronx, New York, confirmed the connection between MSG and what was now popularly being called Chinese restaurant syndrome (CRS). The team tested wonton soup from a Chinese restaurant where two patrons had suffered a reaction. A prominent theory of Chinese restaurant syndrome is that it was caused by wonton soup made with MSG, consumed at the beginning of a meal on an empty stomach. Schaumburg and his colleagues fed wonton soup to two individuals with self-proclaimed MSG sensitivities who then reported the symptoms of CRS. Using this scenario as their starting point, they fed 56 volunteers doses of MSG-laden chicken broth. The participants drank this broth first thing in the morning, on an empty stomach. Another thirteen participants were administered MSG intravenously in doses up to 125 mg. Some people showed signs of the "syndrome"—burning sensation on the skin, facial pressure, chest pain, and headache—at 3 grams, for others, there were no symptoms even over 20 grams.

I tried a version of this experiment myself. I woke up on a recent sunny, summer morning and rolled out of bed. Instead of my morning cup of tea, I dissolved a heaping tablespoon of MSG in a cup of warm water, and drank it down before breakfast. Frankly, it turned my stomach, and I felt weird enough that I had to go back to bed. But I took my reaction with a grain of salt—so to speak. The FDA currently estimates that the average American consumes 0.5 grams of MSG as an additive per day; so even the 3 grams in the Schaumburg study is *a lot* more than anyone would reasonably consume in an entire day, let alone in one meal. And MSG is rarely consumed in the conditions I replicated: it's used as a flavor enhancer, which means that it's usually consumed with food, not on an empty stomach. The report's authors acknowledged that when their study participants had food in their stomachs, it delayed or stopped the effects altogether.

But "Monosodium L-Glutamate: Its Pharmacology and Role in the Chinese Restaurant Syndrome" had a huge problem: preconceived bias. It didn't test to find out *if* MSG caused Chinese restaurant syndrome; the scientists assumed it did. Its goal was to discover at what quantities MSG caused the symptoms. At the time, no one challenged their underlying claim. And after the study's publication, the resulting press coverage solidified the relationship in the public's mind between MSG consumption and adverse side effects.

At the time, though, no one took Chinese restaurant syndrome seriously. It was seen as the result of overindulgence—like a hangover. The *New York Times* reported on MSG in 1968, interviewing Chinese restaurant owners and patrons alike. A restaurant-goer from the Bronx said that "three times he had experienced a tightening of the face and temple muscles, numbness, weeping, and even fainting, after eating 'in my favorite Chinese restaurant.'" None of these symptoms kept this guy from his favorite Chinese meal, however—although he admitted he thought that sodium, not MSG, was to blame for his CRS. A Chinese restaurateur pointed out that he and his family ate Chinese food three times a day and never suffered any signs of the syndrome. Only one of the restaurant owners interviewed acknowledged that a few of his guests—"three or four among thousands and thousands of customers"—had ever exhibited anything resembling Chinese restaurant syndrome.

Actor Lorne Greene, one of the stars of the hit TV Western *Bonanza*, was hospitalized in 1972 with what he claimed was the Chinese restaurant syndrome.

"I had had a light breakfast that day and practically nothing for lunch, and my wife and I went out to a Chinese restaurant for dinner, and the food was *de-goddamn-licious*," he told the *New York Times*. "Shrimp, beef, fried and sizzled, and like an idiot I put some more soy sauce on the rice, and that stuff is *filled* with monosodium glutamate." Greene collapsed as he was leaving the restaurant, but recovered fully and lived to eat Chinese food another day.

Public attitude toward MSG took a sinister turn with the studies of medical doctor and professor John Olney, who conducted experiments by injecting MSG directly under the skin of baby mice. The mice developed brain lesions as well as "stunted skeletal development, marked obesity, and female sterility." Olney pointed out that five of the seven scientists responsible for the FDA review of MSG's safety had either worked for or lobbied on behalf of MSG manufacturers and major consumers. Drs. Olney, Schaumburg, and Byck, plus activist Ralph Nader (yes, that Ralph Nader), lobbied the FDA to get MSG removed from the "Generally Recognized as Safe" list. "Anything that can cause brain damage in animals is dangerously toxic," Olney told the *New York Times* in 1977.

Olney's critics accused him of fearmongering, arguing that his study bore no relation to the human consumption of MSG. The irony of Olney's experiment is that glutamic acid is the most common neurotransmitter in the human brain; the brain manufactures this amino acid to form nerve connections that help us learn and remember. When MSG is consumed, none of it reaches the brain. Humans have a blood-brain barrier: a semipermeable cell wall that regulates which chemicals are absorbed into the brain. The brain doesn't want any extra glutamic acid getting in, because it's happy making its own.

After Olney's study, and his active presence in the press, "No MSG" signs began appearing in the windows of Chinese restaurants. These restaurants were villainized for using monosodium glutamate, despite the fact that fifty million pounds of MSG was manufactured in America in 1976, and currently appears in brands as wide reaching as Kraft and Kentucky Fried Chicken.

As I pieced together the evidence against MSG—scanning through forty-year-old medical studies and news articles—I realized we had developed a fear of "chemicals" that persists to this day. But this fear has little basis in actual science. Today more scientists, and a small coterie of chefs, are speaking up for this much-maligned chemical.

The movement began in 1993, when L. Tarasoff and M. F. Kelly of the University of Western Sydney in Australia conducted a review of all the previous studies of MSG. They focused on an extremely problematic issue: MSG had a distinctive flavor. In previous double-blind studies, when MSG was administered versus a placebo, it was very easy for test subjects to tell whether or not they were getting MSG based on its taste. This oversight potentially influenced the test results.

Tarasoff and Kelly performed a new test that used capsules filled with MSG to bypass the taste, and test subjects also drank milk and ate their choice of muesli bars afterward (apricot and coconut, tropical fruits, three fruits, black currant, apple, or peppermint chocolate chip, if you were wondering). Nearly the same percentage of participants had reactions to MSG as to the placebo: 15 percent to the MSG pills and about 14 percent to the placebos. Their conclusion was clear: "The present study led to the conclusion that 'Chinese Restaurant Syndrome' is an anecdote applied to a variety of postprandial illnesses; rigorous and realistic scientific evidence linking the syndrome to MSG could not be found."

Today, there's a double standard when it comes to the perception of MSG. If it's in Chinese takeout, it's called MSG, and it's likened to poison. But when MSG is utilized by high-end American chefs and brands, it's referred to as "umami," and it's celebrated as revolutionary. Although Ikeda named this taste umami in 1907, the designation wasn't accepted officially by the scientific community until 2000, when taste receptors on the tongue were specifically identified for glutamate. Umami became the fifth official taste, alongside sweet, salty, bitter, and sour.

Since then, the word has been adopted by chefs and high-end food makers as a safe alternative to saying MSG. But the most important fact I've learned about MSG is that many foods I love, and that chefs cook with, contain naturally occurring MSG—or umami, depending on who you're asking.

Take, for example, kombu dashi—the broth Ikeda used in his experiments. According to a 2008 *New York Times* article on kombu dashi, "The Secret's Out as Japanese Stock Gains Fans," chef Eric Ripert uses it at Le Bernardin, one of the most highly decorated restaurants in New York City. "He complements Kumamoto oysters with dashi gelée, finishes mushrooms with the stock, and brushes it on raw fish before layering on olive oil and citrus," the article noted. Per Se and Jean-Georges, two other high-end NYC restaurants, also feature kombu dashi in their seafood dishes. "Kelp and bonito are loaded with umami, the taste of mouthwatering savoriness," the *Times* wrote.

Umami Burger, a popular New York restaurant chain featuring "gourmet burgers and craft beer," uses the combination of salt and glutamate-heavy ingredients to create supersavory burgers. Its signature Umami Burger is topped with Parmesan cheese (1.0 to 2.7 percent free glutamate), shiitake mushrooms (0.7 percent), roasted tomato (0.14 to 0.26 percent), caramelized onions, and an "umami ketchup." Remember that sodium and glutamate together in a liquid or emulsion is just the same as consuming crystallized monosodium glutamate.

Some chefs skip over these natural sources of umami and go straight for a dash of MSG—just as cooks did a century ago. Mission Chinese, chef Danny Bowien's "Americanized Oriental" restaurant in San Francisco, proudly put MSG shakers on the tables. Zakary Pelaccio, a chef and former owner of Fatty Crab in Manhattan, admitted his love of MSG to the *New York Times* in 2008. In his own cooking, he'll add MSG straight: "Too much MSG, and you get that harsh, acrid taste, but get it just right, and that dish will sing." Chicago-based chef and cookbook author Grant Achatz, owner of the restaurants Alinea and Next, uses MSG in his home cooking. Along with salt and black pepper, MSG is one of his kitchen staples. "If you gave me those three items, I could make anything taste good," he said. Although he added that many would hate him for just saying he likes MSG.

The most outspoken pro-MSG chef is David Chang. Trained as a ramen cook in Japan, he opened his first restaurant in New York, Momofuku Noodle Bar, in 2004. He's now owner of eight restaurants in New York alone, runs his own research-and-development department, and has won multiple James Beard Foundation awards. Chang doesn't use powdered MSG in his restaurant. But you will find squirts of Kewpie mayonnaise, which comes from Japan and contains MSG. He also uses kombu dashi, as well as other umami-rich ingredients, and supports an extensive fermentation program in his R&D department built on creating foods with high amounts of glutamic acid.

At the 2012 MAD Symposium in Copenhagen (*mad* is the Danish word for food), Chang practically scolded the audience for the stigma surrounding MSG.

"I can think of no other food ingredient or additive, at least in Western culture, that is as vilified, that is basically a pariah, as much as monosodium glutamate," he said. "There are a lot of people who hate Asian food. There are a lot of people who hate our food at Momofuku. There recently was a guest, that came in a couple months ago, and was complaining to the staff that we were adding MSG to our food. She was angry, she was so angry. She was saying she had headaches, she was sweating, heart palpitations, basically Chinese restaurant syndrome. She was allergic to MSG." He continued, "I wanted to, the next day, say on the menu, 'If you think you're allergic to MSG, please assume that we do put MSG in our food.' Because all evidence suggests that MSG is not harmful to you."

A growing group of foodies support pro-MSG chefs like Chang, and J. Kenji López-Alt is leading the pack. Kenji was an editor at *Cook's Illustrated* magazine and headed America's Test Kitchen—the part of the magazine that does rigorous food tests, like the head-to-head vanilla extract challenge—before assuming the role of managing culinary director of the food blog *Serious Eats*. His book *The Food Lab: Better Home Cooking Through Science* applies the scientific method to the kitchen to create fool-proof recipes. Like me, he comes from a family of scientists, and it's obvious in his work.

Kenji grew up in a Japanese American household: his mother emigrated from Japan in the late 1960s; her parents followed a decade later. In his house, there was always a shaker of MSG on the table, alongside the pepper and the salt. His grandma used it to season rice, eggs, and soup, and his mom added it to her dumplings. MSG was just another condiment to Kenji.

Kenji considers MSG in all its forms valuable tools in his kitchen. He'll use MSG when he's making traditional Japanese recipes, but alternately, he'll also flavor a stock with a Parmesan rind or the heel of a prosciutto, which are rich in glutamic acid. "Sometimes I want to put garlic powder on my pizza instead of fresh sliced garlic," he told me when I spoke to him over the phone one morning. He was making eggs in his West Coast kitchen, while I sipped tea on the East Coast. "I wouldn't say that necessarily makes one better than the other, it's just different things for different needs and different times," he explained. He described MSG as having a one-dimensional flavor, while something like a kombu dashi, on the other hand, is more complex.

Kenji has even included MSG as an ingredient in a few of his recipes in his James Beard award-nominated column in *Serious Eats*, "The Food Lab." But he often gets pushback on these entries: emails accusing him of trying to poison people by using "chemicals" in his cooking. "Most of the time, it's pretty easy to ignore those things, because it comes from people who are scientifically illiterate, which is no fault of their own," he said. It's part of his job—and mine—to educate.

He has sympathy for those who claim to experience symptoms from MSG consumption, despite the fact that science proves otherwise. "Anecdotally, people do claim to get reactions and I don't think it's right to completely dismiss all those," he said. "You can't say someone doesn't get a headache. Maybe it's psychosomatic; but there's something going on."

He pointed out to me a very simple explanation for the symptoms of Chinese restaurant syndrome, one that even Dr. Kwok had theorized in the now-infamous 1968 letter to the *New England Journal of Medicine*. Since MSG is a salt, when you eat it in combination with table salt, it's easy to overconsume sodium. And that will leave you bloated and sick.

But Kenji's sympathies have a limit. "I don't know very many people who claim to get reactions from Doritos the way they get reactions from Chinese food."

If you think you might have an MSG sensitivity, you have to avoid not just food with added MSG but also all the foods I've mentioned in this chapter: everything from Japanese cuisine, to Parmesan cheese, to breast milk. However, if you have consumed these foods and have not experienced a reaction, then you *don't* have an MSG sensitivity. My own MSG consumption is now quite a bit more than that of the average American. Before writing this chapter, I never actively cooked or seasoned with MSG. Now with each bite of homemade soup or stew, I think to myself, "You know what would make this taste better?" The answer is always MSG. Every grocery store product that proclaims proudly, "No MSG!" I see as a missed opportunity, and think longingly of my vintage bottle of Wyler's Meat Tenderizer.

I often wonder what Kikunae Ikeda would have thought about the MSG controversy that gripped America in the 1970s, and the lingering doubts that persist to this day. Would he have been surprised by the trouble his discovery caused? He had created MSG with the intention of benefitting mankind. And he—like my brother, like any organic chemist—understood the science, and knew it to be harmless.

When I talked to Kenji, he felt that trying to convince people MSG was safe wasn't important in terms of a healthy diet. You can eat it or not—it will make no difference.

"But it's important in the sense that dispelling any sort of mistruth is important," he said. And I agree.

A fear of "chemicals" has become a sickness in American food culture, one that defies logic and is based solely on emotion. But in the country's culinary centers there is a rebellion, made up of chefs, food writers, and scientists. And as a result of their work, I've already noticed a subtle change in public opinion. Five years ago, while planning a talk on MSG with Soma, fans told me they would come but wouldn't eat the food samples we cooked with MSG. But now, when I rattle off my eight flavors for inquisitive foodies, when I get to MSG, instead of a protest, I'll get a sly smile. "Oh yeah . . . MSG is great," they'll tell me, hesitantly. We pause for a moment, recognizing a comrade in the MSG crusade.

Umami Finishing Salt

To honor Dr. Ikeda and his discovery, I made my own MSG from scratch in my home kitchen, using Dr. Ikeda's original "recipe." This is "natural" MSG, as homemade as a chocolate chip cookie. There are other chemicals in there, accounting for the color, ocean-like smell, and briny taste. But it has the unmistakable tongue-coating umami sensation that Ikeda identified more than a century ago. The complexity of this salt's flavor is even more delicious than commercial MSG.

Yield: makes about ½ cup

2 ounces kombu
½ cup table salt

1. Make the kombu dashi. Gently wipe the kombu with a damp paper towel. Place in a pot with 4 cups of water. Allow the kombu to soak for 3 hours. Add salt and simmer over gentle heat for about 30 minutes, and then discard the kombu.
2. Raise heat to medium-high and reduce dashi until about 90 percent of the liquid has evaporated, about 60 minutes, scraping down the salty

residue from time to time. You should have about 3$\frac{1}{2}$ ounces (a scant $\frac{1}{2}$ cup) of sediment with a bit of liquid.

3.   Pour sediment and liquid into a shallow glass baking dish and place in a 250-degree oven. The finishing salt is done when the salts crystallize and all of the liquid has evaporated. The size of the baking dish will determine how long evaporation and crystallization take. The larger the dish, the greater the surface area, and the quicker the evaporation. An 8 × 8-inch baking dish took about 90 minutes.

Sriracha

Sriracha

THE OCTOBER AFTER my visit to the Gaya plantation, I made a pilgrimage to Irwindale, California, to visit the mecca of hot sauces, the Huy Fong Sriracha factory.

Although some might consider Sriracha a food fad, I don't think it's going away anytime soon. And it's because Sriracha might be the perfect hot sauce for American tastes. It has a winning balance of vinegar and sugar, combined with salt and garlic. It's made with fresh jalapeño peppers, so it's comparatively mild (about half as hot as Tabasco), which makes it accessible to more palates. Sriracha's slightly thick texture is another advantage: as a topping, it stays where you put it. You can engineer every bite of eggs, for example, to be exactly as spicy as you want it. And when used as a sauce for meats, it coats with an incomparable aptitude.

And then there's its unmistakable bottle. A bottle of Sriracha looks like the peppers it's made from: the clear plastic shows off the bright red sauce, which contrasts with its green cap. The front is printed with the now-iconic rooster logo—the Chinese zodiac symbol of the sauce's inventor—and the back is covered in text, written in multiple languages, giving the packaging an air of exoticism.

The story of Sriracha is a quintessentially American story. Our food is a mash-up of people and influences from all over the planet. Sriracha combines cuisine from France and Thailand with the dreams of a Vietnamese refugee named David Tran, but it's produced entirely in Southern California. The garlic comes from Gilroy, peppers from a nearby farm just north of Los Angeles, and they're processed together in the factory in Irwindale.

Sriracha has seen a meteoric rise in popularity since it was first produced by Huy Fong Foods in 1980. The hot sauce industry as a whole is one of the ten fastest-growing industries in the United States, generating over $240 million dollars in sales annually. In 2014, sales of bottles of Sriracha hot sauce reportedly exceeded $60 million dollars. But that number was probably underreported, and when you factor in the money that Huy Fong makes licensing its name to products that include Sriracha (like Giants' Sriracha-flavored sunflower seeds, Country Archer Sriracha Beef Jerky, and Rogue Sriracha Hot Stout) their net worth is far higher. The company has never had a year of declining sales, despite never spending a penny on advertising. And it has other hot sauce companies running scared: Tabasco introduced its own version of Sriracha to try to compete.

My first request to tour Huy Fong was politely but firmly declined. With the surge in the sauce's popularity, plenty of fanatics were emailing love letters to gain admittance to the source. My heart sank when I received a reply to my request: "Dear Sarah, Thank you for your interest in our products! We strive to make the best sauces using quality ingredients in every bottle. In regards to your interest, unfortunately, we do not offer tours in our facility. Sincerely, Customer Service." What would I do? I had a book to write!

Luckily, my friend Gabe happened to be visiting from Cleveland, attending to contacts in New York City. He's a confectionary packaging salesman, and as far I as I can tell, his job involves receiving a lot of free candy. But he has also made lots of cold calls to companies that might be looking for new boxes.

"Call the company after hours," he told me. "Listen to the mailboxes. See if you can figure out who you need to talk to directly. Get their extension."

I did have a name from the few news articles where reporters had clearly been inside the factory: Donna Lam, executive operations officer. I phoned at four in the morning West Coast time and listened carefully to the company directory. When I found Donna's mailbox, I left an enthusiastic and sincere plea. By that afternoon, she had called me back, thrilled to have me visit. I had landed the much-coveted factory tour.

The morning of the interview, I ate mediocre eggs and hash browns in my hotel room, longing for some Sriracha to improve upon them. I was nervous. I navigated the notoriously messy Los Angeles highways in my rental car (which, compared with driving in New York City, I actually found quite orderly). When I rolled up to the Huy Fong factory in Irwindale, it looked sleeker and more corporate than the Holiday Inn I had left that morning. I was expecting low-slung industrial; I got cool earth tones and a little fountain spraying jets of water in front of a chrome Huy Fong logo.

When I swung open the front door of the office, I smelled the delicious, subtle scent of garlic; when I mentioned this smell to the receptionist, she said that she didn't even notice it anymore. Donna Lam, tall, sleek, and chic, in tidy clothes and flawless makeup, soon came out to shake my hand, and led me upstairs to a conference room. Huy Fong is a family affair: Donna is the sister-in-law of Sriracha's creator, David Tran.

"David said we can show you the whole factory," she said. And an instant later, David was in the room shaking my hand. He wore a white T-shirt emblazoned with the famous rooster logo. At the age of sixty-eight, there was still a bounce in his step and a twinkle in his eye.

"In the past, we've been worried about a competitor maybe taking our designs and copying the sauce." Donna shrugged and looked to David. "But now . . ."

"I don't have a competitor," David said firmly. "You can see everything," he said, widening his hands for emphasis. "The whole factory."

The whole factory was enormous; over 650,000 square feet of floor space, it had opened only a few months before I visited. But Donna estimated that because of increasing demand for the hot sauce, they would outgrow the building's capacity in less than ten years.

When asked about this growth, David attributed it to one thing: "The Americans like *spicy* food."

Contrary to the popular stereotype, Americans *do* like spicy food. It's in our biology. Much like chili powder and curry powder, Sriracha gets us a little bit high every time we eat it. The capsaicin in its jalapeño peppers triggers heat receptors in our mouths, and our brains release endorphins as a response. The experience is addictive, so we repeat it again and again with spicier and spicier food. Two hundred years ago, black pepper was considered hot; now a jalapeño hot sauce is universally loved.

And hot sauce has had a long history in the United States. The earliest bottles of hot pepper sauce were being sold in Massachusetts in 1807, made from cayenne peppers. Americans have topped off their meals with Tabasco since 1868, and the sauce's success created a deluge of knockoffs by the end of the nineteenth century. But these spicy sauces are often divisive: you love them or you hate them. None has reached the same degree of acceptance as Sriracha.

The original Sriracha sauce, which later inspired David's Sriracha, was created in Si Racha, Thailand. A hot red chili sauce called Sriraja Panich, it was invented in 1949 by a woman named Ms. Thanom Chakkapak. Whenever she is referred to—in news articles, documentary videos, or even by the employees of her company—she is always called by her full name: Miss Thanom Chakkapak. I don't know why, but it's awesome. Sriraja Panich is made using garlic and finger-shaped peppers called *prik chi faa*, along with vinegar, sugar, and salt. It's fermented in casks before bottling. Sweet and vinegary, the sauce has a consistency slightly thicker than that of Tabasco. It's peppery without being particularly hot. In Thailand, it's a popular condiment for fresh seafood and *khai jiao*, a wok-fried omelet.

Thai Omelet

Eggs are beaten with fish sauce for a deep umami flavor, and rice flour is added to make the edges extra crispy. The result is like a savory funnel cake. It can be served with a filling of pork, chicken, or pad thai, but I think it's best with simply a squeeze of Sriracha. Recipe adapted from Leela Punyaratabandhu for *Serious Eats.*

Yield: serves 1 to 2

2 large eggs
$1/2$ teaspoon lime juice
1 teaspoon Thai fish sauce
1 tablespoon water
1 tablespoon rice flour
$3/4$ cup plain vegetable oil
Sriracha, for garnish
Basmati rice, if desired

1. Combine eggs, lime juice, fish sauce, water, and rice flour in a medium bowl. Beat with a fork until frothy. If the flour forms a few lumps, break up as many as possible with your fingers.
2. Heat the vegetable oil in a small (6-inch) pot or a round-bottom wok set over medium-high heat until lightly smoking. Hold the egg bowl about a foot above the pan and pour the egg mixture into the oil in one go.
3. The egg mixture will immediately puff up. Do not disturb it. After 20 seconds, flip the omelet using a large slotted spoon, a spider, or a

metal spatula. Let the other side cook for another 20 seconds. Remove the omelet from the pan, garnish with Sriracha, and serve immediately over cooked basmati rice.

Srirajah Panich was exported to countries around Southeast Asia, including South Vietnam, where it became a popular condiment for southern-style pho. Pho is the unofficial national dish of Vietnam—pronounced like *fuh* if you're Vietnamese, and more like *foh* if you're American.

Some of the origins of pho can be found in French cuisine. Vietnam was under French rule for nearly a century, from 1859 to 1954, and was known as French Indochina. Before the French takeover, beef was not a common cooking ingredient: cattle were considered more valuable as farm labor. But French colonists, who might have missed beef stew from home, began using the animals for food. Pot-au-feu, which translates literally as "pot in the fire," is a classic French dish where different cuts of beef—and sometimes pork or chicken—are boiled with seasonal vegetables in a rich broth of beef marrow, onions, garlic, and herbs. The broth is served as a first course, followed by the meat, with highly flavored accompaniments such as pickles and hot mustard. When this French dish was prepared in Vietnam, it evolved into pho, a broth of beef bones and charred vegetables, very similar to a pot-au-feu broth, and served with rice noodles and boiled beef along with highly flavored accompaniments like hot sauce.

In 1954 Vietnam was partitioned into north and south regions, after the end of French colonial rule. Pho in South Vietnam got a little fancier than in the North. Different meats were added, such as tripe or beef meatballs, and it was served with a plate of accoutrements that the diner could add to taste: bean sprouts, thorny cilantro, Thai basil, lime, hoisin sauce, and Srirajah Panich.

It was David Tran's experiences with Ms. Thanom Chakkapak's chili sauce, or one of the legion of sauces that replicated it, that inspired him to create his own hot sauce.

David was born in 1945 in what would shortly become South Vietnam. His brother owned a pepper farm in Long Binh, an agricultural area just north of Saigon. During the Vietnam War, David said, the market was bad for peppers: the area was a major site of conflict. David decided to try to make a chili sauce to sell instead. This is a timeless agricultural trick: by processing the crop, it became more valuable and didn't spoil. Grain can be turned into alcohol, fruit into preserves, and peppers into hot sauce.

Although Tran's original recipe was inspired by hot sauces like Sriraja Panich, his was different. He used cooked chilies, oil, and galangal—a rhizome that belongs to the ginger family, with an incense-like spiciness. It was a family business: his brother grew the peppers, David ground them, his father-in-law washed reused jars acquired from a nearby US Army base, and his brother-in-law filled them with the sauce. The family sold batches of the sauce to jobbers: middlemen who would then sell to restaurants and shops. The sauce became a popular condiment for roast dog amongst the Vietnamese. Hot sauce was also used by American servicemen to spice up bland MREs; it's likely that some of David's sauce made its way onto army bases.

Tran and his family made ends meet with their hot sauce business during the war, but life got more difficult in the war's aftermath. When the United States pulled out and Saigon fell in 1975, the North swept in to unify the country. The new Socialist government wanted to decapitalize commerce. David's family was considered Sino-Vietnamese, or Hoa, an ethnically Chinese group that made up much of Vietnam's middle class, as business owners and merchants. The North Vietnamese army closed businesses, seized property, and confiscated money—much of which was owned by Sino-Vietnamese families. Additionally, as political relations between China and Vietnam soured—a result of ongoing border skirmishes and Chinese protests of the treatment of the Sino-Vietnamese—Chinese living in Vietnam were systematically targeted and ostracized by the government. They were fired from their jobs and subjected to security checks. Many were forcibly relocated into previously unsettled areas called "New

David Tran

Economic Zones," where food shortages and poor sanitary conditions resulted in a rapidly rising death rate. The forced relocation policy and closing of many businesses left an economic vacuum in its wake. Vietnam's economy began to collapse.

By 1978, the government was forcibly expelling ethnic Chinese from the country, while simultaneously charging each person about $11,500 for the "privilege" to leave. Some refugees fled overland, but more left in small fishing vessels or decrepit ocean freighters. Approximately two-thirds of the refugees that fled Vietnam after the war were ethnically Chinese, and by 1979, sixty thousand refugees from Vietnam were arriving in other countries each month, with an unknown number dead at sea. These waves of postwar refugees became known as the "boat people."

David felt no ties to his ethnic homeland of China, but he knew he was unwelcome to stay in the country where he was born. His successful chili sauce business allowed him to save enough money to pay for his family's escape out of Vietnam. The way out was dangerous. As a precaution against disaster, the family divided into four groups with four different destinations outside of Vietnam: Hong Kong, Indonesia, Malaysia, and the Philippines. David Tran and his immediate family boarded a rusting and dilapidated Panamanian freighter named the *Huey Fong*. The ship was packed with over three thousand refugees, more than twice the ship's recommended capacity. The deck was crammed with luggage and people of all ages, standing shoulder to shoulder or sleeping in piles.

The ship approached Hong Kong on December 23, 1978. It was intercepted by British immigration officials and was ordered to turn around immediately. Instead, the ship dropped anchor in international waters and waited for over a month. The ship's captain, Shu-Wen-shin, claimed that the refugees threatened to kill him if he left for another port.

An American newspaper article reported on the situation aboard the cramped vessel: "'Children crying from hunger and women weeping for fear of dying'. . . more than half the refugees on the *Huey Fong* are 'either sick or totally exhausted. Some of them can hardly walk, others cannot talk, and still others vomit all the time.'"

In January 1979 Hong Kong declared itself a "first port of refuge." The British government decided to harbor incoming refugees and, in partnership with the United Nations, quickly relocate them across the world. The *Huey Fong* was finally allowed to land thirty-one days after it first set sail. Refugees, including David and his family, were brought ashore for a medical inspection and then interned in a refugee camp.

By 1980, America had absorbed over 230,000 Vietnamese refugees. Special laws were created that expanded Vietnamese immigration quotas and prioritized Vietnamese refugees over other immigrants for entry. David and his family arrived in Boston the first week of January 1980. Can you imagine—from Vietnam to Boston in the dead of winter? All David could think was that he needed a job to support his family in America. He knew that hundreds of thousands of Vietnamese refugees were flooding into the United States, and they would want the comfort of foods they knew from home. They would need a pepper sauce like the one David had made in Vietnam.

David called his brother, who was relocated across the country, in Los Angeles. David asked if there were red peppers in LA. His brother said yes. David packed up his family and headed across the country.

For his new hot sauce, David decided to use fresh chilies, unlike the cooked sauce he made in Vietnam. Not cooking the chilies cut down on production time. David scoured the supermarkets, testing chilies, and attempted a hot sauce from local green jalapeños. Although jalapeño peppers naturally ripen to a bright red hue, a ripe red jalapeño is a sight seldom seen on grocery store shelves. Green jalapeños are generally sold in the States because they are more profitable: they can be harvested earlier, so they save production costs, and they can be held longer in stores before they go bad. But David thought the green hot sauce wasn't right—he felt a hot sauce must be red.

He approached a vegetable vendor about buying up his red jalapeños.

"They sort them from the green ones. Nobody want the red chili—no market," David told me. "They threw it away. So I get them."

He blended the red chilies with salt, sugar, vinegar, and garlic. By February 1980, one month after he landed, David was in business.

David dubbed his new sauce Sriracha *Hot* Chili Sauce and named his company Huy Fong, after the *Huey Fong*, the boat that brought him out of Vietnam. He sold Sriracha to a few grocery stores in LA's Chinatown. From the first day he started production, he couldn't make enough hot sauce to meet demand. Since then, Sriracha sales have grown by double digits every year.

The current Sriracha factory produces 7,500 bottles hourly. When I visited Irwindale, after David told me that I could see the entire production, I slid on a hairnet and jumped into a golf cart with Donna. David rolled off in his own cart (his name was on the hood, on a gold placard) to oversee his business. David designed and customized the system by which the fresh peppers are turned into Sriracha, and tinkers with the machines himself when they're not working. I had arrived right smack in the middle of their busiest time for production: the pepper-processing season.

"We have to process the same day," Donna told me during my tour. "We want it as fresh as possible, so we capture it right after it's picked."

Each bottle of Sriracha can vary in color and flavor: early-season peppers are more orange and spicy; late-season peppers are bright red and sweet. Despite producing several millions of bottles of Sriracha each year, Huy Fong's sauce retains the variations of a small-batch product. During a class I taught to Sriracha fanatics at the Brooklyn Brainery, one student told me his father collects Sriracha bottles like vintages of fine wine, appreciating the subtle differences between each one.

"Our customers call and ask, 'Why can't you keep it consistent?' Well, it's a natural product: the color, the heat, the juiciness. We don't want to fool around with it," Donna said. "We do it fresh. We do it California."

Semitrucks arrive at the factory, each pulling two trailers with green metal mesh sides, filled to the top with jalapeño peppers in all shades of green, red, and brown. They each dump forty tons of produce into giant metal hoppers attached to the back of the factory. From the hoppers, the peppers are fed via conveyer belts to a washing station inside the factory. The mud that is cleaned off them is valuable topsoil that is shipped back to the farm.

The next stop: massive grinders, which puree the peppers into what Huy Fong calls its basic chili mash. Donna led me through a separate set of doors to reach this room: it's closed off and carefully ventilated, because the capsaicin released by the grinding peppers can be an irritant to the eyes, nose, and throat. I breathed in and coughed, but felt relief as soon as we left the room.

Once the chilies are ground, they're mixed with salt, vinegar, potassium sorbate (which inhibits the growth of nasties such as mold), and sodium bisulfate (which maintains the brilliant red color). Because these ingredients are added before storage, Huy Fong's products are considered unfermented—as opposed to Srirajah Panich, which is intentionally aged and fermented to develop the flavor. The thick chili mash is squirted into blue food-safe barrels and stored. By November, they have enough chili mash stashed away for an entire year's worth of Sriracha production.

Rounding the corner into the Sriracha storage room is like viewing the last scene in *Raiders of the Lost Ark*. More than three-quarters of the entire factory is dedicated solely to storage. A mini forklift lifted a blue barrel full of chili paste into place; that blue barrel was but one in an ocean of blue barrels, housed in what seemed like an infinite warehouse. It was awe inspiring.

Three products are made at the Huy Fong factory from the basic chili mash stored in those blue barrels: the chili mash itself is sold as Sambal Oelek; when garlic is added, it's called Chili Garlic. Sriracha sauce is the chili mash pureed to a slightly smoother finish, with garlic, sugar, and xanthan gum added. The latter is a thickener that stops the sauce from separating. Without it, the jalapeño juices would float to the top, while the seeds and skin bits would sink to the bottom.

The finished Sriracha is squirted into Huy Fong's iconic bottles, which are also made in the factory. There is a soothing how-it's-made-ness to watching the heated plastic shaped and printed on the automated assembly line, filled with red sauce, and capped with a green squeeze top. These bottles are grouped by the dozen and packed into boxes to make their trips to adoring fans in every corner of the country. Each year, the supply of Sriracha is sold out before it's even produced: Huy Fong fills orders for distributors who handle the nitty-gritty of getting it across the country.

A few months after my visit, the Tran family decided to open their factory doors to anyone who wanted to see their process. Now any fan who is willing to make the pilgrimage to Irwindale can step inside and learn how the sauce is made. The tours are booked full months in advance, which speaks to Sriracha's popularity.

As I was led through the expansive factory, I wondered how David's hot sauce went from a handmade, small-time operation in 1980, to the multimillion-dollar business it is today.

It began with the Vietnamese refugee community. Sriracha was originally targeted at new Vietnamese immigrants, and the sauce became an important part of the transition of Vietnamese refugees to their new homes in America. I came across a heartwarming example of its importance one day on my Facebook feed. If you've ever been on Facebook, you're aware of #tbt, or Throwback Thursday, where people post photos of themselves or their families from the past. One day I saw an adorable photo of my old college friend Doan Buu at five years old. Doan's whole family had fled Vietnam in the final stages of the war; he was the first of his siblings to be born in America. In the photo—from about 1985—he's standing with three cousins behind a monumental pile of fried chicken at a summer party in Kansas City, Kansas. Dead center in the photo was the unmistakable Sriracha bottle—just five years after David started making it in LA.

Other than with fried chicken (which Doan told me "is beloved by Vietnamese people; at least my family"), Doan remembered Sriracha being used in his household almost exclusively for pho—the French-influenced beef and noodle soup popular in Vietnam. In the 1980s, pho restaurants popped up in cities that supported large concentrations of Vietnamese refugees, such as LA, DC, and Houston. The pho restaurants quickly became popular outside of the Vietnamese communities; within a decade, local English-language papers and magazines were publishing reviews and recommendations of pho restaurants. And pho was an easy dish for Americans to love. In the words of Mai Pham, Vietnamese American chef and cookbook author: "Most of the ingredients are very familiar. It's fresh and not so spicy. Visually it's easy to see. It's not mysterious."

Sriracha's popularity stems from these pho restaurants, particularly the eateries that popped up in the LA area. Sriraja Panich was the most important condiment for pho in Vietnam, and in America, it was replaced by locally produced Huy Fong Sriracha. The easily recognizable bottles sat on the tables in pho restaurants, first in LA and then across the country.

I was first introduced to pho, and to Sriracha, in Washington, DC, around 2006. When I'd bus to the District for a weekend of partying with friends (like our late-night antics at Ben's Chili Bowl), the visit would always conclude with a Sunday morning stop at Pho 75 in Arlington, Virginia. The restaurant featured long, cafeteria-style tables in a drop-ceilinged room with a few Asian-ish decorations on the wall. I would watch my worldly DC friends turn their steaming hot pho broth pink with Huy Fong Sriracha. Taking their lead, I tentatively squirted a few dabs in my own bowl. Previously intimidated by the brutal burn of hot sauce, I found Sriracha mild enough that it added a pleasant zing. And every time I went back, I confidently added a little more Sriracha than on the previous visit.

One of the earliest mentions of Huy Fong's Sriracha in print is in a review of this very restaurant in the May 1987 edition of the *Washingtonian* magazine, just seven years after David and his family landed in America and began making the sauce. The review describes Pho 75 as "plain as a post," so it seems the locale hasn't changed much in thirty years; but neither has the food. "The *pho* is delicious as served," the reviewer wrote. "However, Pho 75's largely Vietnamese clientele invariably adjusts its flavor by adding a generous squeeze of lemon, a bit of hoisin sauce, a few drops of nuoc mam, and a squirt of bright-red, garlic-suffused Sriracha chili sauce. Plain or seasoned to taste, this is a most worthy *pho*."

Sriracha's appearance in Vietnamese dining establishments—where it was noticed by American patrons—was a crucial step in this flavor becoming an integral part of American cooking. Looking at Sriracha's growth since then illustrates how a flavor goes from exotic to mainstream in modern America. The Center for Culinary Development in Emeryville, California—which works with clients to develop successful food products—has developed a "Trend Mapping techinique," a five-stage system that maps food trends, like Sriracha, as they become part of American culture.

According to the CCD, "In stage one, the flavor appears in 'foodie' dining establishments." Frequently, an ingredient might be used by the immigrant kitchen staff first: Sriracha was spotted being used by Asian workers in San Francisco fine-dining restaurants in the early 1990s; from there the hot sauce began to transition to the dining room and into the meals of the American clientele. In 1997 the *New York Times* reviewed Asia de Cuba, a tiki-Asian-Latin-fusion restaurant in the Murray Hill neighborhood of Manhattan: "Now, our waiter is introducing us to our condiments: a mildly spicy pineapple relish, a clear potent habanero-oil-and-vinegar mixture, and a large bottle of splashy red chili sauce. 'This is sriracha, from Vietnam,' he says. Actually, sriracha is the famous chili sauce of Thailand, but it's a fine point." Both the reviewer and the waiter were wrong—or they were both halfway right. I suspect it was a bottle of good ol' California Sriracha.

In stage two, gourmet magazines and foodie-focused blogs cover the trend, and it might start appearing in gourmet food stores. A major turning point for Sriracha came when *Bon Appétit* magazine declared it the Ingredient of the Year in 2010, calling it "[t]he secret ingredient in dishes served at both four-star restaurants and neighborhood mom-and-pop spots." *Cook's Illustrated* declared Sriracha the best all-purpose hot sauce in 2012, and praised Sriracha's viscosity, balanced saltiness, mild heat, bright flavor, and slight sweetness. In its taste test, Sriracha beat America's oldest and most beloved brands—including Tabasco and Frank's RedHot.

In stage three, a new food appears on the menus of conventional chains such as Applebee's and the Cheesecake Factory. In Sriracha's case, it appeared in chain restaurants at almost the same time it saw widespread coverage in food media. P. F. Chang's was the first to use it as an ingredient in sauces and dips in 2000, but Applebee's gave it menu billing in 2009 with a Sriracha-mayonnaise dipping sauce for fried shrimp.

In stage four, recipe websites feature the ingredient, as well as women's magazines that aren't solely food focused. Both *Martha Stewart Living* and the Food Network Blog asked "Have You Tried Sriracha?" in 2011. Martha Stewart noted, "The sauce's popularity has soared in the United States recently—Sriracha has made the jump from the condiment caddy at Asian restaurants to home-kitchen counters." The Food Network commented on Sriracha's cultlike fan base and mentioned its popular Facebook page. The blog post also illustrated its quick crossover from a pho condiment to its place among American foods: "It seems logical to squirt this crimson sauce on egg rolls, stir-fry, and noodle dishes, but save some for burgers, fries, pizza, and tuna salad too."

In the last stage, number five, the food or flavor appears in chain retail stores and fast-food establishments. That means it has officially gone mainstream. Sriracha can now be purchased in Walmart, while Subway introduced a Sriracha sub sauce in 2013. The same year, it was one of the three finalist flavors in the Lay's "Do Us a Flavor" competition, but suffered a controversial loss to Cheesy Garlic Bread. (At least it was controversial for me—I think the Sriracha chips are better.)

Sriracha went from a niche product for Vietnamese immigrants to the American mainstream in thirty years. Its success has exceeded David

Tran's expectations; in fact, he didn't have any expectations at all when he began. He simply thought, "Oh, I'll just make it and see how it goes."

It went very, very well. Although David began by buying unwanted peppers from the local farmers' market, Sriracha sales quickly outgrew what LA's Wholesale Produce Market could supply. Today all the peppers that make Sriracha come from one supplier: Underwood Ranches, run by Craig Underwood and his farm manager Jim Roberts. From Labor Day until Thanksgiving, six hundred tons of ripe, red jalapeño peppers are trucked from Craig's farm to the Sriracha bottling plant every day. They travel from field to factory in under three hours.

The day after my visit to Huy Fong headquarters, I met Craig in the middle of SoCal farm country, north of Los Angeles. The drive was all panoramic vistas of dry, craggy hillsides and rolling acres of fruit tree–covered farmland. My appointment with Craig was at eight in the morning, so the sun still sat low in the sky as I drove, its light beaming through the hazy dust kicked up by massive farm machinery. I waited for him at a pull-off along the highway that cut through the farm country. When Craig's truck rolled up, we shook hands, and I climbed in the passenger seat. I had to politely ask his elderly dog, Jally (short for Jalapeño Pepper), to move to the back seat. She complied, grumpily.

Craig was the very image of an all-American farmer: rugged boots and a trucker hat worn low over his white hair. He's a fourth-generation farmer, but thanks to his twenty-five-year partnership with David and Huy Fong Foods, the family farm has boomed like never before. It all started in 1988, when Craig was looking for new business and wrote David a letter.

"I asked if we could grow peppers for him," Craig said. David, whose business had outgrown the farmer's market supply, thought partnering directly with a farm might be a good idea. "David said sure, so we grew him fifty acres. Next year, we'll be at two thousand acres." Underwood Farms and Huy Fong have a "lovely partnership," in Craig's words—one that is incomparable in the industry. "Usually farmers and processors are advisories," Craig explained. "Our goals are the same as David's: we're trying to make a really good product as cheap as possible."

Craig took me out to his fields, flush with Technicolor red jalapeños. Craig and David have changed the landscape of this valley: the area used to be all orchards—oranges, mostly. The money coming in from Sriracha allowed Craig to pay a higher rent for farmable land, so they beat out other agriculture for acreage. At the current rate of Huy Fong's growth, Craig adds two hundred to three hundred acres of land to grow peppers every single year. Keeping up with its rate of growth is difficult. Not only do they add acreage every year, but new machinery, infrastructure, and employees. And Sriracha's growing popularity shows no signs of waning.

Our pickup truck pulled up alongside a field where pickers—Hispanic men and women—harvested jalapeños. Craig pulled over to talk to one of his managers. He spoke with his warm, SoCal accent, but chatted about wages and the picking schedule in fluent Spanish.

Two dozen hand pickers were working in the field. Each picker squatted with a white Home Depot–style bucket, ripping the peppers from the plants with both hands. They shuffled forward down the row, plant to plant, filling the bucket at a furious pace. Once the bucket was full, they stood up and ran—and I mean, really hustled—to a tractor trailing a few carts. The bucket of peppers was dumped into a cart, and the workers ran to a staff member who held a hole punch. A card—like an old-time clock card—was safety-pinned to the picker's shirt or hat. This style choice was to save the time of fussing to pull it out. The overseer punched a hole for every bucket, and at the end of the day, they were paid based on how many buckets they had picked. If they ran and squatted and picked for six or seven hours a day; they could make between $12 and $20 an hour. A good picker took home around $120 a shift, but the work was grueling.

However, in a few years, most of the hand pickers will be replaced by new machines. In another distant field, I could see the hulking machines. They're former tomato pickers, customized to handle the peppers. No one produces peppers in the quantity of Underwood Farms, so they had to find machines they could fit to the work.

"At the rate Huy Fong is growing, we would not be able to find enough people to pick," Craig told me. "It's literally impossible. . . . It's harder and harder to find skilled people. Even during the [economic] downturn, we had nobody asking for jobs. Zero."

A recent study performed by the University of California, Irvine, and Temple University showed that while the number of low-skilled jobs in the United States has remained the same in the past twenty years, the number of workers to fill them has dropped by twelve million. Access to educational opportunities and lower birth rates in America has allowed first-generation Americans to move away from physically demanding jobs such as farm labor. And with restrictive immigration laws preventing the entry of new immigrants, the study calls the lack of labor "a real and growing threat to US economic growth."

As a farmer, Craig spends all of his days working alongside immigrants. He blames his difficulty finding good employees on restrictive immigration policies designed by anti-immigrant politicians. "It's easy to blame your problems on immigrants because we've done it with the Chinese, we've done it with the Irish . . ." He sighed with frustration as we sat in the cab of his truck, looking out over the jalapeño fields. "Whenever there's a downturn in the economy, everyone turns to immigrants and says, 'You know, you're to blame!' I can guarantee you that nobody working here is taking a job away from somebody who would like to be employed."

And without immigrants, and more specifically refugees like the Tran family, America wouldn't have Sriracha.

Craig dropped me back off at my car, and I drove away from his farm, northward, toward San Francisco. I'd swing by Gilroy, the Garlic Capital, before visiting the Angel Island Immigration Station, the Chinese Historical Society of America, and, finally, seek out Punjabi food in Yuba City. The stretches of road I drove were more rural than I had ever imagined

California could be. I suddenly understood how California could waver and fight on political issues; it's both the urban centers of Los Angeles and San Francisco and the rural farms where more than half of America's produce is grown.

The experience made me realize how diverse we are as a nation. Each of the places I've visited, and the stories I've explored, made up a patchwork quilt in my mind. I visualized the swatches of fabric delicately sewn over a hanging classroom map of the United States. Here, behind this patch, are Boston's farsighted traders and businessmen, bringing in ships with hulls filled with black pepper. Here, when I pull up this corner, are the German immigrants who settled around San Antonio, whose taste for spicy local chili inspired the creation of chili powder. And here, sewn around Southern California, a refugee from Vietnam made a Thai-style chili sauce that's produced by Mexican labor and has seduced a nation. It's a story more American than apple pie.

The Spicy Zeig

This drink was first mixed for me late, late, late one night at my apartment. I was amazed at the balanced flavors of the three ingredients: savory, spicy, and sweet. It's named after its creator, a dear friend.

Yield: serves one

2 ounces vodka
Dash dry vermouth
2 to 3 drops Sriracha

Shake well with ice; strain into a martini glass.

Epilogue

The Ninth Flavor

AS I NEARED the end of my research, I got a call from Jaya Saxena, a reporter from *Serious Eats*. She asked if she could interview me for her column, Back of the House, in which she highlights unique food jobs. Apparently, my job—historical gastronomist—fit the bill. My intern Jill and I had already planned a day of recipe testing, so we invited Jaya to drop by while we worked. She watched as we whipped up a weird 1860s cream soda, made with eggs and baking powder; roasted James Beard's Chicken with 40 Cloves of Garlic; and tempered white chocolate for Warm Vanilla Cakes. Jaya asked for the historical dates of the recipes; I think she expected that they had all been written in the distant past. But the recipe for the vanilla cakes was from 2001.

"Because so much has changed about the way we eat in the past thirteen years," she said, with a bit of an eye roll. Then she caught herself. "Wait: Has the way we eat changed in the last thirteen years?"

Absolutely. The American kitchen is not static; it's cumulative, and it evolves. Ten years ago, I had not heard of Sriracha, and now it is in every refrigerator I open (at least, those refrigerators stocked by millennials). And in the next decade, or the next century, our cuisine will continue to change. Which means a new flavor will earn a permanent place in Americans' hearts and stomachs.

All it takes is a special event that creates an interest in a flavor, followed by increased availability paired with a biological preference. I wondered: Which flavor might earn its place in American kitchens next? I began my search for my ninth flavor. And the best place to peep into the future of food is at the epic Summer Fancy Food Show in New York City.

Each year, the event sprawls across several floors of the Jacob K. Javits Convention Center in Manhattan, an enormous glass building modeled architecturally after the 1853 New York Crystal Palace exhibit—another trendsetting event that, in its time, illustrated the future of food, technology, fashion, and more.

Several months after my interview with Jaya, I walked out onto the floor of the Summer Fancy Food Show. The Javits Center is a mile walk from the nearest subway station, so it made for a sultry trek through the heat. By the time I stumbled through the glass doors, I was certain I was going to burst into flames. But then someone handed me a free coconut water, hung a press pass around my neck like a Hawaiian lei, and all was well.

When I stepped into the vast hall where more than 2,500 exhibitors displayed their wares, I had Jaya's question in my mind: How had our food changed in the last decade, and how was it going to change in the next? The Fancy Food Show was on it: new brands, new products, new foods, new flavors—free samples. Most of the products displayed sat somewhere between stage one and stage two, according to the Center for Culinary Development's five-step process: somewhere between foodie dining establishments and food-focused blog coverage. It was here that food trend spotters came to find the next big thing, but the goal of most of the exhibitors was to land a contract with a major retailer like Whole

Foods. Nationwide distribution meant a huge change of fortune for many of these new companies. Other booths—such as Nielsen-Massey, which sells the Gayas' Mexican vanilla—were established brands there to connect with their clients and distributors.

I roamed the endless aisles and scarfed up cubes of free cheese. I paid special attention to a section reserved for first-time exhibitors but also looked for patterns throughout the hall: there were Malabar black pepper pork "clouds," Japanese-curry jerky, bourbon-barrel-aged vanilla; Sriracha chocolate bonbons, and caramels that were "accented with the pleasing saltiness and rich umami of Japanese miso," according to their packaging. America's eight flavors were all there, often used in creative new ways.

Tea had a huge presence at the show, from displays of gorgeous whole tea leaves, to a bevy of chai-flavored products. But the most significant tea trend I noticed was for matcha, a finely powdered green tea from China, also traditionally used in Japanese tea ceremonies. At the show, the Republic of Tea, a pricy but commonly available tea brand, released its own Matchia tea, a blend of matcha and chia seeds. Ito En and Teapigs were also pushing their own versions of the tea. Interestingly, matcha didn't first appear in America as a drink but as a flavoring (and coloring) for baked goods.

It might have been in the Paris bakery of Sadaharu Aoki that matcha was first used in pastries. Aoki, a Japanese patissier who opened his first shop in the Seventh Arrondissement of Paris in 1998, became known as a quirky chef who used traditional Japanese ingredients in classic French pastries. Matcha's bold green color appeared in his cakes, tarts, macaroons, and even croissants. As cookbook author David Lebovitz described the trend, "It was if someone hit the switch one day, and all of a sudden a flash of electric-green took Paris by storm. You couldn't walk by a patisserie without seeing something sweet and shockingly green standing out among the more traditional-looking pastries in the lavish window displays." Matcha arrived in New York in the early 2000s, either in French or Japanese bakeries; it's unclear. But because America has a history of emulating both of these cultures, I'm not surprised that the trend caught on.

In 2001 Martha Stewart's holiday cookies special issue magazine described a recipe for Green Tea Shortbread Leaves, which incorporated green tea, saying it "gives buttery shortbread a mild, somewhat exotic flavor, as well as a delicate tint." Matcha appeared by name in 2015 in *Martha Stewart Living* in a recipe for Green Tea Crepe Cake, as an ingredient in the pastry-cream filling. The recipe is a blend of French techniques and Japanese ingredients, much like Aoki's work.

And recently, I walked past Le Pain Quotidien, a chain bakery, on the south side of Bryant Park in Manhattan. It had a sign out front that said, "Try Our New Matcha Muffins!" Afterward, on a hunch, I searched "matcha" on Walmart's web page. A year ago, I got no hits. As of this writing in 2016, Walmart offers over a dozen matcha products, from the traditional green tea, to matcha caramels, to matcha green tea sea salt.

It's likely that matcha tea's purported health benefits have fueled the growing trend, as has increased immigration from Asia. Although matcha is a strong candidate for a ninth flavor, it remains to be seen whether or not it becomes a universal part of American cuisine. But more than two hundred years after dumping tea into Boston Harbor, Americans seem ready to put down the coffee cup and give tea another chance.

Even Starbucks serves a green tea Frappuccino, but it is the originator of another, bigger trend: pumpkin spice. In January 2003 the coffee company began to brainstorm special seasonal flavors to follow the success of its holiday peppermint mocha drink. Peter Dukes, Starbucks' director of brand management, headed the project. In early taste tests, pumpkin spice didn't garner a lot of enthusiasm. But Dukes felt there was something unique there—especially because there were no other pumpkin-flavored products on the market at the time.

The Starbucks developers decked out a test lab with Thanksgiving paraphernalia to get them in the mood and ate dozens of pumpkin pies to hit on the right flavor combination. They finally settled on a version that focused on pumpkin pie spices such as ginger, cinnamon, nutmeg, mace, and clove rather than pumpkin itself. Starbucks test-marketed the pumpkin spice latte in two cities in 2003, and the drink sold so well that the company could not keep up with demand. "Within the first week of the market test, we knew we had a winner," Dukes recalled. "Back then, we would call store managers on the phone to see how a new beverage was doing, and you could hear the excitement in their voices." Starbucks launched the flavor nationwide the following year and has sold over two hundred million pumpkin spice lattes since.

Following the success of Starbuck's invention, many other brands began to release their own pumpkin-spice-flavored foods beyond coffee drinks. At the Fancy Food Show, there were pumpkin spice caramels, pumpkin caramel praline popcorn, and pumpkin spice extract—as well as pumpkin spice tea, hot chocolate, and portable almond milk pumpkin spice lattes. But major brands also have released their own pumpkin-spice-flavored products, from M&M's to Oreos to vodka. Nineteen percent of restaurant menus in the Northeast feature at least one pumpkin-spice-flavored item and in 2012, pumpkin-spice-flavored foods did $290 million in sales.

This love of pumpkin spice makes it a strong candidate for a ninth flavor, and our affection for it is linked to nostalgia as well as science. Pumpkin pie has been a part of American cuisine since at least the eighteenth century, and McCormick debuted its pumpkin pie spice blend in 1934. But if you tried to mix together just the spices of a pumpkin pie, you wouldn't get the same satisfying experience of a Starbucks latte—or a slice of pumpkin pie. In pumpkin spice flavoring, up to eighty different chemicals replicate the flavor and textural experience of a slice of pumpkin pie. The spices are represented by their major chemical components, such as eugenol for cloves and vanillin for vanilla. Additionally, there are lactones for a creamy sensation, ketones for buttery notes, cyclotenes for burnt-sugar notes, and pyrazines to replicate the toasted tastes in the top layer of baked pie. Together these chemicals make our brains think, "Oh! Pumpkin pie!" But if you're horrified by all of the "chemicals" going into your pumpkin spice latte, keep in mind that an actual slice of pumpkin pie contains over 350 chemical compounds, *including* the 80 that go into pumpkin spice flavoring.

Another trend I spotted at the Fancy Food Show was smoke. It's a flavor that's close to my heart, reminding me of the fire-infused flavors of the foods I cooked at my museum job in Ohio. Smoky flavors appeared in chips, nuts, and other snack foods, paired with salt and spice, like hickory-smoked cheddar popcorn and smoked okra pickles. But it was almost as popular in sweet as it was in savory: I also spotted smoked chocolate chips and smoked cola gumdrops. And there were products to help the enthusiastic amateur cook: home smokers small enough to fit on a fire escape.

The easiest way to infuse open-fire flavor in food is with liquid smoke. It is actually smoke, from hardwood burned at high temperature, that is run through a condenser—cooling the hot vapor quickly so that it forms a liquid, like when you breathe onto a cold windowpane. The liquid is collected and concentrated. My fellow foodie J. Kenji López-Alt, who spoke with me about MSG, made it himself once with a homemade condenser and said that the result was better than anything in the store. Used broadly commercially, liquid smoke is already in the kitchens of advanced home cooks who want to achieve a certain bacon-ness.

The prominence of smoke in American food made it a good candidate for the ninth flavor in this book, but I also noticed a deluge of flavors from the Middle East at the show. The United States has spent much of the past quarter century with military in and out of the Middle East, and our involvement there has also caused a wave of immigration to our shores. As with chili after the Mexican War, soy sauce after World War II, and maybe even hot sauce after the Vietnam War, military personnel often sought out the foods and flavors they experienced abroad when they returned. The new immigrant population that arrived after these wars also had a need for the ingredients they knew from home. Their food preferences seeped into American mainstream markets and restaurants, and then into blogs and cooking shows.

I have seen war propagate new food trends historically, but I wanted to find out if it was still true in the twenty-first century. I talked to an old high school friend, Stan, who, as a marine, has done one tour of duty in Iraq and four in Afghanistan. He told me that in Afghanistan, he lived and worked closely with the Afghans, and often ate in local restaurants, ordered food from town, or feasted at big parties on base where a local would cook long-grain rice in huge cauldrons, as well as lamb and fresh naan bread.

Even while still in Afghanistan, Stan and his fellow marines adapted the foods they ate. "We would absolutely bastardize the culture," he remembered, "and rather than eat like an Afghan, we'd roll heaps of kebab meat in the chewy, fresh naan and eat that shit like a huge burrito."

When Stan returned to the States, he told me he found himself eating naan, instead of pizza, as comfort food, in addition to being the voice that suggested going to the kebab place, when friends or family wanted Panera. "If I could make the shit myself, I would," he added. "But that's the thing with partial assimilation: we learn to enjoy the flavor but never have the time or the language to learn the way the locals make it." The food, transported to the United States, continues to evolve. It is used in new ways by Americans, and over time, it becomes removed from its foreign roots.

Middle Eastern influences appeared all over the Fancy Food Show. Cumin was featured by name in many Middle Eastern and Indian products such as curries and stews, but also in a lot of flavored New England cheeses. Za'atar, a spice blend with thyme, sesame seeds, salt, and sumac (a bright red berry that adds a citrus flavor) appeared in yogurt and tahini dips, as well as being packaged on its own. And cardamom, popular in Middle Eastern sweets, had made the crossover into American-style desserts such as lime and cardamom frozen yogurt, green tea coconut cinnamon cardamom mints, and in a cardamom chai-spiced pumpkin butter.

Another prominent flavor of this trend is one that Americans of two hundred years ago would have been very familiar with: rose water. It's often paired with cardamom to create floral, citrusy flavors typical of Persian, Turkish, and other Middle Eastern cuisines. In 2010 the *New York Times* ran an article titled "Rose Water Adds a Subtle Kick," which featured a recipe for a grilled rosewater pound cake that was reminiscent of the cakes I had baked from early nineteenth-century cookbooks. The article's author, John Willoughby, gave the flavor its historic due: "Taking a cue from 18th-century bakers, substitute rose water for the vanilla in cupcakes, puddings, or scones."

As America's cultural makeup changes, this old flavor is becoming new again. Sometimes a flavor comes full circle—but this time around, rose water is carving out its own niche, side by side with vanilla.

In the midst of my day prowling the aisles at the Fancy Food Show on the hunt for the next big flavor trend, I sat down in the press lounge with Kara Nielsen, a professional food trend spotter. She got her start as a pastry chef and a culinary educator in the 1990s; Kara referred to being a foodie twenty years ago as an "amateur sport."

"Those of us who were in love with food usually got jobs in the food business, and we would sort of feed off each other, going to different cities, checking out new places to eat," Kara told me. It was a lot harder in an era before blogs, Yelp, and Instagram—harbingers of the now-widespread foodie culture.

Her love of the latest food trends turned into a career in trend spotting, which is what led her to the Fancy Food Show. I asked her how a new flavor becomes a trend.

"It's meeting a need," she said. What determined those needs? "Society. You know, these societal changes push on you and change your values, and as your values change, your needs change."

She gave the new trend for eco-friendly green living as a prime example. "You've got guilt factor, because all of a sudden you realize you're contributing to the landfill in a way you never knew before. All of a sudden, that Styrofoam cup is just the grossest thing ever because society has told you it's a gross thing."

Kara said there are many different factors that drive societal change, and therefore change the way we eat: science, medicine, travel, immigration. I'd seen each of these factors at work shaping the flavor of America's food in the past. Science and technology brought us vanilla and MSG; medicine has fueled the trend for curry and garlic; travel helped us fall in love with chili powder and soy sauce; and immigration brought us Sriracha, among many other food trends. I believe these same trends will continue to influence the flavors of our food in the future. And looking forward is a little bit like soothsaying: the flavors that Americans choose to add to their pantries will say something about who we are as a country.

Since researching the stories in this book, I've gained an immense pride in American food—which I believe is the most complex and diverse cuisine on the planet. Our lack of strict tradition has allowed us an unparalleled freedom to create, grow, and transform. Whichever flavor comes next, its taste and scent will represent more than just good food; it will represent the people who cook with it. In America, we have an infinite number of national identities—but these eight flavors are common to us all.

Acknowledgments

I AM GRATEFUL to be rich in supportive friends and family, and I want to acknowledge the many people who had a hand in this book.

First of all, to my mother, Karen Lohman, who made me into the independent, creative person that I am. She has been there to listen to me talk through ideas; she has been my researcher, my baked-goods recipe tester, my proofreader, and the first one to see each of these chapters. She has done hundreds of other tasks for me, and without her support, this book would not exist. Always honest, her encouragement means the world to me.

Next to my editors at Simon & Schuster: Michael Szczerban, who plucked me from obscurity and told me I should be writing a book. Then, to Emily Graff, who picked up the reins and saw this project to its conclusion.

My agent, Wendy Sherman, and her entire office: the former for negotiating this incredible opportunity, the latter for both their support and squealing in delight when I brought them historic Christmas cookies.

Jill Paradiso started as my intern at the beginning of this process and cooked through nearly every recipe in this book with me. She took on research projects and formatted endnotes before coming on as my official recipe tester and one of my fact-checkers. Her work, support, skill as a chef, and friendship were integral to the completion of this book; I cannot thank her enough.

There are a few scholars and researchers not mentioned in this text but without whom vast sections of this book could not have been written: thanks to Sean Basinski, Randy Clemens, Dr. Pesach Lubinsky, Bob Plager, Scott Weiner, and Dr. Steven Witherly for their time and input.

To my team of intrepid fact-checkers: Charlotte Purser Arnold, Kathleen Fletcher, Meghan Gerlach, Andrew Gustafson, Tammy Hart, Miranda Knutharth, Victoria Marin, Grace McGookey, Laura Nesson, Jay Popasopilus, Anna Rasche, and Brooke Borel, for her tutelage.

To the Lower East Side Tenement Museum and the Brooklyn Brainery, who have always supported my career.

And to the army of friends who tracked down citations, went on adventures, housed me, fed me, hugged me, and more: Christina Chan, Sarah Conrad, Madeline Earp, Laureen Fredella, Will Heath, Dan Hendrock, Judy Levin, Sarah Litvin, Nina Mehta, Sarah Tomasewski, Andrew Torrens, Jess Tsang, Tanya Washburn, Maggie Weber, Emily Fellner Zeig, Melissa Zhang, and especially Pat McHugh and Erin Hopkins McHugh, without whom I would not have gotten through 2015.

And lastly, to everyone who has ever been brave enough to accept my invitation to come over for a historical dinner.

Notes

Introduction: History Has a Flavor

PAGE

xv   *Eight to twelve chemicals*: Talk by Jack Fastag, "Flavor Lab at MOFAD Lab," at the Museum of Food and Drink, Brooklyn, NY, November 19, 2015.

xvi   *Together salty, spicy, cheesy*: Ibid.

xvi   *The physiological signals*: "Frontal Lobes," on the website of the Centre for Neuroskills, accessed March 2, 2016, www.neuroskills.com/brain-injury /frontal-lobes.php.

One: Black Pepper

1   *United States is the largest*: Peter J. Buzzanell, Rex Dull, and Fred Gray, "The Spice Market in the United States Recent Developments and Prospects," United States Department of Agriculture Economic Research Service, 6, http://www.ers.usda.gov/media/304145/aib709a_1_.pdf.

1   *According to Al Goetze*: "Black Pepper Field Report," FoodReference.com, accessed March 7, 2016, www.foodreference.com/html/a-blk-pepper-fr108 .html.

1   *Americans use more*: "U.S. Spice Consumption," accessed May 22, 2016, http:// www.ers.usda.gov/data-products/food-availability-(per-capita)-data-system .aspx.

4 *Pepper vines were first*: Harold McGee, *On Food and Cooking: The Science and the Lore of the Kitchen* (New York: Scribner, 2004), 427.

4 *When pepper berries ripen*: Henry N. Ridley, *Spices* (London: Macmillan, 1912), 287.

5 *In the final stage of the process*: K. P. Prabhakaran Nair, *Agronomy and Economy of Black Pepper and Cardamom: The "King" and "Queen" of Spices* (Amsterdam: Elsevier, 2011), 52.

5 *The pepper berries are turned*: Frederic Rosengarten, *The Book of Spices* (Wynnewood, Pa.: Livingston, 1969).

6 *And Lampong pepper*: Regina Schrambling, "Black Gold: Globally Sourced Varietal Peppercorns Bring Sweet-Hot Nuance to Every Dish," *Los Angeles Times,* January 3, 2007, http://articles.latimes.com/2007/jan/03/food/fo-pepper3/2.

7 *Although the recipe's name*: Karen Hess, *Martha Washington's Booke of Cookery and Booke of Sweetmeats* (New York: Columbia University Press, 1995), 200.

10 *That wasn't uncommon*: David L. Ferguson, *Cleopatra's Barge: The Crowninshield Story* (Boston: Little, Brown, 1976), 17.

10 *The incident was seldom*: Ibid., 22.

11 *With this bit of information*: George Granville Putnam, *Salem Vessels and Their Voyages: A History of the Pepper Trade with the Island of Sumatra* (Salem, Mass.: Essex Institute, 1922).

11 *Carnes's ship, the* Rajah: Ibid., 10.

11 *When the ship returned*: James Duncan Phillips, *Pepper and Pirates; Adventures in the Sumatra Pepper Trade of Salem* (Boston: Houghton Mifflin, 1949), 14.

11 *Blond and blue-eyed*: Ferguson, *Cleopatra's Barge*.

11 *When a ship like the* America: James D. Gillis and Henry Whipple, *Sailing Directions for the Pepper Ports on the West Coast of Sumatra, North of Analaboo: To Accompany a Chart of that Coast* (Salem, Mass.: Salem Gazette Press, 1839).

13 *The Acehnese adorned themselves*: William Marsden, *The History of Sumatra, Illustrated* (London: J. McCreery, 1811), 46.

13 *In reality, the Acehnese*: Ibid., 146.

14 *"They were very much surprised"*: John Crowninshield, *John Crowninshield in the* America III *at Sumatra, 1801*, ed, Howard Corning, Essex Institute Historical Collections, vol. 80, no. 16 (1944): 153.

14 *When John was ready*: Ferguson, *Cleopatra's Barge,* 26.

14 *If the pepper crop failed*: Ridley, *Spices*, 297.

14 *When the Americans arrived*: Marsden, *History of Sumatra,* 46.

15 *Consider that in 1802*: Stanley Lebergott, "Wage Trends: 1800–1900," in

Trends in the American Economy in the Nineteenth Century (Princeton, N.J.: Princeton University Press, 1960), 482.

15 *The pepper sold for*: Putnam, *Salem Vessels*, 11.

15 *It's no surprise*: Ferguson, *Cleopatra's Barge*, 26.

15 *"They were all marked"*: Ibid., 35.

16 *George wrote to them*: Ibid., 71.

16 *As more ships sailed*: Robert Booth, *Death of an Empire: The Rise and Murderous Fall of Salem, America's Richest City* (New York: St. Martin's Press, 2011), 44.

16 *But by 1830*: Ridley, *Spices*, 299.

16 *The last boatful of pepper*: National Park Service signage at the customhouse in Salem, Massachusetts, June 2012.

17 *alkaloids in black pepper's piperine*: Dr. Gregory Lohman, interview by the author, October 2013.

17 *I was amazed to find*: "Food Bacteria-Spice Survey Shows Why Some Cultures Like It Hot," *Cornell Chronicle*, March 4, 1998, www.news.cornell.edu /stories/1998/03/food-bacteria-spice-survey-shows-why-some-cultures-it-hot.

21 *McCormick & Company*: "Historic Milestones and Passionate Flavor Discoveries," McCormick & Company, accessed April 14, 2014, www.mccormickcor poration.com/Our-Company/History.aspx.

21 *Fannie Farmer's 1896*: Fannie Merritt Farmer, *The Boston Cooking-School Cookbook* (Boston: Little, Brown, 1896).

22 *In the two decades*: U.S. spice consumption spreadsheet.

Two: Vanilla

29 *Only the twenty species*: Kenneth M. Cameron, "*Vanilla* Phylogeny and Classification," in *Handbook of Vanilla Science and Technology*, ed. Daphna Havkin-Frenkel and Faith C. Belanger (Oxford, UK: Wiley-Blackwell, 2010), 249, http://onlinelibrary.wiley.com/book/10.1002/9781444329353.

29 *The Mayas took advantage*: Dr. Pesach Lubinsky, interview by author, December 14, 2013.

30 *Plantations proliferated by 1760*: Jonathan D. Sauer, *Historical Geography of Crop Plants: A Select Roster* (Boca Raton, Fl.: CRC Press, 1993), 204; Emilio Kouri, *A Pueblo Divided: Business, Property and Community in Papantla, Mexico* (Stanford, CA: Stanford University Press, 2004), 10.

31 *In the eighteenth century*: Jeri Quinzio, "Asparagus Ice Cream, Anyone?" *Gastronomica* 2, no. 2 (Spring 2002).

31 *He was possessed*: Maira Kalman, "And the Pursuit of Happiness: By George," *New York Times*, December 31, 2009.

32 *He brought with him*: Gene Zechmeister, "James Hemings," Monticello.org, July 11, 2012, www.monticello.org/site/plantation-and-slavery/james-hemings.

32 *While in France*: Ibid.

32 *Jefferson transcribed*: "Jeffersonian Dinners," Monticello.org, accessed March 23, 2014, www.monticello.org/site/research-and-collections/jeffersonian-din ners.

33 *The recipe has been credited*: Lucia Stanton, "Adrien Petit," Monticello.org, revised April 29, 2011, by Anna Berkes, www.monticello.org/site/jefferson /adrien-petit.

34 *He also bought*: Anna Berkes, "Ice Cream," Monticello.org, June 28, 2013, www.monticello.org/site/research-and-collections/ice-cream.

34 *"It costs about 24s."*: "From Thomas Jefferson to William Short, 28 July 1791," Founders Online, on the website of the National Archives, accessed March 2, 2016, http://founders.archives.gov/documents/Jefferson/01-20-02-0340.

36 *Only on extremely rare*: Tim Ecott, *Vanilla: Travels in Search of the Ice Cream Orchid* (New York: Grove Press, 2005), 85.

37 *All the vanilla orchids*: Lubinsky, interview by author, December 14, 2013.

37 *In all likelihood*: Ibid.

38 *He went on to note*: C. Morren, "On the Production of Vanilla in Europe," in *Annals of Natural History; or, Magazine of Zoology, Botany, and Geology*, vol. 3, ed. W. Jardine, P. J. Selby, Dr. Johnston, and Richard Taylor (London: R. and J. E. Taylor, 1839), 5.

38 *Edmond was born*: "*Registre Edmond Albius*," accessed March 2, 2016, https:// schoolsontheslaveroute.files.wordpress.com/2014/05/registre-edmond-albius .jpg.

38 *When he was old enough*: Ecott, *Vanilla*, 91.

38 *Of Edmond, he wrote*: Jean Pierre Rambosson, *Histoire et Légendes des Plantes Utiles et Curieuses* (Paris: Firmin Didot, Frères, Fils et Cie., 1869), 331.

39 *Edmond was celebrated*: Ibid.

42 *Edmond Albius died*: Ecott, *Vanilla*, 107.

42 *He agreed to return*: Zechmeister, "Hemings," www.monticello.org/site/plan tation-and-slavery/james-hemings.

42 *A few months later*: Annette Gordon-Reed, *The Hemingses of Monticello: An American Family* (New York: W. W. Norton, 2008), 550.

42 *Hemings . . . had committed*: Zechmeister, "Hemings," Monticello.org, www .monticello.org/site/plantation-and-slavery/james-hemings#footnote14_cllztp2.

42 *Jefferson called it*: "James Dinsmore," Monticello.org, www.monticello.org
/site/plantation-and-slavery/james-dinsmore.

43 *It is behind these walls*: Sauer, *Historical Geography of Crop Plants*, 204.

44 *When these chemicals*: Chaim Frenkel, Arvind S. Ranadive, Javier Tochihuitl
Vázquez, and Daphna Havkin-Frenkel, "Curing of Vanilla," in *Handbook of
Vanilla Science and Technology*, 83.

44 *When the curing process*: Ibid., 95.

46 *In 1847*: Eliza Leslie, *The Lady's Receipt-book: A Useful Companion for Large
or Small Families* (Philadelphia: Carey and Hart, 1847), 126.

46 *The resulting vanilla*: Arvind S. Ranadive, "Quality Control of Vanilla Beans
and Extracts," in *Handbook of Vanilla Science and Technology*, 151.

47 *Humanity's desire for*: "Vanilla," *Spices: Exotic Flavors & Medicines*, on the
website of History & Special Collections, Louise M. Darling Biomedical
Library, UCLA, accessed March 23, 2014, http://unitproj.library.ucla.edu
/biomed/spice/index.cfm?displayID=27.

47 *Vanillin was first*: H. Korthou and R. Verpoorte, "Vanilla," chap. 9 in *Flavours
and Fragrances: Chemistry, Bioprocessing and Sustainability*, ed. R. G. Berger
(Berlin: Springer, 2007).

47 *It's water soluble*: "Fire and Spice," General Chemistry Online!, last modified
August 17, 2015, http://antoine.frostburg.edu/chem/senese/101/features/cap
saicin.shtml.

48 *Castoreum was also*: Melissa Locker, "Your Vanilla Ice Cream May Actually
Smell Like Beaver Butt," *Time*, October 3, 2013.

48 *Today vanillin is*: Korthou and Verpoorte, "Vanilla."

48 *If I used one*: "Vanilla Extract," on the website of America's Test Kitchen, accessed March 2, 2016, www.americastestkitchen.com/taste_tests/455.

48 *As I've noted*: Patrick G. Hoffman and Charles M. Zapf, "Flavor, Quality, and
Authentication," in *Handbook of Vanilla Science and Technology*, 164.

48 *But imitation vanilla*: "Vanilla Extract," www.americastestkitchen.com/taste
_tests/455.

49 *An ice cream trade journal*: Samuel H. Baer, "Vanilla," *Ice Cream Trade Journal*
4, no. 1 (January 1908): 49.

49 *In the 1960s*: Joseph Dunn, "Madagascar Eyes U.S. Vanilla Mart: Change in Ice
Cream Label Laws Could Help Island," *New York Times*, November 8, 1959.

50 *Although the technology*: "AmCan Food Division," accessed March 25, 2014,
www.amcan.fr/Pages-Eng/legislation_vanillin-Eng.htm.

50 *The dessert became*: Pierre Franey, "60-Minute Gourmet," *New York Times*,
October 16, 1985.

50 *But ever since the mid-1990s*: Patricia Tennison, "Tahiti Vanilla Stands Out in Flavor, Aroma," *Chicago Tribune*, April 9, 1987.

51 *It's purely cosmetic*: Ecott, *Vanilla*, 11.

51 *Humans and other primates*: Felix Buccellato, "Vanilla in Perfumery and Beverage Flavors," in *Handbook of Vanilla Science and Technology*, 235.

51 *Every American consumes*: Wolfgang Veit and Carol Scovotti, "The Market for Vanilla in Germany and the United States," *Export Opportunity Surveys* (August 2012): 9.

51 *All that vanilla*: Patricia Rain, "Is Fair Trade Vanilla Really Fair?," on the website of the Vanilla Company, last modified July 26, 2013, http://vanilla .com/fair-trade-vanilla.

51 *With no standardized price set*: Richard J. Brownell Jr., "Fair Trade—The Future of Vanilla?" chap. 7 in *Handbook of Vanilla Science and Technology*.

Three: Chili Powder

58 *Chili powder gets us*: Simon Cotton, "Spicing Up Chemistry," on the website of the Royal Society of Chemistry, accessed May 27, 2014, www.rsc.org/Edu cation/EiC/issues/2006May/SpicingupChemistry.asp.

59 *American residents of New Spain*: Margaret Swett Henson, "Anglo-American Colonization," Texas State Historical Association, https://tshaonline.org /handbook/online/articles/uma01.

61 *Customers sat*: Marian Martinello, *The Search for a Chili Queen: On the Fringes of a Rebozo* (Fort Worth: Texas Christian University Press, 2009), 3.

61 *The tourists called*: Molly Heilman, "She's Chili Queen for a Night," *San Antonio Light*, March 9, 1941.

61 *The depiction gave*: Nikki Silva and Davia Nelson, *Hidden Kitchens: Stories, Recipes, and More from NPR's The Kitchen Sisters* (Emmaus, Penn.: Rodale Books, 2005), 36.

62 *But at the chili stands*: Jeffrey M. Pilcher, *Planet Taco: A Global History of Mexican Food* (New York: Oxford University Press, 2012), 229.

63 *The card read*: Marian L. Martinello, *Chili Queen: Mi Historia* (Fort Worth: Texas Christian University Press, 2015).

65 *Although Texas isn't*: T. R. Fehrenbach, "San Antonio, TX," Texas State Historical Association, www.tshaonline.org/handbook/online/articles/hds02.

65 *It's given both*: Katy Vine, "Auf Wiedersehen to a Dialect," *Texas Monthly*, July 2013.

65 *It expanded*: "Remembering the Long Lost Germans of Texas," *All Things Considered*, National Public Radio, aired May 19, 2013.

66 *Texas is always*: Illustration by James Wells Champney, "San Pedro Springs— The Germans Have Established Their Beer Gardens," in Edward King, *The Great South; A Record of Journeys in Louisiana, Texas, the Indian Territory, Missouri, Arkansas, Mississippi, Alabama, Georgia, Florida, South Carolina, North Carolina, Kentucky, Tennessee, Virginia, West Virginia, and Maryland* (Hartford: American, 1875), 158.

66 *It changed hands*: Suzanne Ashe, "Historic Disagreement," *New Braunfels* (TX) *Herald-Zeitung*, April 19, 2007; "The Phoenix Saloon History," accessed April 1, 2014, www.thephoenixsaloon.com/fullhistory.php.

66 *He opened the café*: Gebhardt Mexican Foods Company Collection—A Virtual Collection, on the website of the University of Texas at San Antonio Libraries, accessed March 2, 2016, http://webapp.lib.utsa.edu/Gebhardt.

67 *He filed a patent*: "A Guide to the Gebhardt Mexican Foods Company Records, 1896–1988," *Gebhardt Mexican Foods Company Collection,* on the website of the University of Texas at San Antonio Libraries, accessed April 1, 2014, www.lib.utexas.edu/taro/utsa/00029/utsa-00029.html#adminlink.

67 *Finally, Gebhardt added*: William Gebhardt, Food Compound and Method of Making Same, US Patent 646,558, filed July 30, 1897, and issued June 28, 1898, www.google.com/patents/US606624?dq=gebhardt+1897&hl=en &sa=X&ved=0ahUKEwjXheKWsrTJAhWBQD4KHa9YB7MQ6AEIH DAA.

67 *But when he attempted*: Gebhardt: *Mexican Foods Company Collection*, http://webapp.lib.utsa.edu/Gebhardt.

70 *In* The Great South: King, *The Great South*, 162.

70 *The famous novelist*: Stephen Crane, *Prose and Poetry* (New York: Library of America, 1984), 716.

71 *The situation would*: Pilcher, *Planet Taco*, 126.

71 *Another law banned*: Marci R. McMahon, *Domestic Negotiations: Gender, Nation, and Self-Fashioning in US Mexicana and Chicana Literature and Art* (New Brunswick, N.J.: Rutgers University Press, 2013), 38.

71 *She insisted that her chili*: "S.A. 'Queens' Say Chili Is Sanitary," *San Antonio Light*, September 18, 1941, 16-A.

72 *The Action Line editor's*: "Action Line," *San Antonio Light*, October 26, 1967.

76 *Everyone made a big to-do*: John Raven, "The History of Chili Cook-offs Part Two: Chili Competition Erupts in Terlingua," Traditional Texas Food, accessed April 1, 2014, www.texascooking.com/features/april2007_chili_cookoffs2.htm.

76　*In the* Corpus Christi Caller-Times: Garth Jones, "No Chili Decision: Great Cookoff Well-Seasoned by Humorists," *Corpus Christi* (TX) *Caller-Times*, October 22, 1967.

77　*While cooking*: Ibid.

Four: Curry Powder

87　*one of the most ethnically diverse*: Lisa L. Colangelo, "Queens One of 'Most Diverse Places on Earth,' New Figures Show," *Daily News*, July 12, 2009, http://www.nydailynews.com/new-york/queens/queens-diverse-places-earth-new-figures-show-article-1.430744.

87　*over 130 languages are spoken*: Sam Roberts, "Listening to (and Saving) the World's Languages," *New York Times*, April 29, 2010, http://www.nytimes.com/2010/04/29/nyregion/29lost.html?_r=0.

88　*Currently, around two million*: "Profile of General Population and Housing Characteristics: 2010," United States Census Bureau, 2010 Census, accessed May 23, 2014, http://factfinder2.census.gov/faces/tableservices/jsf/pages/productview.xhtml?pid=DEC_10_DP_DPDP1&prodType=table.

89　*The most well known*: Julie Sahni, *Classic Indian Cooking* (New York: William Morrow Cookbooks, 1980), 35.

90　*There's also* Sambar podi: Ibid., 39.

90　*Turmeric contains*: "Spicing Up Chemistry," www.rsc.org/Education/EiC/issues/2006May/SpicingupChemistry.asp; American Chemical Society, "India's 'Holy Powder' Finally Reveals Its Centuries-Old Secret," PressPac, April 15, 2009, www.acs.org/content/acs/en/pressroom/presspacs/2009/acs-presspac-april-15-2009.html#P69_5923.

90　*Additionally, it might help*: Lauren K. Wolf, "Turmeric-Derived Compound Curcumin May Treat Alzheimer's," *Chemical & Engineering News* 90, no. 31 (July 30, 2012).

90　*British soldiers*: Lizzie Collingham, *Curry: A Tale of Cooks and Conquerors* (New York: Oxford University Press, 2006), 133.

93　*Glasse and Randolph both*: Ibid., 141.

94　*They headed toward*: Vivek Bald, *Bengali Harlem and the Lost Histories of South Asian America* (Cambridge, Mass.: Harvard University Press, 2013), 32.

95　*His last name indicated*: The Ismaili, website of the Ismaili Muslim Community, accessed May 18, 2014, www.theismaili.org.

95　*Soon Smile moved*: "Hotel Cecil, London (1896–1930)," Facebook page,

accessed May 20, 2014, www.facebook.com/pages/Hotel-Cecil-London
-1896-1930/179693868745485.

95 *The largest in Europe*: Advertisement, *Harper's Weekly*, May 13, 1905, 699.

95 *It advertised that*: Ibid.

97 *It remained a popular*: "Louis Sherry Dies; Famous Caterer," *New York Times*,
June 10, 1926.

97 *Lieutenant Colonel Newnham-Davis*: Nathaniel Newnham-Davis, *Dinners
and Diners: Where and How to Dine in London* (London: Pall Mall, 1901),
32.

97 *He had his own station*: "A Chef from India," *Daily Iowa State Press*, November
18, 1899, 7, http://newspaperarchive.com/us/iowa/iowa-city/daily-iowa-state
-press/1899/11-18/page-7?tag=ranji+smile&rtserp=tags/?pf=ranji&pl=sm
ile&page=3.

99 *Another is Murghi Rain*: "Item: Hotel Flanders Indian Room Dinner and Afternoon Tea Menu," on the website of the Historical Society of Pennsylvania Digital Library, accessed May 20, 2014, http://digitallibrary.hsp.org/index
.php/Detail/Object/Show/object_id/11323.

99 *In this preparation*: "Sindhi Style Fish," on the website of Nitu Didi, accessed
May 20, 2014, http://nitudidi.com/2012/07/26/sindhi-style-fish-sayel-fish.

100 *The fish and potatoes*: "Bombil Batata Bhaji," VahRehVah.com, September 28,
2007, www.vahrehvah.com/bombil-batata-bhaji-1#.U3338a1dW7j.

102 *The same year that Smile*: "Journey to a New Land," on the website of Becoming American Museum, accessed May 22, 2014, www.punjabipioneers.com
/exhibits/Journey.

102 *They came from Punjab*: "Faith and Culture: Sikhism," on the website of Becoming American Museum, accessed May 22, 2014, www.punjabipioneers
.com/exhibits/Faith.

102 *The* San Francisco Chronicle: *The San Francisco Chronicle*, April 6, 1899, 10.

103 *Cheap labor from Asia*: Karen Isaken Leonard, *Making Ethnic Choices: California's Punjabi Mexican Americans* (Philadelphia: Temple University Press,
1992), 19.

103 *They were often married*: Ibid., Chapter 2.

103 *An English paper said*: "The Clubman: The 'H.A.C' in America—Eccentric
Dinners at Sherry's—Old Fashions in Uniforms," *The Sketch: A Journal of
Art and Actuality* 43 (October 14, 1903): 438; "The Feeding of Our Boys at
School—Drinking the King's Health in Water," *The Sketch: A Journal of Art
and Actuality* 43 (July 22, 1903): 4.

103 *In any case*: "Ex-Waiter, Not a Prince," *New York Times*, November 8, 1901.

103 *He wore at least*: "The Clubman: The 'H.A.C' in America—Eccentric Dinners at Sherry's—Old Fashions in Uniform," *The Sketch* 43.

104 *If Sherry's had indeed*: "Forty-Eighth Congress, Session II, Chapters 161–164, 1885," accessed May 20, 2014, http://library.uwb.edu/guides/usimmigration/23%20stat%20332.pdf.

105 *At the time, immigration*: "First Congress, Session II, Chapter 3, 1790," accessed May 20, 2014, http://library.uwb.edu/guides/usimmigration/1%20stat%20103.pdf.

106 *The* Washington Post: "Prince of India Is Here," *Washington Post*, September 15, 1907.

106 *Making lace*: "Rose Schlueter," Ancestry.com, accessed May 21, 2014, http://trees.ancestry.com/tree/69049230/person/30192384434.

106 *In October 1907*: "Prince Smile Has a Happy Mission," *Indianapolis Sun*, October 22, 1907.

106 *In Pittsburgh*: Charles Fellows, *The Menu Maker: Suggestions for Selecting and Arranging Menus for Hotels and Restaurants with Object of Changing from Day to Day to Give Continuous Variety of Foods in Season* (Chicago: Hotel Monthly Press, 1910).

106 *Rochlitz was called*: "A Chef-Prince Weds an American Girl," *Kansas City* (MO) *Star*, August 7, 1912.http://newspaperarchive.com/us/kansas/kansas-city/kansas-city-star/1912/08-07/page-10?tag=ranji+smile&rtserp=tags/?pf=ranji&pl=smile

107 *"Boston is entertaining"*: "Secret of Beauty Out: Indian Prince Prepares His American Bride's Food," *Racine (WI) Journal News,* June 3, 1913, http://newspaperarchive.com/us/wisconsin/racine/racine-journal-news/1913/06-03/page-14?tag=ranji+smile&rtserp=tags/?pf=ranji&pl=smile.

107 *In 1914 she was cast*: " 'Dancing Around' Next: Winter Garden's New Show to Open October 5th—Al Jolson to Head Cast," *New York Times*, September 24, 1914.

108 *Local papers began*: Lee and Yung, *Angel Island*, 150.

108 *Those who wanted*: Ibid., 149.

108 *It officially excluded*: "Sixty-Fourth Congress, Session II, Chapters 27–29," accessed May 22, 2014, http://library.uwb.edu/guides/usimmigration/39%20stat%20874.pdf.

108 *The Indian men*: "Living in California," on the website of Becoming American Museum, accessed May 22, 2014, www.punjabipioneers.com/exhibits/California.

109 *In the 1920s and 1930s*: Bald, *Bengali Harlem*, Chapter 5.

109 *A Punjabi Sikh*: "Komagata Maru," on the website of Becoming American Museum, accessed May 22, 2014, www.punjabipioneers.com/exhibits/Komagata.

109 *But the US Bureau*: "Not All Caucasians Are White: The Supreme Court Rejects Citizenship for Asian Americans," History Matters, accessed May 22, 2014, http://historymatters.gmu.edu/d/5076.

110 *The loss of income*: "Louis Sherry Dies," *New York Times*.

110 *A notice appeared*: "Legal Notices," *The Brooklyn Daily Eagle*, May 31, 1937, 15.

113 *before moving to*: Raposo, Jacqueline, "Homeward Bound: Chef Floyd Cardoz Returns to India," *Serious Eats*, January 27, 2014.

114 *In 1999* New York Times: Florence Fabricant, "Tabla Is Closing," *New York Times*, September 30, 2010.

114 *"This is American food"*: Ruth Reichl, "Restaurants; American Food, Indian Spices," *New York Times*, February 24, 1999.

114 *Tabla closed in 2010*: Fabricant, "Tabla Is Closing," *New York Times*.

114 *He most recently*: Ryan Sutton, "The Meyer Magic Is Missing at Floyd Cardoz's White Street," Eater (New York), November 11, 2014, http://ny.eater.com/2014/11/11/7195049/white-street-restaurant-review-floyd-cardoz.

115 *What's more*: David Sax, *The Tastemakers: Why We're Crazy for Cupcakes but Fed Up with Fondue* (Philadelphia: Public Affairs, 2014), 200.

116 *The law abolished*: 1965 Immigration and Nationality Act, Pub. L., 89-236, 79 Stat. 911, on the website U.S. Immigration Legislation Online, University of Washington-Bothell, accessed May 23, 2014, http://library.uwb.edu/guides/usimmigration/1965_immigration_and_nationality_act.html.

Five: Soy Sauce

119 *Soy sauce is*: Roberto A. Ferdman and Ritchie King, "Ketchup Isn't the King of American Condiments. Mayonnaise Is," Quartz, last modified January 29, 2014, http://qz.com/172019/ketchup-isnt-the-king-of-american-condiments-mayonnaise-is.

120 *Wan Ja Shan is*: "About Us: Factory Visit," on the website of Yamasa Corporation, accessed March 5, 2016, www.yamasausa.com/about-us/#factory_visit.

120 *It's made in Kentucky*: "Kentucky Bourbon Soy Sauce—America's Heartland," YouTube, accessed March 5, 2016, www.youtube.com/watch?v=wBx1HCnzdoE.

121 *Chinese soy sauce*: Jenny Lee-Adrian, "Do You Know Your Soy Sauces?" *Serious Eats* (blog), last modified, March 29, 2011, www.seriouseats.com/2011/03 /do-you-know-your-soy-sauces-japanese-chinese-indonesian-differences .html.

121 *Jiang is the ancestor of miso*: Masayuki Machida, Osamu Yamada, and Katsuya Gomi, "Genomics of *Asergillus oryzae*: Learning from the History of Koji Mold and Exploration of Its Future," *DNA Research* 15, no. 4 (August 2008).

122 *This mixture becomes*: William Shurtleff and Akiko Aoyagi, *History of Koji— Grains and/or Soybeans Enrobed with a Mold Culture (300 BCE to 2012)* (Lafayette, CA: Soyinfo Center, 2012), 581.

122 *And its thing is*: Matthew Orion Oyola, "The Chemistry of Soy Sauce," ChemistryIsLife.com, accessed March 5, 2016, www.chemistryislife.com/the-chem istry-of-soy-sauce.

122 *Soy sauce is high*: "Basic Report: 16123, Soy Sauce Made from Soy and Wheat (Shoyu)," National Nutrient Database for Standard Reference Release 28, on the website of the US Department of Agriculture (USDA) Agricultural Research Service, accessed March 5, 2016, https://ndb.nal.usda.gov/ndb/foods /show/4860?fgcd=&manu=&lfacet=&format=&count=&max=35&offset= &sort=&qlookup=16123.

123 *After a few days*: Harold McGee, *On Food and Cooking: The Science and the Lore of the Kitchen* (New York: Scribner, 2004), 499.

123 *A British immigrant*: T. Hymowitz and J. R. Harlan, "Introduction of Soybean to North America by Samuel Bowen in 1765," *Economic Botany* 37, no. 4 (October 1983).

123 *Only affluent Americans*: Shurtleff and Aoyagi, *History of Soy Sauce*, 7.

124 *Since soybeans*: Andrew F. Smith, *Pure Ketchup: A History of America's National Condiment, with Recipes* (Columbia: University of South Carolina Press, 1996), 17.

124 The Cook Not Mad: *The Cook Not Mad* (Watertown, N.Y.: Knowlton & Rice, 1831), 87.

124 *These soy sauce knockoffs*: Shurtleff and Aoyagi, *History of Soy Sauce*, 250.

124 *The names for*: Ibid., 7.

126 *There was a tiny*: *Appetite City*: "Chop Suey," video "Chinatown," Four Pounds Four, accessed March 7, 2016, www.fourpoundsflour.com/appetite -city-chop-suey.

126 *Families sent sons*: Lee and Yung, *Angel Island*, Chapter One.

126 *The work these Chinese*: Ibid., 115.

127 *By the time California*: *Remembering 1882: Fighting for Civil Rights in the*

Shadows of the Chinese Exclusion Act, Chinese Historical Society of America, Museum & Learning Center, 2007), www.civilrightssuite.org/1882/index .php/iID/174, 6.

127 *By 1852, there were*: Ibid., 6.

127 *by 1870*: "Exposing Historic Musical Racism," accessed March 5, 2016, www.modelminority.com/joomla/index.php?option=com_content&view =article&id=467:exposing-historic-musical-racism-&catid=40:history& Itemid=56.

127 *He was from*: Scott D. Seligman, "Wong Chin Foo Chronology," accessed March 5, 2016, www.firstchineseamerican.com/chronology.htm.

128 *Wong soon embarked*: Ibid.

128 Harper's Weekly, *in 1877*: Scott D. Seligman, *The First Chinese American: The Remarkable Life of Wong Chin Foo* (Hong Kong: Hong Kong University Press, 2013).

128 *He gave American readers*: Scott D. Seligman, "Everything but Rats and Puppies: Wong Chin Foo Introduces Americans to Chinese Food," *Cleaver Quarterly* (Summer 2014).

128 *He even taught*: Ibid.

129 *According to a* New-York Tribune: Andrew Coe, *Chop Suey: A Cultural History of Chinese Food in the United States* (New York: Oxford University Press), 110.

129 *"An American yesterday"*: *Remembering 1882*, 8.

131 *In 1863, Chinese*: William Wei, "Key Issues," The Chinese American Experience: 1857–1892, accessed March 5, 2016, http://immigrants.harpweek.com /ChineseAmericans/2KeyIssues/!KeyIssuesTopPage.htm.

131 *California Chief Justice*: *Remembering 1882*, 9.

131 *This law banned*: Lee and Yung, *Angel Island*, 75.

132 *The reporter uncovered*: "Mott-Street Chinamen Angry. They Deny That They Eat Rats—Chung Kee Threatens a Slander Suit," *New York Times*, August 1, 1883.

132 *In 1884 he wrote*: "Chinese Cooking. Wing Chin Foo's Account of His Countrymen's Customs. The Oriental and Occidental Cuisine Compared. Plain Viands and Mysterious Dishes," *Brooklyn Daily Eagle*, July 6, 1884.

132 *He wrote that*: Renqiu Yu, "Chop Suey: From Chinese Food to Chinese American Food," in *Chinese America: History and Perspectives 1987* (San Francisco: Chinese Historical Society of America, 1987), 89.

132 *But Renqiu Yu*: Ibid.

133 *In cooking,* za sui: Ibid.

134 *By 1903, there were*: Jennifer 8 Lee, *The Fortune Cookie Chronicless: Adventures in the World of Chinese Food* (New York: Twelve, 2008).

134 *According to the* New-York Tribune: "Chinese Takeout," *Lunch Hour NYC*, on the website of the New York Public Library, accessed March 5, 2016, http://exhibitions.nypl.org/lunchhour/exhibits/show/lunchhour/icons /chinese.

136 *In one letter, he wrote*: Seligman, *First Chinese American*.

137 *Japanese immigrants*: Lee and Yung, *Angel Island*, 114.

138 *While Ellis Island*: Ibid., 57.

138 *Under this exception*: Ibid., 116.

139 *The sushi was*: Ibid., 117.

139 *It is used*: *The Kikkoman Way of Fine Eating: Discover a New World of Flavor with Brewed Soy Sauce* (Tokyo: Kikkoman Shoyu., 1973), 16.

140 *In 1949, 251,000 gallons*: William Shurtleff and Akiko Aoyagi, "History of Soy Sauce, Shoyu, and Tamari," on the website of the Soyinfo Center, accessed March 5, 2016, www.soyinfocenter.com/HSS/soy_sauce6.php.

140 *In 1972, as business*: "Make Haste Slowly: The Kikkoman Creed," on the website of Kikkoman Sales USA, accessed March 5, 2016, www.kikkomanusa .com/creed.

140 *It was the first*: Ibid.

142 *Reporter John Birdsall*: John Birdsall, "The End of 'Ethnic,'" last modified June 5, 2012, www.chowhound.com/food-news/117226/the-end-of-ethnic -food.

142 *thirteen Japanese restaurants*: Susan Miyagi Hamaker, "Michelin Guide 2015 Awards Stars to Japanese Restaurants in New York, JapanCulture-NYC, last modified September 30, 2014, www.japanculture-nyc.com/2014/09/30 /michelin-guide-2015-awards-stars-to-japanese-restaurants-in-new-york; Gabe Ulla, "The 14 Most Expensive Tasting Menus in America," Eater, last modified January 28, 2013, www.eater.com/2013/1/28/6489897/the-14-most -expensive-tasting-menus-in-america.

142 *Only two Chinese*: Patty Lee, "The 15 Best Value Michelin-Starred Restaurants in NYC," Thrillist, last modified on December 3, 2015, www.thrillist .com/eat/new-york/michelin-star-restaurants-in-nyc-cheapest-new-york -options.

143 *Wally Tang*: Ligaya Mishan, "Nom Wah Tea Parlor," *New York Times*, April 12, 2011.

143 *He inherited*: Ibid.

144 *At Nom Wah*: "'Touch the Heart' with Nom Wah & Fung Tu," panel

discussion with Jonathan Wu, Jeff Yang, and Wilson Tang, Museum of Chinese in America, May 22, 2014.

144 *After getting off to*: Pete Wells, "Restaurant Review: Fung Tu on the Lower East Side," *New York Times*, May 12, 2015.

Six: Garlic

150 *The Gilroy Garlic Festival*: Pauline Adema, *Garlic Capital of the World: Gilroy, Garlic, and the Making of a Festive Foodscape* (Jackson: University Press of Mississippi, 2009), 25.

150 *Garlic is a potent*: Harold McGee, "The Chemical Weapons of Onions and Garlic," *New York Times*, June 8, 2010.

150 *A clove of garlic*: McGee, *On Food and Cooking: The Science and the Lore of the Kitchen* (New York: Scribner, 2004), 312.

151 *But keep in mind*: Ibid., 208.

151 *The resulting chemical*: ScienceDaily, "Chemists Shed Light on Health Benefits of Garlic," news release, January 31, 2009, www.sciencedaily.com /releases/2009/01/090130154901.htm.

151 *But allicin also*: McGee, *On Food and Cooking*, 311.

151 *A dash of raw garlic*: Ted Jordan Meredith, *The Complete Book of Garlic: A Guide for Gardeners, Growers, and Serious Cooks* (Portland: Timber Books, 2008), 31.

151 *The potent flavor*: McGee, Harold, "The Chemical Weapons of Onions and Garlic," *New York Times*.

151 *These are related*: McGee, *On Food and Cooking*, 313.

152 *Additionally, consuming garlic*: "Hydrogen Sulfide Is Responsible for the Vasoactivity of Garlic," *Life Extension News* 11, no. 1, January 2008, www .life-enhancement.com/magazine/article/1932-hydrogen-sulfide-is-responsi ble-for-the-vasoactivity-of-garlic.

152 *Different garlic varieties*: McGee, *On Food and Cooking*, 313.

153 *It is no surprise that*: Hayley Boriss, "Garlic Profile," website of the Agricultural Marketing Resource Center (AgMRC), last modified April 2014, www .agmrc.org/commodities__products/vegetables/garlic-profile.

154 *By the late nineteenth century*: Thomas H. Kinnard, "Treatment of Painful Hemorrhoids," *Eastern Medical Journal* 7, no. 1 (January 1887): 148.

154 *"Garlic is said to be"*: Brooklyn Daily Eagle, April 20, 1879, http://bklyn.news papers.com/image/50349150/?terms=Garlic.

154   *It* might *have lowered*: Block, *Garlic and Other Alliums*, Chapter 5.6.

154   *And, in a double-blind study*: P. Josling, "Preventing the Common Cold with a Garlic Supplement: A Double-Blind, Placebo-Controlled Survey," *Advances in Therapy* 19, no. 4 (July/August 2001): 189–93, www.ncbi.nlm.nih.gov /pubmed/11697022.

154   *Its proven antifungal*: Block, Eric, *Garlic and Other Alliums*, Chapter 5.5.1.

155   *Carême was born*: Florence Fabricant, "This Is One Celebrity Chef You Won't Find on TV," *New York Times*, May 19, 2004.

155   *In 1792 his parents*: Ian Kelly, *Cooking for Kings: The Life of Antonin Carême, the First Celebrity Chef* (New York: Walker, 2003), 31.

155   *He cooked for*: Ibid., 167.

155   *Carême's 1833 cookbook*: Antonin Carême, *L'art de la cuisine française au dix-neuvième siècle: Traité élémentaire et pratique* (Paris: Imprimeur-Unis, 1847), 251.

158   *One visitor to*: Lawrence R. Schehr and Allen S. Weiss, *French Food: On the Table, on the Page, and in French Culture* (London: Routledge, 2001), 46.

159   *"There's an unsurpassed"*: Michael Bauer, "Restaurant Review: Berkeley's Chez Panisse Still on Top," *San Francisco Chronicle*, February 15, 2014.

159   *Carême died*: "Antonin Carême: First Celebrity Chef," *All Things Considered*.

159   *Good ol' Mary*: Mary Randolph, *The Virginia Housewife: Or, Methodical Cook* (Baltimore: John Plaskitt, 1836), 29.

160   *He listed garlic*: François Tanty, *La cuisine française: French Cooking for Every Home, Adapted to American Requirements* (Chicago: Baldwin, Ross, 1893).

160   *used garlic in only*: Fannie Merritt Farmer, *The Boston Cooking-School Cookbook* (Boston: Little, Brown, 1896), 288.

160   *Four million Italians*: "Immigration . . . Italian: The Great Arrival," on the website of the Library of Congress, accessed April 21, 2014, www.loc.gov /teachers/classroommaterials/presentationsandactivities/presentations/immi gration/italian3.html.

160   *Widespread poverty*: Bolton King and Thomas Okey, *Italy To-Day* (London: J. Nisbet, 1901), 130.

161   *A 1901 study*: Ibid.

161   *But the average*: Bureau of Labor Stastistics, "1901," in *100 Years of U.S. Consumer Spending: Data for the Nation, New York City, and Boston*, accessed April 21, 2014, www.bls.gov/opub/uscs/1901.pdf.

161   *In 1900, during*: "An Italian Wedding in South Brooklyn," *Brooklyn Daily Eagle*, July 15, 1900.

161   *Originally, it might*: Mario Carbone, interview by author, March 3, 2013.

163   *It appeared in*: Bertha M. Wood, *Foods of the Foreign-born in Relation to Health* (Boston: Whitcomb & Barrows, 1922), 32.

163   *He continued*: Daniel Okrent and Harris Lewine, eds., *The Ultimate Baseball Book: The Classic Illustrated History of the World's Greatest Game* (New York: Houghton, Mifflin, 2000), 209.

164   *Nearly thirty thousand*: Charles Glass, *Americans in Paris: Life and Death Under Nazi Occupation* (London: Penguin, 2010), 1.

166   *In 1945 James Beard*: Luke Barr, *Provence, 1970: M.F.K. Fisher, Julia Child, James Beard, and the Reinvention of American Taste* (New York: Clarkson Potter, 2013), 79.

166   *He delighted in eating*: Ibid., 80.

166   *In 1945 while Beard*: Adema, *Garlic Capital of the World*, 55.

169   *From France*: Odile Redon, Françoise Sabban, and Silvano Serventi, *The Medieval Kitchen: Recipes from France and Italy* (Chicago: University of Chicago Press, 2000), 165–67.

169   *Today Americans*: "Census 2000 Brief," The United States Census Bureau, June 2004, 2.

169   *A study in the*: B. Teucher et al., "Dietary Patterns and Heritability of Food Choice in a UK Female Twin Cohort," *Twin Research and Human Genetics: The Official Journal of the International Journal for Twin Studies* 10, no. 5 (October 2007): 734–48, www.ncbi.nlm.nih.gov/pubmed/17903115.

170   *Some scientists believe*: "Baby's Palate and Food Memories Shaped Before Birth," *Morning Edition*, National Public Radio, aired August 8, 2011.

170   *But a preference*: J. A. Mennella and G. K. Beauchamp, "The Effects of Repeated Exposure to Garlic-Flavored Milk on the Nursling's Behavior," *Pediatric Research* 34, no. 6 (December 1993): 805–8, www.ncbi.nlm.nih.gov/pubmed/8108198.

170   *Today there are*: "2015 Top 100: Restaurant Chain Countdown," on the website of *Nation's Restaurant News*, June 18, 2015, http://nrn.com/top-100/2015-top-100-restaurant-chain-countdown#slide-85-field_images-136081.

Seven: Monosodium Glutamate (MSG)

177   *Reporter Julia Moskin*: Julia Moskin, "Yes, MSG, the Secret Behind the Savor," *New York Times*, March 5, 2008.

178   *The city first started*: Elizabeth Royte, "Less Than Barren," POV Borders Environment, accessed July 15, 2014, www.pbs.org/pov/borders/2004/talk/er_185.html.

179 *This broth, kombu dashi*: Ole G. Mouritsen and Klavs Styrbaek, *Umami* (New York: Columbia University Press, 2014), 66.

179 *Depending on the variety*: Jeffrey Steingarten, "Why Doesn't Everybody in China Have a Headache?," in *It Must Have Been Something I Ate: The Return of the Man Who Ate Everything* (New York: Vintage Books, 2002), 91.

179 *This broth was prized*: Harris Salat, "The Secret's Out as Japanese Stock Gains Fans," *New York Times*, October 14, 2008.

179 *For much of Japan's*: Henry Smith, "Raw Fish and a Hot Bath: Dilemmas of Daily Life," in *Learning from Shōgun: Japanese History and Western Fantasy* (Santa Barbara: University of California, 1980).

181 *Ikeda, a recent graduate*: Ohkoshi Shin-ichi, "Notable Alumni: Kikunae Ikeda (Discoverer of 'Umami')," on the website of the University of Tokyo School of Science, accessed March 6, 2016, www.s.u-tokyo.ac.jp/en/research/alumni /ikeda.html.

181 *Although he dressed*: "Docudrama Commemorating the Centennial of the Discovery of Umami," accessed July 9, 2015, www.youtube.com/watch ?v=geleAcDxObo.

181 *"I was abashed"*: Ibid.

181 *"There's a commonality"*: Kikunae Ikeda, "On the Taste of the Salt of Glutamic Acid," in *Proceedings of the 8th International Congress in Applied Chemistry* 38 (1912): 147.

181 *"It is usually"*: Ole G. Mouritsen and Klavs Styrbæk, *Umami: Unlocking the Secrets of the Fifth Taste* (New York: Columbia University Press, 2014), 22.

182 *He noticed it*: Ohkoshi, "Notable Alumni: Kikunae Ikeda," www.s.u-tokyo .ac.jp/en/research/alumni/ikeda.html.

182 *What Ikeda had discovered*: Mouritsen and Styrbæk, *Umami*, 24.

183 *They're sometimes called*: John Mahoney, "The Notorious MSG's Unlikely Formula for Success," BuzzFeedNews, August 16, 2013, www.buzzfeed.com /johnmahoney/the-notorious-msgs-unlikely-formula-for-success.

184 *In a speech*: Ikeda, "On the Taste of Salt," 147.

185 *If a highly nutritious*: Jordan Sand, "A Short History of MSG: Good Science, Bad Science, and Taste Cultures," *Gastronomica: The Journal of Critical Food Studies* 5, no. 4 (Fall 2005): 38–49, doi: 10.1525/gfc.2005.5.4.38.

185 *In America, MSG*: Mahoney, "Notorious MSG's Unlikely Formula for Success."

185 *The resulting slurry*: Ibid.

185 *Ajinomoto partnered*: Sand, "Short History of MSG," 41.

185 *MSG had been designed*: Ibid., 41.

186 *Some of the Chinese*: Ibid., 43.

186 *Nearly every recipe*: Leon Huang, *Selected Chinese Recipes* (Hong Kong: Fortune, 1968).

187 *Ajinomoto introduced*: Sand, "Short History of MSG," 44.

187 *Though the* New York Times: "Origin of Aji-no-moto," *New York Times*, September 13, 1950.

187 *Another* Times *columnist*: Jane Nickerson, "The Beginner's Spice Shelf," *New York Times*, June 5, 1955.

188 *By 1969, fifty-eight*: Ian Mosby, "'That Won-Ton Soup Headache': The Chinese Restaurant Syndrome, MSG and the Making of American Food, 1968–1980," *Social History of Medicine* 22, no. 1 (2009): 133–51.

188 *I came to this belief*: "Chicken in a Biskit Original Crackers, 8-Ounce Units (Pack of 6)," Amazon.com, accessed March 6, 2016, www.amazon.com /Chicken-Biskit-Original-Crackers-8-Ounce/dp/B000F9XB8O.

189 *The US Food and Drug Administration*: Gary Taubes and Cristin Kearns Couzens, "Big Sugar's Sweet Little Lies," *Mother Jones*, November/December 2012, www.motherjones.com/environment/2012/10/sugar-industry-lies-cam paign.

190 *One letter described*: Mosby, "'That Won-Ton Soup Headache.'"

190 *A prominent theory*: Steingarten, "Why Doesn't Everybody in China Have a Headache?"

190 *Schaumburg and his colleagues*: Herbert H. Schaumburg, Robert Byck, Robert Gerstl, and Jan. H. Mashman, "Monosodium L-Glutamate: Its Pharmacology and Role in the Chinese Restaurant Syndrome," *Science* 163, no. 3869 (February 21, 1969): 826–28.

191 *A restaurant-goer*: Richard D. Lyons, "'Chinese Restaurant Syndrome' Puzzles Doctors," *New York Times*, May 19, 1968.

191 *Only one of the restaurant*: Ibid.

191 *"I had had a light"*: Mosby, "'That Won-Ton Soup Headache.'"

192 *"Shrimp, beef, fried and sizzled"*: Klemesrud, "The Man Who Struck it Rich with *Bonanza*," *New York Times*, October 8, 1972, D23–24.

192 *"Anything that can cause"*: Patricia L. Raymer, "That Won-Ton Soup Headache," *New York Times,* April 20, 1977.

192 *The irony of Olney's*: Dr. Stephen Witherly, interview by author, April 11, 2014; Mouritsen, and Styrbæk, *Umami*, 25.

192 *These restaurants*: "Kraft Smart Search," accessed May 23, 2016, https:// smartsearch.kraftfoods.com/Search/results.aspx; "Kentucky Fried Chicken Food Allergies and Sensitivities," accessed May 23, 2016, https://www.kfc .com/nutrition/food-allergies-and-sensitivities.

193   *This oversight*: L. Tarasoff and M. F. Kelly, "Monosodium L-Glutamate: A Double-Blind Study and Review," *Food and Chemical Toxicology* 31, no. 12 (December 1993): 826.

193   *Tarasoff and Kelly*: Ibid.

194   *"He complements"*: Salat, "The Secret's Out."

194   *chef Danny Bowien's*: Allie Pape, "Mission Chinese Food Now Has MSG Shakers on Its Tables," Easter (San Francisco), last modified October 3, 2014, http://sf.eater.com/2014/10/3/6905209/msg-shakers-mission-chinese-food-sf.

194   *In his own cooking*: Moskin, "MSG, the Secret Behind the Savor."

195   *Although he added*: "Grant Achatz on MSG, Salt & Pepper," Vimeo, accessed March 6, 2016, https://vimeo.com/81167347.

195   *At the 2012 MAD*: "M.A.D. Food Co.: About," on the website of M.A.D. Food Co., accessed March 6, 2016, http://www.madfeed.co/video/msg-and-umami/.

Eight: Sriracha

202   *The hot sauce industry*: "Hot Sauces," America's Test Kitchen, accessed March 6, 2016, www.americastestkitchen.com/taste_tests/255-hot-sauces.

202   *In 2014, sales of*: Lauren Doucette, "Sriracha: A Brief History of the World's Most Popular Hot Sauce," Fork + Plate, last modified August 5, 2015, http://forknplate.com/2015/08/05/sriracha.

202   *But that number was*: Roberto A. Ferdman, "The Highly Unusual Company Behind Sriracha, the World's Coolest Hot Sauce," Quartz, last modified October 21, 2013, http://qz.com/132738/the-highly-unusual-company-behind -siracha-the-worlds-coolest-hot-sauce.

202   *And it has other*: "The Best-Selling Condiments in the U.S.," Bloomberg, accessed March 6, 2016, www.bloomberg.com/ss/10/10/1007_bestselling_condi ments/14.html.

204   *The earliest bottles*: "A Brief History of U.S. Commercial Hot Sauces," accessed May 1, 2014, www.fieryfoodscentral.com/2008/12/27/a-brief-history -of-us-commercial-hot-sauces/.

204   *Americans have topped*: Ibid.

204   *A hot red chili sauce*: *Sriracha: A Documentary Film by Griffin Hammond*, Vimeo, accessed March 7, 2016, https://vimeo.com/ondemand/sriracha/80617133.

204   *It's fermented*: Ibid.

206   *Vietnam was under*: "Vietnam-History," accessed May 1, 2014, http://asia.isp .msu.edu/wbwoa/southeast_asia/vietnam/history.html.

206 *Before the French takeover*: "The History and Evolution of Pho: A Hundred Years' Journey," LovingPho.com, last modified December 29, 2015, www .lovingpho.com/pho-opinion-editorial/history-and-evolution-of-vietnamese -pho.

206 *The broth is served*: James Beard, *Beard on Food: The Best Recipes and Kitchen Wisdom from the Dean of American Cooking* (New York: Bloomsbury, 1974), 16.

206 *When this French dish*: Andrea Nguyen, "History of Pho Noodle Soup," Viet World Kitchen, October 31, 2008, http://vietworldkitchen.typepad.com /blog/2008/10/the-evolution-of-pho.html.

206 *Different meats were added*: Ibid.

207 *David was born*: Frank Shyong, "Sriracha Hot Pepper Purveyor Turns Up the Heat," *Los Angeles Times*, April 12, 2013.

207 *David decided to try*: John T. Edge, "A Chili Sauce to Crow About," *New York Times*, May 19, 2009; David Tran, interview by author, October 2, 2013.

207 *The family sold batches*: Edge, "Chili Sauce."

207 *The sauce became*: Ibid.

207 *The North Vietnamese army*: Theresa C. Carino, "Vietnam's Chinese Minority and the Politics of Sino-Vietnam Relations," accessed May 1, 2014, http:// www.ibiblio.org/ahkitj/wscfap/arms1974/Book%20Series/TheImageOfGod IM/IOGIM-vietnam.htm.

207 *Many were forcibly*: Ibid.

209 *By 1978, the government*: "David Tran Has Beaten Greater Odds Than Srirachapocalypse," on the website for the documentary film *Sriracha*, December 20, 2013, http://srirachamovie.com/post/70622620438/david-tran-has-beaten -greater-odds-than.

209 *Some refugees fled*: Yuk Wah Chan, ed., *The Chinese/Vietnamese Diaspora: Revisiting the Boat People* (New York: Routledge, 2011).

209 *Approximately two-thirds*: "E. Vietnam and the Ethnic Chinese After 1975," Online Archive of California (OAC), accessed May 13, 2014, www.oac.cdlib .org/view?docId=hb138nb08w;NAAN=13030&doc.view=frames&chunk .id=ss2.10&toc.id=ss2.10&brand=oac4.

209 *As a precaution*: Edge, "Chili Sauce."

209 *An American newspaper*: Associated Press, "Vietnamese Take Over Ship, Refuse to Leave Hong Kong," *Toledo* (OH) *Blade*, December 27, 1978.

210 *In January 1979*: Chan, *Chinese/Vietnamese Diaspora*.

210 *By 1980, America*: Hataipreuk Rkasnuam and Jeanne Batalova, "Vietnamese Immigrants in the United States," on the website of the Migration

Policy Institute, August 25, 2014, www.migrationpolicy.org/article/vietnamese
-immigrants-united-states.

210 *David and his family*: Edge, "Chili Sauce."

211 *He blended the red chilies*: Ibid.

211 *Since then, Sriracha sales*: Roberto A. Ferdman, "The Highly Unusual Company Behind Sriracha, the World's Coolest Hot Sauce," Quartz, October 21, 2013, http://qz.com/132738/the-highly-unusual-company-behind-siracha-the -worlds-coolest-hot-sauce.

211 *The current sriracha factory*: Ibid.

212 *Once the chilies*: Michaeleen Doucleff, "Sriracha Chemistry: How Hot Sauces Perk Up Your Food and Your Mood," *The Salt*, National Public Radio, aired February 24, 2014.

214 *In the 1980s*: Rkasnuam and Batalova "Vietnamese Immigrants in the United States," www.migrationpolicy.org/article/vietnamese-immigrants-united-states.

214 *And pho was*: Nguyen, "History of Pho Noodle Soup," http://vietworld kitchen.typepad.com/blog/2008/10/the-evolution-of-pho.html.

215 *"The* pho *is delicious"*: *Washingtonian* 22, 1987, 196.

215 *According to the CCD*: Kelsey Blackwell, "Restaurant Flavors Impact Retail Product Trends at the Summer Fancy Food Show," on the website of New Hope Network, July 11, 2011, http://m.newhope360.com/news-amp-analysis /restaurant-flavors-impact-retail-product-trends-summer-fancy-food-show.

215 *Frequently, an ingredient*: Caleb Hannan, "Sriracha Hot Sauce Catches Fire, Yet 'There's Only One Rooster,'" *Bloomberg Businessweek*, February 21, 2013.

216 *P. F. Chang's was*: Edge, "Chili Sauce."

217 *He's a fourth-generation*: Craig Underwood, "Huy Fong Sriracha," *Edible Ojai & Ventura County*, May 1, 2013, http://ediblenetwork.com/ojai/online-maga zine/huy-fong-sriracha/.

217 *It all started in 1988*: Ibid.

217 *"Usually farmers"*: Craig Underwood, interview by author, October 2014.

219 *A recent study*: Lauren Fox, "Business Groups Not Backing Down on Immi-grant Reform," *U.S. News & World Report*, March 27, 2014.

219 *And with restrictive*: Ibid.

Epilogue: The Ninth Flavor

223 *Aoki, a Japanese patissier*: David Lebovitz, *Ready for Dessert: My Best Recipes* (Berkeley, CA: Ten Speed Press, 2012), 220.

223 *"You couldn't walk"*: Ibid.

224 *In 2001 Martha Stewart's*: "Green Tea Shortbread Leaves," Martha Stewart, accessed March 6, 2016, www.marthastewart.com/316840/green-tea-short bread-leaves.

224 *Matcha appeared*: "Green Tea Crepe Cake," Martha Stewart, accessed March 6, 2016, www.marthastewart.com/1124574/green-tea-crepe-cake.

224 *But Dukes felt*: Lisa Fleischer, "Pumpkin Spice Latte, the Drink That Almost Wasn't," *Corporate Intelligence* (blog), *Wall Street Journal*, August 30, 2013, http://blogs.wsj.com/corporate-intelligence/2013/08/30/pumpkin-spice-latte -the-drink-that-almost-wasnt.

225 *"Within the first week"*: Fleischer, "Pumpkin Spice Latte"; "Peter Dukes Shares the Story Behind Starbucks First Pumpkin Spice Latte," Starbucks Newsroom, August 24, 2014, https://news.starbucks.com/news/starbucks-first -pumpkin-spice-latte.

225 *"Back then, we would call"*: "Peter Dukes Shares the Story Behind Starbucks First Pumpkin Spice Latte."

225 *But major brands*: Michael Moss, "That Pinch of Pumpkin," *New York Times*, November 12, 2013.

225 *Nineteen perccent of*: "Pumpkin-Flavored Products Growing in Popularity," on the website of the Specialty Food Association, September 16, 2015, www .specialtyfood.com/news/article/pumpkin-flavored-items-more-menus-ever; Moss, "That Pinch of Pumpkin."

225 *Pumpkin pie has*: "Pumpkin-Flavored Products," www.specialtyfood.com /news/article/pumpkin-flavored-items-more-menus-ever.

225 *The spices are*: Dan Charles, "Just What Is in Pumpkin Spice Flavor? (Hint: Not Pumpkin)," *The Salt*, NPR, accessed March 6, 2016, http://www.npr .org/sections/thesalt/2014/11/19/365213805/just-what-is-in-pumpkin-spice -flavor-hint-not-pumpkin.

225 *Additionally, there are*: Moss, "That Pinch of Pumpkin."

225 *Together these chemicals*: Charles, "Just What Is in Pumpkin Spice Flavor?"

225 *But if you're horrified*: Ibid.

226 *The liquid is collected*: "Liquid Smoke," accessed March 5, 2016, www.cooks illustrated.com/taste_tests/395-liquid-smoke.

226 *My fellow foodie*: Ibid.

Bibliography

FOR FURTHER READING, here are some of the major sources I relied on to compile the information in this book.

One: Black Pepper

Booth, Robert. *Death of an Empire: The Rise and Murderous Fall of Salem, America's Richest City*. New York: St. Martin's Press, 2011.

Crowninshield, John. *John Crowninshield in the America III, at Sumatra, 1801*. Edited by Howard Corning. Vol. 80, no. 16. Essex Institute Historical Collections. 1944.

DeWitt, Dave. *The Founding Foodies: How Washington, Jefferson and Franklin Revolutionized American Cuisine*. Naperville, IL: Sourcebooks, 2010.

Farmer, Fannie Merritt. *The Boston Cooking-School Cookbook*. Boston: Little, Brown, 1896.

Ferguson, David L. *Cleopatra's Barge: The Crowninshield Story*. Boston: Little, Brown, 1976.

Gillis, James D., and Henry Whipple. *Sailing Directions for the Pepper Ports on the West Coast of Sumatra, North of Analaboo: To Accompany a Chart of that Coast*. Salem, MA: Salem Gazette Press, 1839.

Hess, Karen. *Martha Washington's Booke of Cookery and Booke of Sweetmeats*. New York: Columbia University Press, 1995.

Marsden, William. *The History of Sumatra, Illustrated*. London: J. McCreery, 1811.

McGee, Harold. *On Food and Cooking: The Science and the Lore of the Kitchen*. New York: Scribner, 2004.

Nair, K. P. Prabhakaran. *Agronomy and Economy of Black Pepper and Cardamom: The "King" and "Queen" of Spices*. Amsterdam: Elsevier, 2011.

Putnam, George Granville. *Salem Vessels and Their Voyages: A History of the Pepper Trade with the Island of Sumatra*. Salem, MA: Essex Institute, 1922.

Ridley, Henry N. *Spices*. London: Macmillan, 1912.

Two: Vanilla

Ecott, Tim. *Vanilla: Travels in Search of the Ice Cream Orchid*. New York: Grove Press, 2005.

Gordon-Reed, Annette. *The Hemingses of Monticello: An American Family*. New York: W. W. Norton, 2008.

Havkin-Frenkel, Daphna, and Faith C. Belanger, eds. *Handbook of Vanilla Science and Technology*. Oxford, UK: Wiley-Blackwell, 2010.

Kourí, Emilio. *A Pueblo Divided: Business, Property, and Community in Papantla, Mexico*. Stanford, CA: Stanford University Press, 2004.

Leslie, Eliza. *The Lady's Receipt-book: A Useful Companion for Large or Small Families*. Philadelphia: Carey and Hart, 1847.

Three: Chili Powder

Arellano, Gustavo. *Taco USA: How Mexican Food Conquered America*. New York: Scribner, 2012.

Martinello, Marian. *The Search for a Chili Queen: On the Fringes of a Rebozo*.

Mexican Cooking: The First Mexican-American Cookbook. Bedford, MA: Applewood, 2002.

Pilcher, Jeffrey M. *Planet Taco: A Global History of Mexican Food*. New York: Oxford University Press, 2012.

Smith, H. Allen. *The Great Chili Confrontation; a Dramatic History of the Decade's Most Impassioned Culinary Embroilment, with Recipes*. New York: Trident Press, 1969.

Four: Curry Powder

Bald, Vivek. *Bengali Harlem and the Lost Histories of South Asian America*. Cambridge, MA: Harvard University Press, 2013.

Collingham, Lizzie. *Curry: A Tale of Cooks and Conquerors*. New York: Oxford University Press, 2006.

Lee, Erika, and Judy Yung. *Angel Island: Immigrant Gateway to America*. New York: Oxford University Press, 2010.

Leonard, Karen Isaken. *Making Ethnic Choices: California's Punjabi Mexican Americans*. Philadelphia: Temple University Press, 1992.

Sahni, Julie. *Classic Indian Cooking*. New York: William Morrow Cookbooks, 1980.

Sax, David. *The Tastemakers: Why We're Crazy for Cupcakes but Fed Up with Fondue*. Philadelphia: Public Affairs, 2014.

Five: Soy Sauce

Coe, Andrew. *Chop Suey: A Cultural History of Chinese Food in the United States*. New York: Oxford University Press, 2009.

The Cook Not Mad. Watertown, NY: Knowlton & Rice, 1831.

The Kikkoman Way of Fine Eating: Discover a New World of Flavor with Brewed Soy Sauce. Tokyo: Kikkoman Shoyu, 1973.

Lee, Jennifer 8. *The Fortune Cookie Chronicles: Adventures in the World of Chinese Food*. New York: Twelve, 2008.

Seligman, Scott D. *The First Chinese American: The Remarkable Life of Wong Chin Foo*. Hong Kong: Hong Kong University Press, 2013.

Shurtleff, William, and Akiko Aoyagi, *History of Koji—Grains and/or Soybeans Enrobed with a Mold Culture (300 BCE to 2012)*. Lafayette, CA: Soyinfo Center, 2012.

———. *History of Soy Sauce (160 CE to 2012)*. Lafayette, CA: Soyinfo Center, 2012.

Yu, Renqiu. *Chinese America: History and Perspectives*. San Francisco: Chinese Historical Society of America, 1987.

Six: Garlic

Adema, Pauline. *Garlic Capital of the World: Gilroy, Garlic, and the Making of a Festive Foodscape*. Jackson: University Press of Mississippi, 2009.

Barr, Luke. *Provence, 1970: M. F. K. Fisher, Julia Child, James Beard, and the Reinvention of American Taste*. New York: Clarkson Potter, 2013.

Block, Eric. *Garlic and Other Alliums: The Lore and the Science*. Cambridge, UK: Royal Society of Chemistry, 2010.

Carême, Antonin. *L'art de la cuisine française au dix-neuvième siècle: Traité élémentaire et pratique*. Paris: Imprimeur-Unis, 1847.

Kelly, Ian. *Cooking for Kings: The Life of Antonin Carême, the First Celebrity Chef*. New York: Walker, 2003.

Randolph, Mary. *The Virginia Housewife: Or, Methodical Cook*. Baltimore: John Plaskitt, 1836.

Tanty, François. *La cuisine française: French Cooking for Every Home, Adapted to American Requirements*. Chicago: Baldwin, Ross, 1893.

Wood, Bertha M. *Foods of the Foreign-born in Relation to Health*. Boston: Whitcomb & Barrows, 1922.

Seven: Monosodium Glutamate (MSG)

Low, Henry. *Cook at Home in Chinese*. New York: Macmillan, 1938.

Mosby, Ian. "'That Won-Ton Soup Headache': The Chinese Restaurant Syndrome, MSG and the Making of American Food, 1968–1980." *Social History of Medicine* 22, no. 1 (2009): 133–51.

Mouritsen, Ole G., and Klavs Styrbæk. *Umami: Unlocking the Secrets of the Fifth Taste*. New York: Columbia University Press, 2014.

Sand, Jordan. "A Short History of MSG: Good Science, Bad Science, and Taste Cultures." *Gastronomica: The Journal of Critical Food Studies* 5, no. 4 (2005): 38–49.

Steingarten, Jeffrey. *It Must Have Been Something I Ate: The Return of the Man Who Ate Everything*. New York: Vintage Books, 2003.

Eight: Sriracha

Clemens, Randy. *The Sriracha Cookbook: 50 "Rooster Sauce" Recipes That Pack a Punch*. Berkeley: Ten Speed Press, 2011.

Chan, Yuk Wah, ed. *The Chinese/Vietnamese Diaspora: Revisiting the Boat People*. New York: Routledge, 2011.

Index

Note: Page numbers in *italics* refer to illustrations.

savory taste (umami), 183; *see also* umami

Savoy, London, 95

Saxena, Jaya, 221, 222

scents, xvi, 51

Schaumburg, Herbert H., 190, 192

Schinus terebinthifolius (Christmas berry or Florida holly), 5

Science, 190

Scooby (dog), 37, 45

seaweed, 185

See-Yu sauce, 134

Serious Eats blog, 196, 205, 221

settlement houses, 161–63

Seychelles, vanilla growing on, 39

shallots, 150

Sherman, Paul W., 17

Sherry, Louis, 95, 103, 110

Sherry's restaurant, New York, 95–99, 104

  closing of, 110

  menu of, 98–99

Shintoism, 181

Shlueter, Rose, 106

Shu-Wen-shin, 209

Simmons, Amelia, *American Cookery* (1796), xvi, 153

Singh Thind, Bhagat, 109–10

Skyline Chili, Cleveland, 74–75

Slate, 1

Smile, Emil and Sara Kididja, 95

Smile, May, 108, 110–11

Smile, Ranji, 88, 94–99, *96,* 127

  as chef, 95–99, 103, 104, 106, 109

  citizenship application of, 105, 110

  cooking demonstrations by, 104–6

  curries made by, 97–99, 102, 106

  curry powders made by, 98

  and Indian immigrants, 103, 104–6

  leaving the US, 110–11

  varying stories about, 103–12

  and women, 106–7, 108–9

Smile, Rebecca, 108

Smith, H. Allen:

  in chili cook-off, 76–77

  New York Chili recipe, 77–78

  "Nobody Knows More About Chili Than I Do," 76

Smith, S. Compton, *Chili con Carne; or, the Camp and the Field,* 60, 61

smoke:

  liquid, 226

  wood, xii, 48

smoke flavor, 226

society, changing, 228–29

sodium, and MSG, 183–85, 189, 191, 194, 197

soil gnats, 3

Soma (Brooklyn Brainery), 88, 152, 183

sour taste, xv, 122, 193

soybeans:

  fermenting, 121–22

  grown in US, 123

soy sauce, xvii, xviii, *118,* 119–45

  in aging tanks, 122–23

  anchovy and stale beer knockoff for, 124

  Bowen's Patent Soy, 123–24, 126

  in Chicken McNuggets, 145

  and Chinese American cuisine, 129, 142, 145

  Chinese style, 121, 143–44; *see also* Chinese immigrants

  and chop suey, 132–34, 136, 137, 142

  Chop Suey recipe (1901), 133–34

  and chow mein, 134–35, 136

soy sauce (*cont.*)

Chow Mein—Latest, 135–36

crafting of, 121

discovery of (eighteenth century), 123

first in US, 123

in Green Bean Casserole, 120

HVP (hydrolyzed vegetable protein) method for, 123, 140

Indonesian *ketjap,* 124

Japanese style, 119, 121–22, 134, 139, 140–42; *see also* Japanese immigrants

jiang as ancestor of, 121, 124

ketchups and catsups as substitute for, 124, 126, 137

Kikkoman factory, 120, 140–42, 187

microbrewed, 120

naturally brewed, 123

pasteurization of, 122

popularity of, 120, 137, 229

production of, 121–23, 185

protein in, 122

saltwater brine in, 122

See-Yu sauce, 134

Soy Sauce Chocolate Mousse with Fruit Compote, 145–47

and sushi, 139

tamari style, 121

umami flavor of, 122

use in American cooking, 124, 126, 128, 133, 137, 140, 141–42, 226

uses for, 139

and Worcestershire sauce, 132, 137

Spain:

conquest of Mexico, 30

monopoly of vanilla beans, 31, 36

Tejas territory of, 58–59

Speaking of Science blog, 177–78

spices, 155

hand grinding of, 93–94

Indian blends of, 89–90, 93

pre-ground, 93–94

pumpkin pie spice, 224–26

spicy food:

antimicrobial properties in, 17–18, 90

biological preference for, 204

heat in, 58, 70

popularity of, 17, 204

Spicy Zeig (drink recipe), 220

Sriracha, xvii, xviii, 150, *200,* 201–20

antimicrobial properties of, 17

from chili mash puree, 212

creation of, 204, 206, 210–11

cultlike fan base of, 216

in flavor competition, 150, 216

in gourmet food stores, 215

hot peppers in, 217, 218–19

and hot sauce industry, 202, 204, 216

Huy Fong factory, 201–4, 211–14, 219

and immigrant laws, 219, 229

as Ingredient of the Year, 215–16

origins in Thailand, 204, 215

and pho, 206, 214–15

popularity of, 202, 215, 217, 218, 222

production of, 212–13

qualities of, 216

in recipe websites, 216

in restaurant chains, 216

Spicy Zeig, 220

Sriraja Panich, 204, 206, 207, 214

Thai Omelet, 205, 206

and Tran, 204, 206–11, 216–18

About the Author

SARAH LOHMAN is originally from Hinckley, Ohio, where she began working in a museum at the age of sixteen, cooking historic food over a wood-burning stove. She graduated with a BFA from the Cleveland Institute of Art in 2005, and for her undergraduate thesis, she opened a temporary restaurant/installation that reinterpreted food of the Colonial era for a modern audience. Lohman moved to New York in 2006 and worked as video producer for *New York* magazine's food blog, *Grub Street*. She left the position in 2009 to launch her own business.

Dubbed a "historical gastronomist," she re-creates historic recipes as a way to make a personal connection with the past. She chronicles her explorations in culinary history on her blog, *Four Pounds Flour*, and her work has been featured in the *New York Times*, the *Wall Street Journal*, and on NPR. Lohman works with museums and galleries around the country to create public programs focused on food, including institutions such as the Lower East Side Tenement Museum; the American Museum of Natural History; the Institute for Culinary Education; and the Museum of Science, Boston. She appeared in NYC-TV's miniseries *Appetite City*, cooking culinary treats from New York's past, and is featured on the Cooking Channel's *Food: Fact or Fiction. Eight Flavors* is her first book.